NEW ORLEANS REMIX

NEW ORLEANS
Remix

Jack Sullivan

University Press of Mississippi / Jackson

www.upress.state.ms.us

The University Press of Mississippi is a member
of the Association of American University Presses.

First printing 2017
∞

Library of Congress Cataloging-in-Publication Data

Names: Sullivan, Jack, 1946– author.
Title: New Orleans remix / Jack Sullivan.
Description: Jackson : University Press of Mississippi, [2017] | Series:
American made music series | Includes bibliographical references and index. |
Identifiers: LCCN 2017017422 (print) | LCCN 2017019445 (ebook) | ISBN 9781496815279
(epub single) | ISBN 9781496815286 (epub institutional) | ISBN 9781496815293 (pdf single)
| ISBN 9781496815309 (pdf institutional) | ISBN 9781496815262 (hardcover : alk. paper)
Subjects: LCSH: Music—Louisiana—New Orleans—History and criticism. | Music—Social
aspects—Louisiana—New Orleans.
Classification: LCC ML200.8.N48 (ebook) | LCC ML200.8.N48 N48 2017 (print) | DDC
781.6409763/35—dc23
LC record available at https://lccn.loc.gov/2017017422

British Library Cataloging-in-Publication Data available

For Robin, David, and Geoffrey,
who keep me in the groove

CONTENTS

ACKNOWLEDGMENTS

I would like to thank Bruce Raeburn, curator of the Hogan Jazz Archive, for his guidance, encouragement, and willingness to share his endless knowledge about New Orleans music. Alaina Hébert and Lynn Abbott were also extremely helpful in sorting out archives and pictures. A personal thanks goes to my longtime friend Jack Belsom, who knows New Orleans opera history in awesome detail and has given lectures to my classes since 1995. The coverage of opera would not have been possible without his scholarship and guidance. I am also grateful to Ben Sandmel, who helped me in the early stages; to David Yaffe, who helped me later on; to Matt Sakakeeny, who shared his research before shaping it into his book on brass bands; to Scott Goldshine, my confidant and alter ego in New York, who provided access to the Rebirth Brass Band and others; and to the many people who helped me arrange interviews, including Mary Fiance Fuss and Paul Siegel.

A special thanks goes to the musicians who welcomed my interviews over several years, often inviting me into their homes, lingering with me after late-night gigs, and giving me a firsthand sense of a NOLA musician's life. It is hard to single anyone out, but I've been especially floored by the generosity of Katja Toivola, Leroy Jones, Wendell Brunious, Kermit Ruffins, Gregg Stafford, Lucien Barbarin, Yolanda Windsay, Phil Frazier, Shammar Allen, Bob and Gerald French, and Richard Moten. The club owners have also been incredibly generous, making me feel like an insider and showing me the triumphs and challenges of the business. I am especially indebted to Cindy Wood, Richard Rochester, Charlie Sims, John Blanchard, Nina Buck, and Nicolas Bazan. For up-to-date knowledge of gigs, customs, and new bands, I'm indebted to my friends Stacy Wojcik and Elizabeth Kalos, both former students who moved down to New Orleans, flipped the student-professor dynamic, and made me their eager student.

This book would not have happened were it not for my superb agent, Valerie Borchardt, who believed in this project from the beginning and gave me the encouragement I needed. Grateful thanks goes to my editor, Craig Gill, and his assistant, Emily Bandy, for their professionalism and patience. Their job was made easier by the long labors of my wife, Robin Bromley, a meticulous editor who read the manuscript and helped me make important decisions.

Portions of this book have appeared in the *Chronicle of Higher Education*, *Opera Magazine*, and the Wexford Festival Opera program book.

NEW ORLEANS REMIX

INTRODUCTION

Since Louis Moreau Gottschalk transcribed African slave drumming in Congo Square, New Orleans has ignited America's hottest sounds. Many books have investigated New Orleans music by reinvoking the "cradle of jazz" myth; NOLA emerges here the way many tourists envision it, as the home of quaint old guys playing Dixieland in Preservation Hall, keeping alive the ghosts of Louis Armstrong and Sidney Bechet. Other books celebrate the laid-back ambiance bequeathed by the French, the exotic world of Lafcadio Hearn and Tennessee Williams, with traditional jazz as the backdrop. Fetishizing the past is a long-standing New Orleans trope—and why not, since its traditions are so seductive and special?

Meantime, far off the mainstream media's radar, the real New Orleans rocks on, supported by an avid local audience. Artists little known to the general public—Marla Dixon, David Torkanowsky, Shamarr Allen, the Pinettes, Topsy Chapman, Aurora Nealand, Tom McDermott, the Brass-A-Holics, to name a few—are pioneering new sounds layered on NOLA traditions. Funk, hip hop, brass bands, zydeco, "hot club" gypsy, and avant-jazz groups are rocking the city in neighborhood bars far from the Bourbon Street tourist scene. Even "neo-traditional" jazz artists like Leon "Kid Chocolate" Brown, Gerald French, and the Shotgun Jazz Band have emerged in startling numbers, making the old sound new for a younger generation. This book addresses what is really happening—every day, not just at Mardi Gras and Jazz Fest—in America's musical capital, presenting the perspectives of contemporary musicians. This is not another book on the history of jazz or Mardi Gras, though it takes a look at Creole songs, French opera, pleasure clubs, marching bands, and other traditions that influence today's sounds. The focus is what has been happening since the 1990s.

The transformations of that decade are dramatic and still very much in place. I've been traveling down to New Orleans from my home in New York since the 1980s, and it was in the '90s that I noticed things really starting to change. Comparing New York to New Orleans, Jason Marsalis, whose family is a microcosm of the changing scene, told me that for a serious musician in the '80s, New Orleans was "not part of the discussion, not even on the table"; the Big Easy was losing many of its finest players to the Big Apple. "Brian Blade, for example, from Shreveport, was in New Orleans; then he went to New York because New York was *the* place. A lot of that was solidified when Wynton and Branford [Jason's brothers] moved to New York, and their careers really took off, and it became, 'That's where you've gotta go.'" Now all that has changed.

New Orleans is not what it used to be, and neither is New York. Thomas W. Jacobsen points out that by the '90s there began to be more work for musicians in New Orleans "than in much larger cities like New York. Not surprisingly then, a significant number of top-notch young musicians moved to town during the period to join an impressive group of local 'young lions' . . . these fine young players were not just playing traditional jazz. The influence of the Marsalis brothers and other young hot shots from the previous decade had a notable impact on the young musicians of the decade."[1] Jacobsen's authoritative account corrects the widespread notion that the big changes in the current scene were all occasioned by Hurricane Katrina. "A lot of people think New Orleans changed because of Hurricane Katrina," says Marsalis, "but Katrina just sped it up. In my own family, everybody, at some point, has taken New Orleans for granted. Even my own father wasn't interested in the more traditional style—though, mind you, he played some great music—until later." The first inkling that New Orleans was transforming came to Jason after his father, who was living in Richmond, came to New Orleans to record a session in Snug Harbor during Jazz Fest: "He doesn't think anything of it; he does the session, he leaves. Then a year later, the record gets released in Japan. Japan! He had no idea that was going to happen. And I remember thinking, 'Local New Orleans is going to be over soon.' He'd gotten used to thinking, 'You do a session, nothing happens. You do a session, nothing happens.'" I told him I thought the biggest change came in the '90s, when I began seeing an eruption of klezmer, free jazz, new trad bands, Brazilian music, and much else. "Yes! No doubt about it! That is true! There were two records I did that showed how different things were. I did a local record, *Los Hombres Calientes, Volume II*, and it was fairly successful—we did some touring and everything. Meanwhile, I did a record with Marcus Roberts on Columbia Records, a major label, and almost no one heard of it, no one knew about it, there wasn't much touring, and that's when I realized New York as the big time was finished.

"After a while, the majors dropped jazz altogether. Now New York is so flooded with people, and it's so expensive to live there, that a lot of guys are saying, 'Screw this. Oh, there's New Orleans!'"[2]

Although the organization of this book is partly chronological, it also reflects the less predictable flow of this improvisational art, a continuum of eclectic experimentation that has been astutely analyzed by drummer Bruce Raeburn, the curator of the Hogan Jazz Archive, in his book on New Orleans style and jazz history.[3] Too often in the past we got tidy chronological accounts, as if the splendid chaos of New Orleans music was a linear phenomenon in which ragtime led to jazz and culminated in bebop. Instead, the music is a surreal stream of happenings that continually echo, mimic, satirize, fold back on, and contradict each other: bop and post-bop, for example, do not necessarily represent "progress" in New Orleans since they sought to dismantle the city's shouters, singers, and swingers; jazz funerals and black Carnival celebrations go back long before jazz was "invented" by Jelly Roll Morton, disrupting the supposed stages in the "history" of jazz; French opera, one of the city's most under-reported contributions, was important in the education of jazz musicians, as was Italian opera, defying the convention that jazz and classical are entirely separate phenomena; and hip hop is not as new as it appears, but is an unexpected riff on Mardi Gras Indian rapping. Even the basic history of the city, indelibly French though the Spanish ruled during most of its colonial period, is one of upendedness and contradiction, the misrule of Mardi Gras. New Orleans reflects a dynamic phenomenon, a mirroring of neighborhood customs, where ensembles traditional and progressive interact freely, playing off each other in a combination of mimicry, inspiration, and parody. The city has always held fiercely onto the old even as it welcomed the new, a secret of its success.

This is fundamentally a book about jazz and brass bands. They came first and are linked with just about every style, no matter how contemporary. Trumpeter Leroy Jones, who grew up admiring James Brown as well as Louis Armstrong, believes that jazz is behind all the genres: "My experience is that the jazz musician is able to play anything. If his orientation is in jazz and swing, he's able to play the other stuff. But if you catch a musician who missed all of that and just came up with rock 'n' roll and '60s music, he'll never get up and swing because it's too complicated, a different type of comprehension. But a jazz player can go and make that gig. The core of jazz is rhythm and syncopation and being able to manipulate rhythms melodically with the same punctuation and articulation. It's the same punctuation. If you have that, you're able to step into other avenues within the genre and other genres as well."[4]

Jazz gets the longest chapter in this book, but like the others, it's a variation on the larger theme of New Orleans music rather than a separate component. Much of the music's charm has to do with its casual resistance to the restrictions of any single genre. "The music is all relative," says Jones. "Just play, just interpret the tune, don't get all choked up and confused about a 'concept.'" For banjoist Chris Edmunds, it's all part of one stream, not just jazz but "funk, Professor Longhair, Fats. We don't really call it different things. We regard it as New Orleans music";[5] for funk master Jon Cleary, "jazz is the first one: that's where it all came from, but these are just labels. The songs I write are all facets of my musical personality. I'm a good sponge. I'm good at absorbing stuff and learning. These styles are not separate from each other; we'll play a shuffle, we'll play a slow blues with jazzy changes, we'll play some funk, we'll play gospel, we'll play R&B—it all comes from the same place: it's all soul music, basically";[6] for Charlie Miller, who grew up on rhythm and blues, played with Dr. John in the '60s, and studied under Leonard Bernstein's first-chair trumpet player at the Manhattan School of Music, "the music is all the same; it just has different names because it comes from different geographies, different places. And then there is the business side: they've been able to divide the music into different styles where they could sell it—record bins with 'blues,' 'New World,' 'reggae'; then they could tell people they could be one kind of fan or another, and people would think that's what they liked, so that's what they would buy. But music is just a spiritual impulse; it can go any way."[7]

As the record bins disappeared, followed by the CD bins, the "genres" blurred even more. Drummer Bruce Raeburn states that the genres "seem like categories, but when you stand back, they bleed over the boundaries into other categories. Willie Tee was a modern jazz guy, but he also did R&B and a lot of other things; he was a principal in the Jazz Workshop; and someone like Zigaboo Modeliste: we think of him as a drummer in the Meters, but if you put him together with David Torkanowsky at Jazz Fest, you're going to hear an excellent, world-class modern jazz drummer as well. And that's the thing: these guys get marketed into categories, but if you track them, they're always breaking out of the categories."

Players in one style have always looked over their shoulders to see what others were doing, incorporating new elements whenever necessary to satisfy new audiences, creating so many "fusions" that the word loses meaning. An eclectic player like George Porter Jr. "can fulfill any assignment," says Raeburn. Musicians seize on different aspects of the tradition to create a personal sound: "They all pick different things to show people they're from New Orleans—it's part of the NOLA ID. They choose whatever has meaning for them."[8]

Singer Charmaine Neville, who was influenced by everyone from the Beatles to Roberta Hunter, is passionate on the subject: "Any kind of music to me is good music. You do it, it's good. And it makes you feel good. That's what music for me is. I know how good I feel, so I want other people to feel good. That's why I perform—because I want them to feel what I feel . . . My mother told me, 'Look, just get out there and do it all. Do it all. Don't be afraid. Do every kind of music you want to do.'"[9] This attitude is to the delight of fans but to the despair of managers and club owners. Snug Harbor, the renowned club on Frenchmen Street, lists Charmaine Neville's regular Monday night performance as "R&B," which is a bit misleading because of her eclecticism, but what else can they do? The label is as good as any.

This does not mean that what Charlie Miller calls "geographies" are meaningless and don't have distinctive profiles and histories. Any tradition—whether jazz, gospel, funk, brass band, zydeco, gospel, or classical—needs to have an identity and a history before it can expand or transcend itself. This book attempts to sort out the more significant genres and subgenres, fluid though they are. The Cajuns and the Mardi Gras Indians, to cite the most obvious examples, have completely separate histories and a fierce loyalty to their traditions. The point is that in New Orleans, because of how gigs happen and how ethnicities have been thrown together, even these have always been relative; and because of recent factors like Katrina, social media, ethnic diversity, and the dramatic incursion of new people seeking opportunities in the city, the population is now more like a gumbo (NOLA's favorite metaphor) than ever.

Any account of the music must examine the unique catalytic power of the city itself. As R&B composer-producer Harold Battiste said thirty years ago: "Musicians come and go, and their creations always seem directed at the city. Because after all is said and done, New Orleans is the star."[10] Why did New Orleans spawn America's greatest vernacular music and why does it still burn so fiercely, long after the great jazz eruptions in Chicago, Kansas City, Memphis, and others have declined or fizzled? How does a tradition happen that is intensely creative for generations, and what elements go into its continuity? Why have so many superb performers—trumpeters from Buddy Bolden to Wendell Brunious, sax players from Sidney Bechet to Donald Harrison, piano bangers from Jelly Roll Morton to Henry Butler, singers from Fats Domino to Topsy Chapman—emerged from the same place? This book seeks answers to these questions through interviews with musicians as well as archival documents from Tulane's Hogan Jazz Archive, the Historic New Orleans Collection, and Lincoln Center's jazz library.

New Orleans is so separate from the rest of America that it continues to be the victim of astonishing misinformation. Many continue to believe the city is barely hanging on since Katrina, and musicians tell me that when they are traveling, people ask them if the city is still flooded. The real flood is the dramatic increase in young musicians coming to the city to seek their fortunes, a phenomenon that is inspiring but also troubling to those trying to save their gigs and protect the New Orleans they grew up with. The immigration issue that rocks world politics takes on a special resonance in New Orleans. The city is experiencing its greatest musical renaissance since the Armstrong era, with many of its founding forms surging back, reinterpreted for a new age, for better or worse. One of the issues this book addresses is whether the new immigrants coming in from places as varied as Nashville and Tokyo are respectful of NOLA tradition or whether they are imposing alien sounds and values.

The reader should not be surprised if he or she continually runs into unfamiliar names. This is not a book about popular rappers like Lil Wayne, though hip hop itself is referenced when it is interwoven into jazz and brass-band gigs, as is the case with groups like the Soul Rebels. In this context, hip hop becomes very different from what one usually associates with the genre. Few artists covered in this book have broken into the national spotlight; the Rebirth Brass Band won a Grammy in 2012, Trombone Shorty was nominated for one in 2011, and Jon Batiste became the bandleader for Stephen Colbert's late night show in 2015—but they are the exceptions. This is true despite the extensive coverage of the scene following Katrina. "A lot of times, people just don't pay attention," says Leroy Jones. "Pops [Louis Armstrong] set a precedent, but there are a lot of great players who didn't get credit, and there continue to be players who don't get the credit they deserve, and they contribute greatly to the music here."[11]

Jones himself exemplifies this neglect; his virtuosity is second to none, but I run into New York jazz musicians all the time who have not heard of him. This volume can only cover a sampling of these artists, hopefully a representative one. I have tried to pick first-class musicians—not hard to find in New Orleans—who represent different attitudes and sensibilities and have sought to weave their voices into a conversation, both within and between chapters, not unlike the call-response dynamic in the music.

I've often been struck by the humility, bordering on self-abnegation, of those I have interviewed. In New Orleans, it's about music, not egos. Bruce Daigrepont, the city's long-standing Cajun master, is typical: "A lot of people say, 'Oh you know there's a category now for the Grammys. You could win a Grammy. You need to jump on the bandwagon.' I don't care about that. That's not important. If I win a Grammy, that would be great. But that's not what motivates me." What does motivate him, he says, is keeping his tradition alive, the songs and "the great musicians I have playing with me."[12] "Nobody is trying to make it big," says banjoist Chris Edmunds. "It's about relaxing, getting to know people, having a good time—not about competing. The musicians here teach each other."[13] This is an age-old tradition. Dave Bartholomew recalls that in the 1940s, people were willing to scrape by "because they wanted to play that music . . . All the musicians I played with in those days, they all wanted to rehearse. They didn't have any 'He didn't come, he come late'—we didn't have that. So the bandleaders had an easy time of it. There wasn't no money anyhow. So you had to really want to be there on your own. You just liked what they were doing."[14]

Allen Toussaint drew a contrast between this intense commitment and the "assembly-line music" that constitutes the mainstream norm: "There are some musics that are the same, and you can just put a different person on that track, on that assembly line. And some do very well; you can make a lot of money. This is the trend: now today she's singing on top of this music, tomorrow he's singing on top, but it's the same thing."[15] The artists I interviewed are not bland enough to make it onto the corporate-pop assembly line, and many have no wish to. Part of this is economics: New Orleans is a city full of musicians but does not have much of a music industry. Still, many musicians are resistant to the whole idea of the pop mainstream. As pianist Eddie Bo puts it, "They *make* 'em superstars. I heard a man on national television singing so far under the key—singing out of tune—while people like Walter ['Wolfman' Washington] never get heard of. They've got some giants, man." Washington is indeed a giant, a highly visible one (he's been doing the same gig at d.b.a. since the '90s), but like Bo lamented, many outside New Orleans have never heard of him. When Bo said this in 1981, he was content to play for himself, for tourists, and for loyal locals who cared about his music: "To worry about getting out there to get people to hear—that's just dead stuff." When he did play "out there" for a large crowd, he worried that the audience was "not going to hear what I'm capable of doing because I won't feel it."[16]

The profound connection between the quality of a performance and the engagement of the audience—a synergy that is more powerful in New Orleans than anywhere I have been—is a central idea in this book. To be sure, New Orleans artists are capable of putting on good shows in places other than their native city, and many tell me they particularly enjoy playing abroad, where they are treated like rock stars. Nonetheless, artists like Bo are convinced they do their best shows in the city because in bigger markets they "won't feel it" and will fail to unleash their full creativity. When I started work on this project, Bo was following the same pattern, playing the happy hour at Jimmy Buffett's Margaritaville (the happiest hour anywhere), along with a few other regular engagements. He was content, he said, to supplement his income by doing local architectural renovation.[17]

This is not to say NOLA performers don't care about recognition. Bo is clearly upset that "giants" like Walter "Wolfman" Washington "never get heard of." There is a poignant tension between a longing for fame and a relief at not attaining it. Singer John Boutte speaks about Jimmy Scott, one of many unrecognized artists: "He had so many great songs, and his life was similar to mine—a little scary, being that close to fame but not really getting there." And yet Boutte gets as close as he needs to. At the 2014 Jazz Fest, he participated in a tribute to Dr. John and was surprised to find himself on a billboard with Bruce Springsteen, Allen Toussaint, the Allman Brothers, the Neville Brothers, George Porter, the original Meters, Zigaboo Modeliste, Irma Thomas, and the Blind Boys of Alabama: "Here I am with all these iconic New Orleans figures and rock 'n' roll guys, singing harmonies with those guys. I had to run from my d.b.a. gig, and I pulled up on my bicycle next to limousines, Rolls Royces and SUVs. And everybody was treating me like I was just one of those cats." When I pointed out that he *is* one of those cats, that people may know about Dr. John and Springsteen but have no idea who Zigaboo is or Irma Thomas or the Blind Boys or George Porter or even the Meters or Toussaint, he paused, then agreed: "They may have listened to the music many times and have no idea. They don't have that big persona—which is a good thing. You've gotta be careful what you ask for: I've never asked for fame. Fame is fleeting like beauty or youth. The only way you're going to keep that up is get plastic surgery. Just grow old gracefully. I just want to keep my health and be happy. I'd had a frustrating day, thinking about what's ahead of me just to get settled again [after Katrina], and somebody said, 'Mr. Boutte, we love you.' That's all you need."[18]

Certain identifiable qualities set New Orleans music apart and are at the center of this book: an unapologetic embrace of melody, an indifference to anything that isn't danceable, a rhythmic displacement that goes back to the history of second lines. But there is another element the book addresses, too, something very hard to pin down precisely because it's so powerful. Most historians place the first music that sounds like New Orleans jazz as erupting at the end of the nineteenth century, but others, like the eminent music historian Henry Kmen, take the origins as far back as the 1840s, when operas and balle masques were as likely to be spilling out into the streets as performed indoors: "Is it not here . . . in the whole overpowering atmosphere of music in New Orleans that the Negro began to shape the music that would eventually be jazz?"[19] Today's music scholars tend to be impatient with something as unquantifiable as "atmosphere," whether overpowering or not. Myths about exoticism, spontaneity, and primitive instinct are dismissed as reactionary clichés. The New Orleans scholar Connie Atkinson, for example, believes they have led to distortion and a denigration of talent: "Musical activities have been marginalized, talent and expertise have been subverted, and cultural activities have been exoticized in a way that denies intelligence and agency." The notion of jazz as a "magic" accident erupting because New Orleans was a port where Africans and Europeans were thrown together comes under particular fire.[20]

Replacing vagaries about magic and exoticism with facts about musical activities and social processes has resulted in a clearer understanding of how the music evolved and how it is constantly in danger of being appropriated and exploited. It certainly helped me understand basic realities, including how players improvise, make a living, and connect with mentors. Does this mean, however, that New Orleans's seductive mythology should be thrown out altogether? Some myths happen to be true, in essence if not in every detail, and anyone who spends time in the city on a regular basis knows it is indeed a space filled with magic and mystery, where words like "primitive" and "exotic" are not out of place. Jason Berry, an authoritative and long-time NOLA observer, cites the elusiveness of the culture, "so close, so beckoning with its aromas and spectacles, yet raising the guard on its elemental mysteries, an essence that defies easy explanations."[21]

Musicians themselves speak repeatedly of the untamable "spirit" of the city, the near-palpable presence of ancestors, the ineffable ambiance that makes the music happen. Indeed, "magic" is a central word in their vocabulary. They disagree on many issues—the meaning of tradition, the musicianship of the new immigrants, the significance of bebop, the definition of funk—but on that fundamental point they are united. Dr. Michael White, for example, acknowledges that "social and economic forces" have shaped New Orleans music, as they do any other, but believes the decisive influence is more intangible: "New Orleans is still a mystical, magical place. Her streets hold the secrets of 10,000 years. Here, cemeteries are the resting places where the practitioners of opera, work songs, symphonies, and the blues danced the bamboula and quadrilles, waltzes and the calinda . . . The 'voice' of Buddy Bolden, the voice that arose from the deepest and most glorious side of human nature and that told all our stories for so long, is an immortal flame to be passed on forever."[22] As jazz guitarist Todd Duke told me: "Music takes on a life of its own in New Orleans."[23] It's a palpable presence, "a living organism," in the words of Chris Edmunds, something that hovers in the humid air, constantly beckoning and bringing people together.[24] It doesn't do to see jazz funerals simply as "cultural plebiscites" and music as a series of "social processes" in need of "demystify-ing." If the old romanticism was exaggerated, the new sociology can be its inversion, another way of avoiding the music.

New Orleans music has a complex energy that is immediately apparent but difficult to pin down because it is simultaneously intense and laid-back, open-hearted and laconic. Sorting this out is daunting. The young artist Eric "Benny" Bloom, for example, wants his trumpet to be "loose" and "clean," "comical" and "thoughtful," words that aren't often strung together, but they define a free-spirited sensibility typical of players I interviewed, a reality that harks back to Armstrong. Bloom knows exactly what he's saying, and anyone who experiences this music firsthand knows that paradox and upendedness, the spirit of Carnival, are the essence of New Orleans music.

Another challenge is covering a fresh talent like Eric Bloom, a newcomer who doesn't sound like anyone else. The difficulty with writing about any-thing contemporary is that things change and a book can become dated quickly. New musicians and ensembles continually erupt out of nowhere, then reconfigure or vanish; rarely has a scene been so volatile and mutable. Yet New Orleans is also the most traditional of cities, the most resistant to change and to all things modern. The counterpoint between old and new is a defining characteristic. Despite the influx of new talent, ineffable realities like those cited above don't alter, and several patterns now seem firmly in place: the brass-band renaissance, the new racial diversity, the surge of female performers, the simultaneous embrace of traditional and modern jazz, the visibility of the Mardi Gras Indians, the proliferation of styles, the resurgence of small clubs. None of this is entirely new, but each has accelerated in the twenty-first century.

One of the most striking changes is the racial diversity of bands. It's hard to wrap one's brain around how different things were not so long ago. Until recently, it was rare to see Asian players, and the mingling of blacks and whites was not as common as one might think. Drummer Barry Martyn remembers coming to New Orleans from England in 1961: "I was the first white musician to join a colored local, as it was called in those days, and caught hell for it. Most of the musicians I play with are black. I was arrested for 'rehearsing with a colored orchestra.' Can you imagine being charged with that? The judge, I believe Judge Bablyon, said, 'See boy, down here we don't mix cream with our coffee. You understand me?'

"And I said, 'Yes sir, I understand, and I'm never going to do that no more.' Bam! '20 or 20—$20 fine or twenty days cleaning up the French Market.' When I got out there, I went back to doing the same thing I was always doing."[25] Trombonist Lucien Barbarin told me that, even as recently as the 1970s, he was the token black player in all-white bands. Now his regular gigs are with musicians who are black and white.

The new visibility of female artists is also a startling change. New Orleans music, like any other, has gender issues. Female singers have always been part of the tradition, but women brass and reed players, until recently, were rare. Clarinetist Doreen Ketchens told me that male players have a difficult time recognizing female talent and try to keep females out of gigs. The horn scene is notoriously male-dominated (a reality in classical music as well), but that is starting to change for the better. The Pinettes, for example, are now one of the most popular brass bands, so much so that they have split into two. To see them live is to realize in a dramatic way the importance of gender: the notes are the same as with male brass bands, but the vibe is profoundly different.

This is part of a larger pattern of inclusion where LGBT artists are surging onto the music scene, a phenomenon that can be traced at least as far back as the early '90s, when bounce, a sub-style of hip hop, emerged in the city and eventually made its way onto HBO's *Treme*. Bounce has mainly straight rappers, but its trailblazers—Big Freedia, Katey Red, Sissy Nobby, and Cheeky Blakk—are proudly gay. Galactic, a pioneering avant-garde funk group that shifts dramatically from album to album, has combined their sounds with those of Allen Toussaint, Trombone Shorty, Walter "Wolfman" Washington, the Rebirth Brass Band, and Bo Dollis, exemplifying the wide spectrum in New Orleans today; when hip hop drum machines and samples are combined with "real" instruments and singers, anything can happen.[26]

It is essential to record the voices of these artists now, not only as representatives of the present, but as windows into the past, since Katrina has washed away so many archives. This is a street art passed down generation to generation, and young musicians are eager to tell their stories—who their mentors were and how the tradition was communicated to them. Michael White warned me that once these witnesses are gone, an entire oral history will pass away. Comparing old Blue Note records and boxing the results into categories has been a way of avoiding the chaotic present of a largely unheralded post-Katrina renaissance.

This is a book about live music. Jazz is an adventure in the moment and can't be captured on recordings. They are valuable as archives, educational tools, and objects of nostalgia, but what they "record" is not the real thing. New Orleans music has an energy that is often snuffed out in a studio. John Boutte believes that "a studio is like a prison. People think they can always do another take. It's better to be on a tightrope without a net. Anybody can make a record." Keith Jarrett, in an often-quoted remark, puts it starkly: "Jazz is there and gone. It happens. You have to be present for it. That simple."[27]

The irony of jazz is that it rocketed to international acclaim just as it was starting up in the early twentieth century largely because recordings were starting up as well—yet recordings contradict what jazz is about. As Nicholas Payton tartly observed, "The idea of recording is not a black aesthetic—to think about, 'Oh, let's record.' In fact, some of the early musicians . . . Buddy Bolden was afraid to record, because he thought it might steal his soul. Black people have more of an oral aesthetic."[28] Ironically, some of the most wonderful recordings today are of Payton himself—as well as Boutte and Jarrett—but none can do justice to the performers heard live. Classical music is also better experienced live, but because it does not rely on improvisation (at least most of the time), a recording can "record" something more essential and real. New Orleans is defined by the anarchy of now; in the neighborhood music bars, you never know what's going to happen next or who will appear on the stage, only that it will happen late. Nor do you know precisely what "type" of music will erupt. It all depends on who shows up, in the band as well as the audience. Players from different styles jam and interchange personnel on a regular basis. Embracing this fluidity is central to understanding the music and the culture. There is a dynamic relationship between audiences and performers, streets and clubs, beats and offbeats, and any one of these things can quickly become another. None of this can be captured on a recording. The visual spectacle is important as well; one needs to see Kermit Ruffins hoisting his beer bottle in a toast or Jon Batiste marching into a set with his magic whistle or the Indians parading in feathered effulgence on Super Sunday.

One does not have to believe that recordings steal people's souls to recognize that they steal the essentialness of hearing this music live; the liveness itself is a kind of soul, a doppelganger that appears when a band is cooking so hot it becomes more than the sum of its parts. Drummers like Shannon Powell or Herlin Riley can turn any band they play with into another entity, and it can only happen in that moment. Now that so much musical reality is virtual, an endless series of YouTube uploads and videos, that soul is more valuable than ever.

Many bands covered in this book frequently come to New York, part of a synergy between the Big Apple and the Big Easy that started before Katrina and increased after it. The hurricane caused unimaginable destruction but also a surge of solidarity and creativity. Some NOLA artists moved to New York in exile but now have apartments there as well as a home in New Orleans, increasing the mutual vibe between two great music capitals.

This phenomenon isn't limited to New York, either; since the flood, all New Orleans music has traveled at an unprecedented rate around America and around the world. New Orleans music has become more popular since the

'90s, but its practitioners are still obscure, a gap this book seeks to address. Jon Cleary remembers that when he moved to New Orleans from England in the early '80s, "not many people knew about it. I was amazed—it was like a diamond in the rough. I developed an evangelical zeal about spreading the word about New Orleans." Cleary has the vantage point of an enraptured émigré: "Coming from the outside, you have the luxury of an objective point of view of New Orleans history and the different threads. Now it's kind of been discovered. It's been subject to all those elements that have changed the entire world. You have the internet; Jazz Fest has become really established. In the time I've been here, the government has promoted New Orleans as a tourist destination in a way that it wasn't when I first came here." "Kind of been discovered" is just right, and indeed, Cleary is a good example. How many R&B or funk fans even know about Jon Cleary, even though his keyboard has rocked the city since the early '80s? Barry Martyn, also from England, points out that the phenomenon is worldwide: when he toured Sweden in the late '60s, "it was bebop country. They were brought up a different way. Now New Orleans-style bands are there."[29] And they're everywhere. Asia, particularly Japan, is a New Orleans jazz center, where players are revered in a way they are not in the US. But again, how many music enthusiasts know about Martyn, who was in New Orleans twenty years before Cleary?

When I first started work on this book, I worried about the willingness of musicians to talk about their art. Billy Collins once mused on the dilemma of getting a poet to speak about poetry: "Poets are notoriously unreliable commentators on their own work, as they should be. Getting a poet to talk about his or her poem is like trying to get a dog to look into a mirror; no matter how well-groomed the poodle, the creatures prefer the smell of something real to their own scentless reflections. A lesson for us all."[30] Musicians prefer the smell of something real as well, and many were initially shy or skeptical about talking. Allen Toussaint said he was wary about interviews, which he found "painful" because interviewers couldn't talk the New Orleans talk and weren't really interested in the music; lesser-known musicians were not used to talking with interviewers at all. Once they warmed up, however, they spoke with humor, eloquence, and a startling humility. I have recorded them in their own voices, without cleaning up profanity or eccentricities of language.

They often talk the way they perform: Leroy Jones with refinement and polish, Kermit Ruffins with garrulous affability, Katja Toivola with unflinching directness, Victor Goines with imperious confidence, Allen Toussaint with mellow sincerity, Jon Batiste with charismatic boisterousness. Phil Frazier speaks in staccato phrases, Germaine Bazzle in sinuous paragraphs. Sometimes the similarity between talking and playing is so close as to be eerie:

Jason Marsalis's speech is full of unexpected spaces and pauses—exactly like his drumming; Aurora Nealand is probing and analytical, like her saxophone and clarinet. Conversations were wide-ranging, and the digressions often turned out to be the gems, but the questions I posed in one form or another were: "How do you view your place in the current NOLA scene, how do you make music, and how do you see yourself in relation to history?" Many seemed to enjoy the opportunity to share, especially about the historical element. As Bruce Raeburn pointed out: "It's a luxury to reflect on the history because what's really happening is that musicians are scrambling for the next gig to make some decent money." Clarinetist Victor Goines told me it's crucial to see beyond the next gig and view oneself in relation to what came before: "Dizzy [Gillespie] used to say you can't know where you're going unless you know where you came from. I like to apply music to life. Knowing the history of what you do is equivalent to looking at old photos of your ancestors, and if you're fortunate enough to look at their faces long enough and concentrate for a long period of time, no matter how different you think you look from them, you'll find one thing in their face that reminds you of you, and that's what the music should always do. It should always remind you of the people who came before you. No matter how avant-garde, how harmonically or rhythmically complex, you need to evoke the spirits of the ancestors each and every time."[31]

As this book aims to show, the ancestors are still very much alive. Native New Orleanians like Goines and Toussaint understand the meaning of the culture in a deep, intimate way, but outsiders, émigrés, and sojourners—Aurora Nealand, James Evans, Jon Cleary, Tom McDermott—bring a fresh, startling perspective. An example is violinist-actress Lucia Micarelli, who in the HBO show *Treme* plays a post-Katrina immigrant musician emerging from the street. Her post-*Treme* story is an eloquent summary of what the music and the culture are about: "New Orleans is a unique place—I don't think there's another city like it, at least not in America. Music and culture run so deep, and the generosity of the musicians blows my mind. It feels to me like they understand the value of tradition and family and passing along the tunes and the stories more than people elsewhere—and as a result, connect emotionally to audiences and each other in a much deeper way. I have so much love for that city, and so much gratitude for the musicians and artists who shared their world with me. My musical horizons were truly broadened by my experience there."[32]

Chapter One

JAZZ CLASSICAL

Opera is jazz's grandma.
—John Boutte

In New Orleans, music is a single, spontaneous flow that washes over normally segregated traditions and genres. Jazz is strongly connected to opera and symphonic music and has been since its origins. Many New Orleans jazz players are comfortable with classical music, including Louis Armstrong, who played with Leonard Bernstein, and Wynton Marsalis, who has tried to usurp the Bernstein mantle himself and has played impeccable performances of the trumpet repertory, from Haydn to Hindemith. (His sultry rendition of Ravel's "Habanera" is peerless.) Marsalis also has written several jazz-classical hybrids, including the multi-genre *At the Octoroon Balls* and the Pulitzer Prize-winning *Blood on the Fields*. Wynton rarely performs as a classical soloist these days, but his brother, saxophonist Branford Marsalis, is taking up where he left off, playing Ravel, Villa Lobos, Milhaud, and Glazunov with the New York Philharmonic and the New Jersey Symphony.

The crosscurrents flow in many directions: Olivia Cook, better known as Olivia "Lady Charlotte" Cook, dreamed of being a classical pianist in the early twentieth century; stymied by segregation, she played jazz on Bourbon Street instead, forming her own band and continuing her career into the twenty-first century. Her favored form was the jazz anthem because it is "close to classical."[1] Antoine Reynaldo Diel studied to be an opera singer but fell in love with jazz and is now one of the most powerful voices on the current New Orleans scene; his opera training helped both his singing and acting abilities: "Being an actor helps you connect with the lyric; it does the job for you."[2] Jon Batiste recently played Chopin in the middle of a late night set at New York's

Dizzy Gillespie Club Coca Cola, a moment that might have baffled New Yorkers but would not surprise those who know New Orleans history and are
familiar with Batiste's education at Juilliard. Batiste likes to point out that he's
not the first: "James Booker would play in the Maple Leaf Bar some of the
most beautiful Chopin you ever heard on a honky-tonk upright piano. And
he would put it in New Orleans blues style—that little bit off, slightly left-of-
center thing that makes everybody dance. Since I'm from that New Orleans
culture, it's not even a conscious decision to do that. I just naturally hear it. It's
part of who I am."[3] Booker himself, an admirer of Ernesto Lecuona, played
"Malagueña" and other piano works as part of his repertory, a perfect match
for his Cuban-inflected style. When John Boutte performed with Trombone
Shorty at Aspen in 2014, he included a jam session featuring Bartók piano
music: "It's so beautiful, right? Everybody that came in said, 'Wow!'"[4] Funk
pianist John Gros, whose mentor was George Porter Jr., was first taught by
classical mentors at Loyola University: "They were huge influences on my
education. I learned how strings blend with the brass, how all the frequen-
cies line up. Classical was very important to me."[5] In his role as educator, Ellis
Marsalis, who performed the Hindemith clarinet quintet for his college jury
("rather badly," he sighs), speaks of the classical chamber tradition and its
connection to the jazz ensemble, especially the quintet: "It's not just five dudes
playing. The quintet in the jazz idiom is parallel to the string quartet in classical music. There's so much music out there for the jazz quintet, but it's been
hit and miss. The quintet can be a means to introduce music both to the musicians and in schools."[6]

This does not mean that the two traditions are the same, only that they are
closely related. "I love classical," says Allen Toussaint, but when I told him that
I heard Debussy and Chopin elements in his solo playing, he had a caveat:
"Yes, but I'm a cat playing it, I'm not very legitimate. That's all right, I still
love it. I love it from my point of view." A bizarre and wonderful example was
Toussaint learning the Grieg Piano Concerto in the wrong key. "I learned it
in B flat minor because my piano was always a half step flat. I compensated
by playing a half step higher, but I didn't know that was what was going on at
the time. Playing along with the recording so I could learn it, I thought this
was right 'cause it sounds like that. I was over twenty before I learned that this
was Grieg's Piano Concerto *in A minor*. I hadn't seen the music, I had just
listened to the records. I did a lot of things like that. I flirted with 'Rhapsody
in Blue'—in the wrong key."[7]

Normally we think of classical as nurtured by vernacular elements—Bach
by church hymns, Haydn by folk dances, Chopin by Polish mazurkas, Dvořák
by spirituals. In New Orleans, the currents flowed both ways. The French

John Boutte. Photograph by Brandon Xeureb, Xistence Photography.

fostered an attitude toward lyricism that created a unified musical sensibility. In French culture, singing was paramount, whether in the opera house or the concert salon, and piano playing was highly valued. Boutte regards his art as rooted in French opera as much as in gospel or black Indian music: "The genres are fluid. They're all part of the New Orleans shelf: jazz, gospel, Pops, the Barbarins, Fats, Smokey Johnson, Little Richard, David Bartholomew, the Mardi Gras Indians, and classical. Remember, New Orleans had the first opera house in America and all-black orchestras in the Creole opera."[8] Opera is part of Boutte's art: "You've got to know the classics. Three years ago, I had the New Orleans Opera Creole singing Leonard Cohen's 'Hallelujah'—seven properly trained African-American opera singers I was using as background. My band asked who was singing? I said, 'Opera singers.' They said, 'What?' I said, 'You've got to realize that opera is jazz's grandma.'"[9]

As Jon Batiste reminds us, opera had a powerful influence on Armstrong's style: "Louis Armstrong was influenced by Luisa Tetrazzini. When he was a child, he would walk around and hear music spilling into the street from the opera house. And when he played his instrument, he wanted to sing like that. He wanted it to be as beautiful and potent as when you hear a beautiful voice. Many things influence someone like Armstrong. People don't expect it, but when you say it, it makes perfect sense."[10]

Numerous musicians in the city see themselves this way: connected to a rich and complex history where an aria and a call-response pattern have equal

Louis Armstrong. Gibson Photographers, Chicago. Courtesy of the Hogan Jazz Archive, Tulane University.

significance. S. Frederick Starr points out that this was true from the beginning: "Armstrong was not an operagoer, but he did not need to be. Whites, black, Creoles of color, and Sicilians in New Orleans all came together under the spell of opera . . . Satchmo viewed opera as a living music and a bountiful well of lyrical inspiration . . . one may speak of Satchmo's bel canto style of trumpet playing, the creation of long lyric lines above the melody. This, too, must be traced to the presence in the New Orleans of Satchmo's youth of several brilliant Sicilian brass bands that carried that tradition into the streets."[11]

Armstrong often warmed up with selections from Italian opera and incorporated snippets from *Pagliacci*, *Rigoletto*, and *Cavalleria rusticana* (which he called "my big thing") in standards like "Tiger Rag." He told Richard Hadlock in an interview that the quartet from *Rigoletto* was one of the earliest numbers he sang and that much of his music "from the olden days" came from "French opera and things like that." His version of "Araby," with the Fletcher Henderson orchestra, incorporated Gounod's *Faust*, including Valentine's farewell aria. The Austro-German repertory crept in as well, especially Von

Suppe's "Poet and Peasant" overture. He was raised as a teenager on Victor Talking Machine Company recordings of the Original Dixieland Band, but "Caruso too, and Henry Burr, Galli-Curci, Tetrazzini—they were all my favorites. Then there was the Irish tenor, McCormack—beautiful phrasing."[12]

During an Italian tour, Armstrong joked that his photographers were eager to shoot him at La Scala next to "those big cats like Verdi and Wagner . . . they wanted that picture to put up in the lobby, me with those big boys there." To Armstrong, Dixieland jazz and Italian opera shared a similar sensuality— "we play 'em both from the heart"—and he was not afraid, in Joshua Berrett's words, to transfer "the bravura gestures of operatic divas to his instrument."[13]

Armstrong was not the only jazz fan of John McCormack. Bunk Johnson imported one of this iconic tenor's most beautiful standards into the trumpet repertory, as Barry Martyn explains: "Who doesn't like opera? How could you not love Caruso, John McCormack? Bunk Johnson was a big fan of John McCormack. He recorded some of his songs. 'Where the River Shannon Flows'—Bunk got that from John McCormack. This is a town where all the influences are tossed around."[14] Such eclecticism has always been part of New Orleans culture.

One of the great unsung stories in American musical history is of the centrality of New Orleans opera, both in the development of jazz and the broader history of opera in America. The late Philip Frohnmayer, professor of music and coordinator of vocal performance at Loyola, said that "New Orleans is an opera town. It's not an odd thing to be an opera singer here. It has a little to do with dressing up and Carnival, and masks, and it's a little bit more laid-back way of life. It allows singers to give their bodies the kind of relaxation that good singing requires."[15] The history, traditions, and lifestyle that make the city conducive to opera are thus the same as the sources of inspiration for other types of music. For jazz players, the laid-backness of the culture makes for better breathing, intonation, and improvisation, and Carnival, with its parades, is the foundation of brass-band music.

In many ways, New Orleans was the opera center in the New World. It was the first American city to have opera seasons, staging its first opera in the eighteenth century and boasting three companies by the mid-nineteenth. The site of important American premieres, it was the subject of enraptured reviews by Walt Whitman, who came to New Orleans to cover the opera scene for the *Brooklyn Eagle* before remaking himself into America's most operatic poet. French opera was directly connected to early New Orleans jazz, as jazz players were often trained by orchestra players from the opera pit. Italian opera was even more popular with early jazz players, who followed Armstrong's lead in importing excerpts from the Italian repertory into jazz

Exterior of the French Opera House, New Orleans. Courtesy of Jack Belsom.

standards. Throughout its history, New Orleans music has been defined by the musical sophistication of Creoles—black, white, and mixed—whose pioneering of jazz was infused with their love of European concert music and opera. Prominent players like the Tio brothers (all clarinetists) mentored jazz players, who later returned the favor by teaching jazz riffs to classical artists. The Tios used the European solfege sight-singing method endorsed by Cherubini and Rossini, thus passing down an important European pedagogy to African Americans who played "by ear."[16]

Opera is not the first thing we think of when we contemplate New Orleans, yet the Crescent City has enjoyed a nearly unbroken operatic tradition since the late eighteenth century. New Orleans's first documented opera, André Grétry's *Sylvain*, was staged at the Théâtre St. Pierre in 1796. In *The World That Made New Orleans*, Ned Sublette posits that the orchestra consisted in part of enslaved players. If he is correct, the participation of African Americans of the lowliest station in elite European performances using Western instruments went back as far as the Spanish colonial period.

From *Sylvain* onward, New Orleans has enjoyed numerous resident companies supplemented by visiting productions from around the world. The French-speaking population was served by the Théâtre d'Orléans, located behind St. Louis Cathedral and led by the visionary impresario John Davis, while a growing English-speaking population enjoyed productions at the

Adeline Patti. Courtesy of Jack Belsom.

Camp Street Theater under James Caldwell. The intense rivalry between the two was good for the city and beyond it as well. To beat the impossibly steamy summer weather, Davis packed his troupe off to New York and Philadelphia, where in midsummer he gave American "premieres" of operas he had already staged in New Orleans.

The total number of important operas the Crescent City staged for the first time in the US is unknown, but even a partial list is mind-boggling. Davis presented Rossini's *La Gazza Ladra, La Donna del Largo, Le Comte Ory*, and *L'Italiana in Algeri* between 1828 and 1833, while Caldwell staged Weber's *Der Freischütz* and Mozart's *Don Giovanni* and *Le Nozze di Figaro*. When Caldwell opened the lavish St. Charles Theatre in 1835, the opera scene heated up even more with US premieres of Bellini's *Norma* and Donizetti's *Parisina*, followed by Davis's staging of Meyerbeer. Within an eight-year period, New Orleans had premiered a dozen works by Donizetti alone.

Two terrible fires brought down the Caldwell empire, but the Théâtre d'Orléans forged on, the catalyst for what Jack Belsom, the premiere scholar of New Orleans opera, calls the Golden Age, a period of unbroken glory that lasted until the Civil War: 109 operas by some thirty-five composers, including American premieres of operas by Rossini, Verdi (twenty-six stagings of *Il Trovatore* in both Italian and French versions alone), Halevy, and Meyerbeer.[17] More new works were mounted in New Orleans than in any city in

America, and according to S. Frederick Starr, the city heard more American premieres than the rest of the country combined. Just before the Civil War brought a sudden, unwelcome intermission to the opera scene, the new French Opera House opened in 1859 on Bourbon Street with Rossini's *Guillaume Tell*, which had premiered in New Orleans in the original French in 1842 (having been incorrectly cited as premiering in New York eleven years earlier); by the early twentieth century, it was staged by the French Opera more than 110 times.[18]

In the nineteenth century, the city attracted America's hottest divas, including Henriette Sontag and Anna de la Grange. A particular favorite was the seventeen-year-old soprano Adelina Patti, who added to her New Orleans pedigree by concertizing with Louis Moreau Gottschalk in Cuba. She appeared in *Lucia di Lammermoor* just before her triumph on the international scene, and in New Orleans in *Il Trovatore* and Meyerbeer's *Le Pardon de Ploërmel* (its US premiere), among others.

The number and importance of productions and artists in this period is hard to wrap one's brain around, but the Civil War and its aftermath brought everything to a fiery halt, along with the rest of the city's cultural life. Even so, opera sustained its stubborn durability; a German National Theatre opened on Baronne Street in 1866, and otherwise depressed New Orleanians were able to enjoy *The Magic Flute* and *Fidelio*. By the 1870s, the French Opera House picked up where it had left off, premiering Thomas's *Mignon*, Lalo's *L'Roi d'Ys*, and Massenet's *Le Cid*. The Wagner flame was slow to ignite in New Orleans (its large German population notwithstanding), but it flared up brilliantly when Walter Damrosch presented three Ring operas along with *Lohengrin*, *Tristan*, and *Die Meistersinger* in a single week in 1895—topped off by a Sunday matinee of *Fidelio*. Even for Damrosch, the founder of Carnegie Hall, this was a remarkable run.

The first years of the twentieth century brought the touring Metropolitan Opera Company to New Orleans with *Parsifal*, while the French Opera House premiered French works, including Massenet's *Don Quichotte*. But the latter burned down, joining the Théâtre d'Orléans, the German National Theater, and the St. Charles, all victims to the city's greatest curse after hurricanes and mosquitoes.

By World War II, aficionados were craving a central venue to finally contain the wonderful but sprawling chaos of New Orleans opera, and in 1943, the New Orleans Opera Association emerged to provide a permanent company with a stable season. Housed in the Municipal Auditorium (unreliable acoustics and all) and later the Theater of Performing Arts (next door to Congo Square, the birthplace of jazz), the association presided over productions of

Interior of the French Opera House, New Orleans. Courtesy of Jack Belsom.

standard repertory and neglected French works as well as modern operas by Menotti, Previn, Musgrave, Floyd, and Heggie.

An impressive stream of stars appeared in New Orleans throughout the twentieth century, just as they did in the nineteenth, beginning with Caruso and continuing with Licia Albanese, Victoria de los Angeles, Montserrat Caballé, Kirsten Flagstad, Mario Lanza (a rare opera appearance in *Madame Butterfly*), Roberta Peters, Placido Domingo, Boris Christoff, Lisa Della Casa, Eileen Farrell, Evelyn Lear, and Beverly Sills, to name a smattering. Since the 1970s, luminaries such as Gary Lakes, June Anderson, Carlo Bergonzi, Erie Mills, and Gran Wilson have flocked to the city. Singers with ties to New Orleans include Norman Treigle, Barbara Faulkner Bernard, LaVergne Monette, Shirley Verrett, Natalia Rom, Jeanne-Michèle Charbonnet, and Elizabeth Futral. Bernard sang with the New Orleans opera for forty-three years in fifty-nine productions. Verrett, a native New Orleanian, battled racism in California as a mezzo in the '60s and went on to become a renowned soprano and music theater star. Rom emigrated to New Orleans from the Soviet Union in 1976 and studied at Loyola University, which has an important opera program, as does Louisiana State University in Baton Rouge.

Not surprisingly, André Previn's 1998 opera, *A Streetcar Named Desire*, was staged in New Orleans. Tennessee Williams is not just a dramatist, but a "serious poet," says Previn, who regards Williams's plays as operas: "The music's missing, but they're operas anyway."[19] Eschewing overt references to jazz, Previn builds jazzy phrases and nuances into an otherwise conventional lyric opera that is sometimes meandering, sometimes eloquent, distinguished mainly for its ending, a repeating trumpet motif over a somber pedal punctuated by a dissonant harp for the doomed heroine's "kindness of strangers" speech. By contrast, Alex North's moody, subjective score for Elia Kazan's 1951 film version of *Streetcar* embraces New Orleans jazz, working it seamlessly into a dreamlike symphonic narrative. This is the first full-blown symphonic jazz crossover piece in the cinema and still the greatest. If Previn is right that *Streetcar* is already an opera without the music, then North's creation of an interior narrative is entirely logical. From the surreal blues and dance music in Blanche's hallucinated reveries to the collapsing glissandi in the rape scene, the orchestral music is vividly operatic; the lyricism of Williams's language provides all the vocal music one needs.

Hurricane Katrina briefly interrupted the opera scene, damaging the Theater of Performing Arts and leading to the cancellation of the scheduled fall productions of *Otello* and *Figaro*. Undaunted, the New Orleans Opera Association mounted a benefit performance on March 4, 2006, that included Domingo, Elizabeth Futral, Frederica von Stade, and Paul Groves. As reported by Jack Belsom, this was "a highly successful" program of arias and ensembles that "drew rapturous applause from 7000 music-starved New Orleanians who crowded the New Orleans Arena."[20] For two years after the storm, productions were staged at Tulane, braving dicey acoustics and a cramped stage; the first production, mounted in October 2007, was *Le Nozze di Figaro*, chosen because of its modest staging requirements. Now the company, renamed Mahalia Jackson Theater of the Performing Arts, is back to four productions a year, with symphonic music played in the Orpheum, the former vaudeville palace resuscitated in fall 2015, with Mahler's Symphony No. 2, the "resurrection symphony," chosen as its opening work.

Opera and jazz obviously spring from different traditions and have separate fan bases, but in New Orleans the two worlds often come together. Bruce Raeburn goes so far as to say that "the essence of jazz resides in the expressive African American vernacular practices that transformed arias or habanera."[21] Players in the New Orleans opera pit and symphony orchestras were important mentors for young musicians who became jazz and brass-band players. (Jelly Roll Morton's teacher, William J. Nickerson, was in an African American symphony orchestra.) Sometimes the line was passed down directly, as in the case of Ray Lopez, cornetist for Tom Brown's Band from Dixieland, whose father played cornet in the French opera. One of the most elegant crossovers is the obbligato of Creole clarinet playing exemplified by Sidney Bechet, whose early musical impressions came from French opera and Caruso recordings, and whose style was nurtured by clarinetists in the French opera orchestra.[22]

The spirit of opera during New Orleans's Golden Age forecast the spirit of jazz. Opera poured out into the streets; singers and musicians of various ethnicities performed at huge outdoor parties, including some at Congo Square. Ethnicities crossed in all directions. Snippets of the Italian repertory became popular items on the street and were picked up by jazzmen like Louis Armstrong, just as habaneras became part of the repertory of King Oliver's Creole Jazz Band, while George Paoletti, an Italian American cornetist who played at the French opera for a quarter of a century, had a gig at Warren Easton High School, where he taught Meyer Weinberg and Louis Prima. Paoletti was one of many Italians who were employed by the French Opera House—there were so many, in fact, that the latter was often called "the Milano Conservatory."[23] Jazz became the great connector, both of ethnicities and seemingly divergent musical traditions. Although opera theaters like the St. Charles were the most opulent in the New World, the formal atmosphere of the opera scene today did not define the form in those days. Under the "order and decency" ethos of the Victorian era, opera in Europe and America was on its way to losing its partying, populist ambiance as well as its public support—but not in New Orleans. The absence of the Puritan ethic in the hedonistic French opera scene was surely a major reason the genre flourished and why so many touring companies were eager to come to "the land that care forgot."

One of the most important progeny of the French opera was Louis Moreau Gottschalk, America's first celebrity composer-pianist. Jon Batiste, a Gottschalk aficionado, says that Gottschalk was "one of the first, if not the first, to blend classical elements in the New Orleans aesthetic. He was the first universal star, a pop star; people loved him, royalty took him around as if he was a god of music—even before Jelly Roll. That's important to remember because lots of people, when they think of New Orleans music, think maybe it's just a party or just a good time in the street or the second line. And it is that, but it's also very deep, introspective musical levels of creation and insight; people who write in the tradition of Beethoven and Bach were also part of their lineage. Jelly Roll was another one—and Sidney Bechet, who wrote an opera. It's all there."[24]

As a boy, Gottschalk studied violin with the concertmaster of the opera orchestra and aspired to be an opera composer in Italy. The smoldering lyricism of Gottschalk miniatures like "Cradle Song" and "The Dying Poet" reflect his saturation in Golden Age opera culture even though his main instrument was the piano.

Even more decisive for his development was the vernacular music he heard as a child. The young "Moreau," as he was called, grew up near Esplanade in the fashionable Creole section at the end of the French Quarter near Congo Square, where the French allowed slaves to practice percussion music and ring dances. He absorbed New Orleans slave drummings and dance forms, forged them into a new form of art, and took them to the music capitals of Europe, where he wowed Chopin, Liszt, Bizet, and Borodin with a combination of Chopinesque glitter, Creole soulfulness, and African rhythm. Nothing like this hybrid had been heard before in either the New World or the Old. His New World sound repealed the squareness of nineteenth-century rhythm and created proto-jazz enclaves in Europe that retain their love of New Orleans music to this day.

A sophisticated aesthetic gleaned from Congo Square slave drumming brought to the Old World by a New Orleans Creole—like so much history in "the land of dreamy dreams," this sounds too good to be true, so naturally some scholars want you to think that it isn't. Debunking NOLA myths is an industry. (Jazz didn't really start in New Orleans; the music is not really jazz; jazz is not really spontaneous.) Recently, S. Frederick Starr, author of the magisterial biography *Bamboula!*, has gone after the Congo Square story. According to the author, there is no evidence the young Gottschalk heard this music in Congo Square, as all those writers have claimed over the past century; he actually heard it indoors from his Saint-Domingue grandmother and maid. The supposition that he heard drummers and dancers is based on the reality that taking one's family to Congo Square on Sundays to hear music was a popular custom for white Creoles like the Gottschalks. Whether he heard them indoors or out (including the music of runaways and curfew violators, as documented by Jean-Pierre Le Glaunec), he imbibed tresillo, habanera, and other Caribbean rhythms; when mixed with Creole songs and Cuban Caribbean cinquillo pounded out on European and Afro-Cuban drums, these quasi-improvisations became a significant kernel of the multicultural mélange later called New Orleans jazz, a mash-up of African and island sounds that rocked music around the world. Mourners at his funeral accurately called him the first Pan American artist.

Gottschalk was not only a composer, but a charismatic virtuoso pianist. Were this not the case, his compositions might never have been programed. In South America, he presided over "monster concerts" allegedly featuring 300 pianos and 600 orchestral players. In Europe, he impressed the musical establishment and their literary counterparts with spectacular technique yoked to a sexy New Orleans persona. When playing solo recitals, he presented the revolutionary New Orleans aesthetic himself; as a New Orleans Creole, he was its ideal personification and executant, sufficiently exotic to be a New World guru yet, as a white Creole, able to champion black music in a racist society.

Gottschalk was Europe's first encounter with a distinctly American musical persona. Gautier wrote that his "songs of the New World have an originality that is full of melancholy, energy, and suaveness and which can carry you deep into fantasy and dreams." Victor Hugo called him a poet "who can enrapture." Like Liszt, whose cadenzas his most difficult piano writing resembles (though he deplored the vulgarity of the Liszt cult), he was a matinee idol and sex object. His mentor at the Paris Opera was Berlioz, who said that Gottschalk "cradles our own disturbing and insatiable desire for the unknown." Berlioz, whose *Damnation of Faust* had its American premiere in New Orleans, viewed Gottschalk the same way Europeans later saw jazz players, as a conjuror of dangerous but irresistible fantasies. Gottschalk was sublimely duplicitous, an artist who only seemed straightforward and easy to read, but, in fact, had a persona that was enormously sophisticated and seductive; he was an artist of "sovereign powers" and "perfect grace" who embodied a "charming simplicity" that "seemed to emanate from a second personality." He knew "precisely how far a fantasy can be carried," yet he had a passionate sincerity. This doubleness, the cool and the sophisticated mingled with the childlike and the uninhibited, was the trademark of New Orleans pianists like Jelly Roll Morton and continues to characterize Eddie Bo, Henry Butler, Davell Crawford, Jon Batiste, and other Gottschalk progeny, who seem innocent and spontaneous one minute, regal and "deft" (to use Berlioz's word) the next.[25]

Gottschalk wrote the extravagantly colorful *Notes of a Pianist*, the first memoir by an international American concertizer. This sprawling, one-of-a-kind multi-genre work combines music criticism, memoir, travelogue, philosophy, fashion, gossip, and politics, the latter marvelously convoluted because Gottschalk was at once a proud Southerner and staunch Unionist.

As composer and prophet, Gottschalk—like Poe, Whitman, and other New World radicals—was more appreciated abroad than in America. "Bamboula," "Le Bananier," "The Banjo," "La Savane," and others became instant hits and continued to haunt Europeans long after the maestro's death. Offenbach transcribed "Le Bananier" for cello and piano; Bizet, whose "Habanera" in *Carmen* is not unlike Gottschalk's, played pieces by "the Creole Chopin" (one of Europe's favorite labels for Gottschalk) as a child. At the 1872 La Scala premiere of *Aida*, three years after Gottschalk's death, critics compared Verdi's music to his. The death itself was characteristically theatrical: Gottschalk collapsed during a rehearsal of his own "Morte!" and never recovered. Again, it seems too good to be true; all he needed was a jazz funeral.

The music lives up to the legend, even a slight thing like "Pasquinade," a startling forecast of ragtime. Spanish and Cuban pieces like "La Jota Aragonesa" and "La Gallina" have an irrepressible peppiness. More ambitious works like "Souvenir de Porto Rico" have a somber, mesmerizing intensity. "Le Bananier" achieved the most notoriety in Europe and has found a small place in the contemporary repertory. Its obsessive focus on a single harmony in the lead idea gives the piece an early place in the evolution of New Orleans "street" style, where musicians riff over a mono-harmonic backdrop. Lesser-known pieces, such as "Manchega," have spicier harmonic turns and more varied rhythms. As for the popular "Bamboula: Danse des Negres," it sounds a bit like Chopin in its perfumed middle section and, more interestingly, a lot like Scott Joplin in its main tune. "La Savane: Ballade Creole" resembles "Skip to My Lou," but as Gilbert Chase first pointed out, it is actually based on a slave song, "Lolotte." We should remember that Gottschalk, though a staunch Southerner, regarded slavery as an abomination; he freed the three slaves he inherited and supported the Union.

The expression of his Civil War views is on raucous display in the battle piece, "The Union," where "Yankee Doodle," "The Star-Spangled Banner," and "Hail Columbia" triumph in a collage Charles Ives might have written had he been a Creole.

Perhaps nothing in the Gottschalk canon is more prescient than his 1858 *Symphonie Romantique: A Night in the Tropics*. The best gloss on the piece is found in *Notes of a Pianist*. Here, Gottschalk displays a sinfully overheated prose not unlike that of Lafcadio Hearn. The tropics, he writes, impart "a voluptuous languor which is contagious; it is a poison which gradually infiltrates all the senses, and benumbs the senses with a species of ecstatic torpor."[26] *A Night in the Tropics* is the musical equivalent of Gottschalk's writing. The cornet solo arcing languidly over shimmering strings inaugurated a new kind of slow music, its melancholy sultriness suggesting early blues.

Even more striking is the Afro-Caribbean rhythm in the Symphonie's "Rhumba" finale, the first hot music for orchestra, a joyous crescendo that is a half-century ahead of its time; the piece is only partly written out, allowing for maximum improvisation, very much the way a jazz score is mapped. (The orchestration calls for anywhere from two pianos to 300 orchestra players, depending on who's available!) This groundbreaking symphony is a tantalizing indication of what Gottschalk might have achieved had appendicitis not claimed him at age forty.

The Banjo, Louis M. Gottschalk. Courtesy of the Louisiana Sheet
Music Collection, Hogan Jazz Archive, Tulane University.

Although Gottschalk was active mainly outside New Orleans (*Night in the
Tropics* was probably composed in Cuba, Martinique, and Guadeloupe), he
did return twice to his native city, first in 1853 when he played ten concerts
(two at the Théâtre d'Orléans with the company orchestra), and a second in
1855, following a long sojourn in Cuba. The archives list several singers from
the troupe participating in these concerts, indicating they were operatic as
well as instrumental events.

Gottschalk gave over a thousand concerts throughout the Americas during his last three years. His enemies ridiculed him as a shallow poseur, much
as Gershwin's detractors did when he introduced African American motifs
into classical music sixty years later. When he died, he vanished from American culture, but in Europe and South America, the energies he set loose lived

on. His influence can be felt in the sambas, tangos, and choros of Brazilian composer Ernesto Nazareth, whose African syncopations resemble those of Gottschalk, and whose music is played by the contemporary NOLA ensemble, the Panorama Jazz Band. He had Creole disciples in the late nineteenth century, and half a century later, Debussy, whose publisher was a Gottschalk devotee and whose teacher, Ernest Guiraud, was a New Orleanian, carried the legacy forward in dances like "Golliwog's Cakewalk" and "La Puerto del vino." One of the first European composers to embrace ragtime and jazz, Debussy viewed the rhythms of the emerging idiom as a liberating antidote to what he regarded as the "pompous outbursts" and "overblown orchestras" of "Wagnermania."[27] Debussy's works come from the end of the nineteenth century, precisely when the first jazz bands were starting up in New Orleans, and continued until the eve of the First World War. He spans the era of minstrel shows and Sousa-infused bands, the immediate precursors of jazz, as well as the Satie-Cocteau period when jazz was all the rage. After Debussy, jazz-classical fusions spread rapidly through Europe, creating a central trope of European modernism in the works of Ravel, Schulhoff, Hindemith, and many others.

One of the most original and visionary composers in the Gottschalk tradition was Frederick Delius, the English composer who based his aesthetic on a memory of black spirituals floating down a swamp, a distant sound he heard on a porch during his youthful sojourn in Florida in the 1880s. His entire output was a Proustian attempt to recapture that ecstatic moment. Gottschalk's most evocative work, like Delius's, was based on euphoric recollections of jungles and bayous in the New World, the breeding ground for Caribbean jazz. The nocturnal cornet in Gottschalk's *A Night in the Tropics* anticipates Delius's faraway horns and choruses in his operas; Gottschalk's languid chromaticism and tangy rhumbas are preludes to Delius's New World style.

Delius's most startling work is the Louisiana Voodoo-tinged opera, *Koanga*, based on the work of a significant New Orleans writer and composed in 1896, just as jazz was emerging, a work interwoven with bluesy flattened sevenths and other specimens of what we now regard as jazz chords. This full-length opera, unaccountably neglected in America's opera houses, is full of Creole and slave-inspired music, including "La Calinda," a seductively syncopated orchestral dance, "He Will Meet Her when the Sun Goes Down," a haunting slave chorus sung over distant banjos (years before Joplin or Dixieland), and "I Hear Palmyra's Voice," a Voodoo hymn to the morning star. *Koanga* is based on the brutal "Bras-Coupe" chapter (initially rejected by Scribner's as "unmitigatedly distressful") from George Washington Cable's novel, *The Grandissimes*. Delius loved the vividness and wildness of American literature, especially that of Twain and Whitman, and Cable's work suited his ideological purposes. A white progressive from New Orleans, Cable presented slavery as a decadent, destructive institution; the mutilated hero is Mioko Koanga (in French, Bras Coupe or "Arm Cut Off") who, in Cable's novel, "made himself into the type of all slavery, turning into flesh and blood the truth that all slavery is maiming." This astonishing piece, which is finally finding its way into the repertory (it was successfully revived at the Wexford Festival Opera in 2015), is a rare specimen of an opera inspired by a New Orleans author as well as by vernacular Creole music.

A far more renowned European composer indebted to New Orleans culture was Igor Stravinsky. His 1918 experiment, *Histoire du soldat*, was inspired by the music-making of Sidney Bechet, which the conductor Ernest Ansermet brought to Stravinsky's attention. (Ansermet called Bechet "an extraordinary clarinet virtuoso, the first of his race to have composed perfectly formed blues on the clarinet.")[28] The timing was perfect since Stravinsky was searching for a new sound to replace his Russian "primitive" style (where could one go after *Le sacre du printemps*?) This tart jazz-classical piece, which precedes Gershwin's *Rhapsody in Blue* and Weill's *Mahagonny*, bears little resemblance to the symphonic jazz of Stravinsky's contemporaries. Missing out on the Paris jazz-bar scene, Stravinsky avoided the faux-Gershwin clichés of the '20s that were to bedevil so many others. Partly because of personnel limitations, the *Histoire* ensemble bears an odd resemblance to a New Orleans jazz band. The slinky fiddle solo suggests New Orleans klezmer and a hint of zydeco; in the finale, the drum set rocks out with a syncopated abandon that no symphonic jazz work ever duplicated, including Stravinsky's own Ebony Concerto. Later, Stravinsky created another Bechet-inspired work, the "Three Pieces for Clarinet Solo." During his symphonic jazz period in the 1990s, Wynton Marsalis took note of all this, using *Histoire* as the model for one of his most striking pieces, *The Fiddler's Tale* Suite.

For symphonic composers in the early twentieth century, jazz was an attractive alternative to the more alienating aspects of modernism. Kurt Weill stated that jazz allowed a contemporary composer to draw a large audience and still maintain the "intellectual bearing of the serious musician."[29] It's not surprising that a composer like Stravinsky, a great innovator who was also a shrewd self-promoter, would embrace an artist like Bechet. With jazz, a composer could be modern and popular at the same time. In the pre-bop era, jazz made the avant-garde irrelevant.

If the greatest innovation came in Europe, the greatest resistance came in America, where tastemakers dubbed jazz an unfortunate fad, at best a temporary degradation, at worst a Negro-Jewish conspiracy against the classical tradition. "American music is not jazz. Jazz is not music," said American taste-maker Paul Rosenfeld, citing its "drug-like" effects and calling it "the folly of the living dead" long before jazz became associated with drug culture.[30] Ironically, jazz's earliest and most fervid champions (along with US dancers and record collectors) were the European composers whose tradition jazz was allegedly tainting. Ravel went so far as to assert that jazz was "the national music of the United states," soon destined to become world music, and taunted Americans for "taking jazz too lightly."[31]

British composer Constant Lambert went further in two selections from his 1934 book *Music Ho!*—"The Spirit of Jazz" and "Symphonic Jazz." These were prescient statements on the subject that have fascinating parallels to the proclamations of Wynton Marsalis. Citing Louis Armstrong as "one of the most remarkable virtuosi of the present day," Lambert heralded a music that bequeathed a new freedom and a new star system, calling jazz an "intoxicating" form, "the most distinguished popular music since Johann Strauss," attaining in form and execution "a far higher level than any previous form of dance music." He believed it to be the most significant symphonic idiom of the twentieth century, capable of fusions only hinted at in Stravinsky's jazz pieces. (Lambert's Delius-inspired *Rio Grande* for chorus and orchestra and his Concerto for Piano and Nine Instruments are his own exquisite contributions to the genre.) Lambert debunked the Noble Savage clichés of jazz, insisting that its complexity is its point. "Though popularly regarded as being a barbaric art, it is to its sophistication that jazz owes its real force," he wrote, and African American jazz is more sophisticated than its white off-shoots: "The superiority of American jazz lies in the fact that the negroes are in touch not so much with specifically barbaric elements as with sophisticated elements." (Stravinsky too preferred jazz as an African American idiom, the expression "of la musique negre. I like it a great deal less in its Anglo-Saxon transcriptions.")[32] Lambert had deep insight into the magic of New Orleans rhythm and its place in music history: "In the best negro jazz bands the irregular cross-accents are given so much more weight than the underlying pulse that the rhythmic arabesques almost completely obscure the metrical framework, and paradoxically enough this 'bar line' music often achieves a rhythmic freedom that recalls the music of Elizabethan times and earlier, where the bar line was a mere technical convenience like a figure or letter in a score." Today, Wynton Marsalis also speaks of traditional jazz as harking back to the improvisational flexibility of early music, though his antecedent is Bach. Marsalis's insistence that real jazz is based on the blues finds a pre-echo in Lambert as well: "The 'hot' negro records still have a genuine and not merely galvanic energy, while the blues have a certain austerity that places them far above the sweet nothings of George Gershwin." (Lambert's strident dismissal of Gershwin is perhaps one reason why *Music Ho!* is so rarely referenced, though many of his contemporaries shared his distaste.) Lambert also resembles Marsalis in his adulation of Duke Ellington, praising him for summing up what was most valuable in the tradition while lifting it to a new level of complexity and richness. Lambert predicted Ellington would turn out to be a greater mover in the history of twentieth-century music than Schoenberg, Hindemith, or other alleged heavy-hitters of the era, and he stated that Kurt Weill would leave a similar mark in opera, calling him "the most successful and important of the Central European composers who have experimented with the jazz idiom." Weill was the great musical poet of the American South, "almost the only composer who can evoke in music the odd, untidy, drably tragic background that is presented to us so forcibly by William Faulkner." Just as *Mahagonny* "sums up the inverted poetry of 'American low life,'" *The Seven Deadly Sins*, where Weill's impoverished female protagonists wander Louisiana and Alabama, achieves "a certain grandeur." For a composer outside the tradition, Weill still has a striking cachet in New Orleans: "Mack the Knife" has become a NOLA standard, in both instrumental and vocal manifestations, and Wynton Marsalis's "September Song" with Sarah Vaughan is one of his suavest early performances.

Rather than arguing about what constitutes "real jazz" and debating whether it was dead or dying, as the Parisian jazz critics were already doing, Lambert analyzed why jazz moves people so deeply and is always so in touch with modern reality. With its ebullient surface and melancholy undertone, jazz is "the constant tenor of our time," both exciting and dangerous, its "intoxicating low spirits" expressing "psychological truth." To the many commentators who disdained the off-beats of jazz as grotesque or abnormal, Lambert had a sweeping retort: "It is the lack of rhythmic experiment in nineteenth century music that is really abnormal ... Without wishing in any way to denigrate the magnificent achievement of the German romantic school from Weber to Mahler, we can without exaggeration say that it is remarkably deficient in purely rhythmic interest. Wagner himself was aware of this failing and admitted it with a deprecatory 'Well, you can't expect everything' air." [33]

Rhythm continues to be a reason so many in the classical world are entranced by NOLA jazz stars. Herbert von Karajan, who admired Louis Armstrong's internal metronome, once told the Vienna Philharmonic that he was on his way to an All Stars concert: "Imagine! Two hours of music, and never once will it slow down or speed up by mistake." [34]

Trumpeter Leroy Jones explains this phenomenon: "My time is solid as the rock. I can dance, and I know what a beat is. If I have cats up there, all they need to do is keep the time; if I kick it, that's where it needs to stay.

"I can take it from there, and anybody else can," Jones continues. "Then you're able to play more and express yourself, and you can breathe because the space is there; it's not frantic. It's not rushing ahead of the time, and it's not dragging behind. This is true of any musical form, which is why a symphony has a conductor. You're not going to get eighty people to feel the beat the same way. So they need to watch somebody; I'm giving it to you—there it is, it's right there. But with jazz musicians, you're not supposed to need a conductor. You have to have that metronome inside you."[35]

The inner metronome is the basis for improvisation and displacement that no metronome can measure. The reverse is true as well; while a symphony orchestra needs a conductor, the exciting maestros, as opposed to those who are boringly literal, have a subtle sense of rubato and swing. These paradoxes explain why a Leroy Jones performance sounds laid-back and relentless at the same time, and why Leonard Bernstein and Gustavo Dudamel can make Mahler swing. Not surprisingly, Bernstein admired Armstrong as an ideal. When the New York Philharmonic appeared with Armstrong in 1956 (for a tribute to W. C. Handy), he told the huge audience that Armstrong's art was something "real" and "noble": "We are only doing a blown-up imitation of what he does."[36]

The NOLA tradition informs many symphonic aesthetics. Shostakovich's charming Jazz Suites from the 1920s are full of bluesy slides and Dixieland tropes. Michael Tippett's "slow blues" in the finale of his 1970 Third Symphony, written in the shadow of the Vietnam War, was inspired by the spirit of Louis Armstrong. The twenty-first century has seen several notable hybrids: George Crumb's 2008 *Voices from the Morning of the Earth* features an inventive riff on "When the Saints Go Marching In," evoking the thunder of a New Orleans jazz funeral, gradually fading away into a ghostly chorus of whistlers (Crumb adds a beat to make the saints march in five, a marvelous bit of rhythmic complexity), while Laura Karpman's multimedia piece from a year later, *Go Tell Your Mama*, samples traditional jazz icons, including Morton and Armstrong, evoking black America's struggle with a white supremacist society. Terence Blanchard's 2013 opera, *Champion*, depicts racism and homophobia in the boxing world. "Together in Harmony," the finale of Barbara Harbach's Tenth Symphony from 2015, features a jubilant brass-band march mixing "St. Louis Blues" with New Orleans jazz polyphony. Wynton Marsalis's epic Third and Fourth Symphonies, *Swing Symphony*, from 2010, and *The Jungle*, from 2016, are so ambitious—incorporating African drumming, ragtime, swing, bebop,

Latin jazz, Bachian fugues, "American pastoral," and much else—that the New York Philharmonic had to cut a movement from each premiere performance. The ever-eclectic Donald Harrison has plunged headlong into classical music, especially in his 2015 orchestral work, *Congo Square*, which mixes rhythms and chants from the Congo Square era with symphonic elements in a rich, shifting tapestry of rhythm and color. This is "not crossover," Harrison insists, but a genuine classical piece that "juxtaposes" African and European elements.[37] For those who prefer an actual jazz piece, he has written *I'm the Big Chief of Congo Square*, which integrates elements of the orchestral work into a score for jazz ensemble.

It's unfortunate that Gottschalk is not around to see the intense crosscurrents he set in motion the day he took "Bamboula" to Paris in 1842. He has never been sufficiently feted in his native country or city, but his time may be coming. America has many composers, from radicals like Edgard Varese to traditionalists like Amy Beach, who were long neglected but eventually given their due.

Gottschalk is unusual in being continually resurrected only to vanish again (as he did in real life, partly because of a sexual scandal, partly because that was his style). Since he is so much earlier than other American masters, the cycle has repeated several times. Lionized in nineteenth-century Europe and South America, he was consigned to oblivion for another half-century until Seymour Solomon, the astute head of Vanguard Records, commissioned Maurice Abravanel, Eugene List, and other diehard Gottschalkians to record *A Night in the Tropics* and several piano pieces, including "Le Bananier" and "La Savane," in a stunning early-stereo LP from 1958, followed by two others in the '60s and '70s. This period also saw the publication of neglected piano works, the republication of *Notes of a Pianist*, and a spate of articles. Another revival of sorts occurred in the '90s with S. Frederick Starr's richly textured biography, *Bamboula!*, and a new spurt of recordings, most notably from Naxos.

The most exciting rise, still relatively miniscule, is occurring in his native city. Although he was America's first international musical celebrity, Gottschalk remains largely unknown in New Orleans. I'm always startled by how many New Orleanians, including players, have never heard of him. Since Katrina, however, things have begun to change. There is now a Louis Moreau Institute in New Orleans that promotes Gottschalk's legacy with performances of Stravinsky, Bartók, and others, including new pieces by up-and-coming composers. Musicians with a world-music sensibility have started playing Gottschalk in clubs throughout the city, in recognition of his singular importance and the sexiness of his compositions. Pianist Tom McDermott, cornetist Connie Jones, clarinetist Evan Christopher, and percussionist Michael Skinkus have created colorful chamber ensembles for Gottschalk pieces like "Danza" and "Manchego." McDermott's languid rubato, Jones's lyrical cornet line, and Skinkus's over-the-edge syncopation bring nineteenth-century New Orleans into the twenty-first. "I must confess that the Gottschalk I play is very adulterated," says McDermott, whose performances are highly improvisatory. "I just take the melody, basically. I play the left hand to some degree, but I improvise on the changes and try to stay in the idiom. I aspire to learn Gottschalk, but these are very difficult pieces. He wrote them to show off his virtuosity." (It's hard to imagine Gottschalk, a legendary improviser, not being delighted by these "adulterations.") McDermott's own art is influenced by Gottschalk, whom he sees as one of the roots of New Orleans jazz, the "Cuban rhythms that go back to Gottschalk, through Jelly Roll, make it into Professor Longhair big time, and continue through Torkanowsky, Henry Butler, Harry Connick Jr., and all those."[38]

Gottschalk would surely have enjoyed these performances, which take his delicate but fiery jazz hybrids and realize their potential as actual jazz. Few things happening in the Crescent City are more lovely and fascinating.

Chapter Two

THE BRASS BANDS: PARTYING AT FUNERALS

In this town, there are no limits.
—Christie Jordain, the Pinettes

The hottest gig in contemporary New Orleans is the Rebirth Brass Band at the Maple Leaf on Tuesday nights. It's been that way since the early '90s, one of the few constants in the Big Easy. Not that the show is in any way orderly; hundreds of locals begin crowding in at 9:30 for a 10 o'clock performance that everyone knows won't start until 11:30 or midnight or whenever all nine Rebirth members wander in from the Tremé. By showtime, it's nearly impossible to bring a drink from the bar at the front into the narrow, New Orleans-red hallway under the stage where the crowd is thronging. Once the band is completely present, they start playing, without introduction, and keep going as one number rockets into another through the night. The club is claustrophobic and hot, with no place to stand comfortably (forget sitting) and little space to dance or drink, though fans manage to do plenty of both.

Few fans care about these discomforts, but those who do can stay for thirty minutes or so and feel satisfied, indeed satiated. Most stay all night, their ears ringing though the next day as they recover from a unique musical high. It's partly the sound itself: blaring, joyful, aggressively direct, yet highly sophisticated in its crisscrossing counterpoint and multilayered chords—stunningly loud, yet rich rather than hard. But it's more than just the music. Essential to the Maple Leaf Tuesday night is the audience, which gives back as much energy as it gets, inspiring the band to keep rocking at all costs. That's why the show is better at the Maple Leaf than, say, Brooklyn Bowl, where I have heard the band do spirited but unremarkable gigs. Phil Frazier, the sousaphone player and leader of the band, told me it's because the audience knows

Phil Frazier, Chadrick Honore, Rebirth Brass Band. Photographs by Brandon Xeureb, Xistence Photography.

the repertory and expects more than just a run-through: "In New Orleans the attitude is, 'We know how good you is, now *show* us how good you is. Even if it's the same songs, it sounds different.'"[1]

These are fierce, loyal fans, full of good music vibes but not especially fond of outsiders. Where they *are* friendly is Sidney's Saloon on St. Bernard Avenue in the Seventh Ward. It's been managed off and on by Kermit Ruffins, who founded Rebirth in 1983 and now has his own swing band. Since 2012, it's become an emblem of the new racial diversity in the city, attracting hipsters as well as old-timers. Ruffins's presence at the bar, as well as the place itself, gives the Rebirth a very different persona from their presence at the Maple Leaf. Sidney's is in a bleak part of the Seventh Ward, by no means recovered from Katrina, a tiny paradise in a big no-man's-land. The place has been around since the 1940s; according to Ruffins, the original owner started it up as a competition with his brother, who owned a church. "I don't know if it's true or not," Ruffins told me, "but it makes a great story."[2]

When Ruffins ran the place, he met you at the bar with hugs and jubilation. Sidney's was then a word of mouth phenomenon. Neighborhood places like this don't market themselves or present "performances." Wednesday night was vaguely Rebirth night, but there was no telling if or when the band would play. As Scott Goldshine, Rebirth's unofficial New York manager, reminded me, Wednesday night at Sidney's wasn't really a gig at all, a place for the band to drink, cut up, and play if they felt like it. ("Do Whatcha Wanna" is Rebirth's signature tune.)

Joints like Sidney's, Little People's, Bullet's Sports Lounge, and Joe's Cozy Corner reflect the traditions of brass-band music, which began in the neighborhoods. The night I went to Sidney's with my American Studies college group, the band came in one by one beginning around 9:30 and finally played at 10:30. Half never showed up at all, but enough did to make a go for us. The sound was leaner and brighter than usual, ringing through the tiny bar out into the empty streets. Instead of the heavy Rebirth bomb, smoking in all directions, it was a lightning bolt, but the basic sound was intact.

That sound moves from the bottom up. As Phil Frazier points out, the band will "start with the tuba, and then bring in the melody, and everybody else would play around it . . . In the past, brass bands would introduce the tunes with the drum."[3] Keith "Wolf" Anderson says, "Anybody'll call out a tune. But tuba can mostly start out a tune if nobody can think fast enough. Tuba is the one that's the backbone."[4] The bass horn and drums must be present, and fortunately Phil's brother Keith, the bass drum player, showed up and gave his all. "The bass drum is the most important thing in the band," Keith insists. "'If the bass is not knocking, the band is not rocking.'"[5]

They were rocking that night, and they kept up a single medley for half an hour, as Frazier set the groove from one song to another. Then they suddenly stopped, leaving a haunting emptiness in the air. I asked Frazier if they could do one more, but the band was leaving; he told me to hold on for the Maple Leaf gig on Tuesday, when we would hear the entire ensemble for hours. The band knew we were coming, and enough personnel had showed up for a gig—that was the essential thing. They had been loyal to us, and loyalty is what matters in the brass-band world.

New Orleans music started in places like Sidney's. "If you look around here," a senior black man told us at the bar, "you see where it all came from." The Rebirth at Sidney's is quintessential New Orleans: the intimacy, the lateness (in every sense), the funky informality, the gradual appearance and sudden vanishing of the band, the unpredictability of who shows up, and the raw intensity of the music. Sidney's also reflects the Big Easy's "easy intermingling of the races," as Tennessee Williams put it in the stage directions for *A Streetcar Named Desire*. The racial and class distinctions between my white, suburban New Jersey group and the locals was stark, but for a brief interval at Sidney's, they vanished. These qualities cannot be created by marketers or managers and would be spoiled if anyone tried.

This is not to say that the tourist or conventioneer package is unimportant; most musicians make their living from these gigs, and the economy of the city has always been based on them. Still, it's important to understand what is essential. Before the promoters, the DJs, and the marketers, there was simply a brass-band parading through a neighborhood and into a barbecue or a bar. That it still happens is why NOLA continues to be a great jazz city, a place where the music breathes as a life force.

Keith "Wolf" Anderson, a veteran of older brass bands, says that he was the catalyst for Rebirth, which was engendered suddenly in the streets: "I started out with Rebirth in '83 . . . I was working at the seafood plant, and I came across these flats on Conti Street on my way to get something at the market. And I heard these kids playing music . . . all kinda crazy, funny stuff . . . it was like they were trying to play jazz, but it was basically school type of music. Then I just went in and started listening to them and said, 'Y'all sound good, you ought to start playing jazz, man' . . . I grabbed Kermit's horn, I grabbed Philip's tuba . . . I grabbed the drums, I grabbed all the instruments to show them their parts, and they tripped out because they didn't know somebody as young as me that knew all those instruments."[6]

The history of Rebirth reflects the fundamental pattern of brass-band music: starting in school, moving onto the streets, blossoming in the clubs, then marching back for neighborhood parties and funerals. Ruffins led his high school group in their first gig at the Sheraton in 1983, then went with them into the French Quarter to play for tips since they were too young to be in the clubs. Calling themselves the Rebirth Brass Band, they were noticed by the agent and promoter Allison Miner, who took a chance and got them a European gig, then a deal with Rounder Records.

According to Keith "Wolf" Anderson, Rebirth, boasting the youngest players of any brass band, set a new tone and established a "new style of music" that bridged the more traditional sound of Olympia and Majestic while exploring the more contemporary vibe of the Dirty Dozen: "Rebirth was like the best of both worlds 'cause we weren't just following Olympia, we were following Dirty Dozen too. So we were doing traditional and more progressive stuff . . . that's probably why our crowd was a little bigger, that's probably why we got popular more." A little bigger grew to much bigger, as crowds for funerals, second lines, and private parties swelled into gatherings in the clubs, first the Glass House, then the Maple Leaf in the mid-'80s.

Even after achieving acclaim, Rebirth continued doing second-line parades, which are named after the rowdy sounds of those who follow behind the first line of players, dancing and partying in the streets with their own improvised percussion and brass ensembles. Some scholars believe second lines are really a straightened-out version of the ring dances in Congo Square; now they are the raucous marchers and players behind the never-ending parades in the city. "We keep that second-line vibe going no matter what," says Phil Frazier, no matter how many new songs they create: "We compose a lot of new songs, but we've been around thirty-one, thirty-two years; we've got a lot of old songs we still do and a lot of new songs we do."[7]

Since second lines are fundamental to the Rebirth aesthetic, odd things happen when the band leaves NOLA. Kermit Ruffins told me that when he took the Rebirth to New York in the early '80s, they did a second line from inside the club out into the street and were immediately surrounded by the NYPD for parading without a license. By the mid-'90s, the Rebirth had a permit, for I remember them coming to New York and parading through the Virgin Record Store near Times Square and down Broadway with my two young sons on their shoulders, their airborne sound ricocheting off the skyscrapers and bringing startled tourists out into the streets. For a moment, the Big Apple became the Big Easy. When the band noticed a lone drummer pounding away on a street island, they crossed over, sat down around him, and listened intently, much as they would in their neighborhood. Afterward, they tried to hail a cab, asking the Pakistani driver in their Tremé accents if he knew the location of the club for their next gig, the Knitting Factory. Chaos ensued. Although they eventually made it down to the Village, they didn't understand the custom in New York of clearing out the place after the first set so the manager can collect more money; once the band started playing, they didn't stop and continued all night.

Kermit Ruffins's affability has set the tone for the group from the beginning, and to this day, he sometimes shows up to cheer or sit in. In the early days, he led the group in local bars like Little People's and Trombone Shorty's, the latter named after the current star, whom I heard playing there when he was eleven years old. Although this is an all-black band, it is so welcoming and personable that it has always attracted a multiethnic crowd, luring lots of young white fans long before brass-band music became fashionable.

Rebirth continues to attract a young crowd even though it's been around since the early '80s; it's because "young people want to get back to something with roots and soul," Phil Frazier believes.[8] Rebirth has created many new tunes since the '80s. Some, such as Kabuki's 2013 song, "Hot Buck-Naked Sex," is so ostentatiously scatological that one wonders if witty jazz euphemisms and double entendres conflating sex and food, sex and deep-sea diving, and all the others, are now irrelevant, literalized for an audience that doesn't need metaphors anymore. Yet the band can also do a compelling G-rated show for family entertainment events. I heard them at the Spoleto Festival in Charleston in a (more or less) formal performance that demonstrated their continued mastery of old marching-band material. It was like hearing a contemporary music group play Brahms—the music is old, but the modern perspective of the players make it sound new.

Bands like Rebirth have a rich but peculiarly nonlinear lineage. Long before jazz ensembles, nineteenth-century amateur brass bands were popular all over America and Europe, playing in villages, churches, and as part of diverse social rituals. What made brass bands in New Orleans different was the insistence of black players on taking white instruments and playing them African style, "incorrectly," with all manner of slides, bluesy sonorities, pentatonic scales, syncopated rhythms, and improvisations. The syncopation and call-response patterns have their origin in the Sunday slave drumming and ring dancing sessions in Congo Square, which began during the French period and extended well into the nineteenth century. European brass instruments and drums added a new layer to African percussion and Creole song, and a brass-band aesthetic gradually emerged.

The triumph of black and mixed-race music was cemented in the early nineteenth century following an eruption of Haitian refugees into New Orleans and another migration of Protestant African Americans from southern plantations. By the late nineteenth century, polkas, waltzes, and quadrilles, popular throughout Europe and America, had taken on a spicier flavor in New Orleans, infused with Creole songs from the islands, the soulful sounds of black spirituals—"the folk music of America," as Dvořák called them in 1892—and the tangy refinement of early ragtime.

Nineteenth-century brass bands had numerous opportunities to develop the "hot" style, as New Orleans has always been an unending spectacle of parades—from church services, funerals, firehouses, social and pleasure clubs, ethnic celebrations, and spontaneous gatherings in bars and outdoor parties, all in addition to Mardi Gras, which was inaugurated by the French in

Jazz Funeral. Photograph by Jack Sullivan.

the eighteenth century. In addition to the sprawling St. Charles Avenue Mardi Gras beloved of tourists, New Orleans has numerous black Indian parades on Mardi Gras Day, each with its own neighborhood tradition and repertory. (See chapter six.)

During the Storyville era, bands began taking the outdoor sound into bordellos and bars, refining it into a tighter aesthetic. By the Buddy Bolden and Louis Armstrong eras, brass bands were like oversized jazz ensembles. New Orleanians, players and audience members alike, did not always distinguish between what was really jazz and what was not—and with the exception of Hot Club intellectuals and similar elites, Europeans didn't either. There were notable holdouts, among them Papa Louis Tio and Manuel Perez's Onward Brass Band, who grumbled about the incursion of "ratty" jazz improvisation into brass-band music, then adapted to it, as New Orleanians have always done when survival is at stake.

Early jazz-oriented brass bands like Tuxedo, Eureka, and Olympia blazed the way for the brass bands of today, becoming what Matt Sakakeeny calls the "mobile version" of jazz, an outdoor spectacle that "transformed the funeral procession into what we now call a jazz funeral."[9] The latter term was not actually coined until the 1950s, but funerals with music have been in existence in New Orleans for a very long time. It's hard to exaggerate their importance. In a jazz funeral, a deceased member of the music community is celebrated by a solemn dirge like "Just a Closer Walk With Thee" or "Old Rugged Cross" that suddenly breaks into second-line dancing in the streets to a syncopated, polyphonic "jazz" version of the same march. The mourners get the wailing and tears over as quickly as decency permits so they can "cut the body loose" and start the party. As Louis Armstrong told Edward R. Murrow in 1956, the second-liners are an encore, "a bunch of raggedy guys, you know, old hustlers and cats and good-time Charlies . . . seems as though they have more fun than anybody because they applaud for Joe Oliver and Manny Perez with the brass band to play it over again, so they get to give this second line, they call it . . . it's really something to see."[10] Keith "Wolf" Anderson calls the second line "a moving block party . . . a moving riot. I mean . . . 'cause the more you move, and the more neighborhoods you run through, you accumulate more and more people . . . it looks like it doubles every neighborhood you get through."[11]

Historian Ned Sublette believes that African American funerals led to what we classify as jazz, but just how it did so is a bit of an enigma: "At some point [black Protestants] began having procession funerals. After a step was taken of adding a brass band to the procession—and I can't put an exact date on when that happened—New Orleans musicians were on the road to something we could call jazz."[12] Sublette's theory is compelling. The jazz funerals I've joined were unforgettable cacophonies of brass bands converging from everywhere, with children dancing on cars and playing trumpets, black and white second-liners singing spirituals together, and rapt moments when the crowd stopped for a massed brass anthem or paraded into a cafe. It's not hard to imagine this sprawling spectacle evolving into a powerful, independent form.

If the exact origins of jazz funerals are mysterious, we do know that the Spanish denounced their early manifestations as disruptive of social order and a breeding ground for slave rebellion. By 1819, observers of African American "funerals with music," like the architect Benjamin Latrobe, were registering their dismay at "excessive distress" counterpointed by "noise and laughter," both equally undignified to those who couldn't comprehend New Orleans's insistence on mourning the deceased while celebrating their lives with "a joyful noise."[13] As Matt Sakakeeny points out: "The music organizes the collective suffering of those at the funeral and the collective pleasure that they anticipate in the shift to up-tempo music. Once the dirge transforms into an up-tempo spiritual, the increase in tempo transforms the emotion from mourning to celebration. Rather than merely accompany the funeral procession, the music structures the entire movement and emotional state of the mourners." Trombonist Bennie Pete of the Hot 8 Brass Band says, "We might be feeling sad or something, but that music and that beat's going to lift our spirit along with the happier time we had with that person. Right then and there—the transition, BAM!—from we mourning him and we grieving over him, to we just thinking about the time we was having fun and laughing loud and partying."[14]

NOLA musicians speak of their departed colleagues as if they are still present, and in the spiritual reality of brass-band music, a sound that hardly ever stops, they continue to live. In *Cities of the Dead*, Joseph Roach states that, in this tradition, "the living defy the segregation of the dead. Their celebration begins at a trajectory of mourning that must be sensed collectively by those present on the occasion, a moment in which the community joyously affirms its renewal in the very act of marking the passing of one of its own ... in these sacred rites of memory, death is not so clearly separated from life."[15] The intensity of the music is such that those in the second-line experience the band as a medium through which the dead body—at least for the duration of the funeral—lives again, arcing upward with the horns as they point toward the sky. "At that time we trying to blow," says Hot 8 trombonist Jerome Jones, "blow him to heaven."[16]

The subject is the occasion for a great deal of New Orleans-style dark humor. Leroy Jones, an original member of the Fairview Baptist Church Christian Marching Band, told me that people have a superstitious ambivalence about jazz funerals; no one wants someone else to drop dead, "but everyone wants to be in a jazz funeral. You can't exactly say, 'Can't wait to see you at the next one.'"[17]

Like many current jazz stars, Jones played in brass bands first, reflecting the history of the two genres. Indeed, many of the city's best jazz players are veterans of brass bands. As Greg Stafford puts it, "The brass band was the breeding ground for all the great jazz musicians who came through New Orleans; most of them played brass-band music. You can go back to Kid Ory, Louis Armstrong, Sidney Bechet. All of those instrumentalists, they played in brass bands all the way up to this stage. It is one of the most significant aspects of the history of the music."[18] How close is brass-band music to jazz now? "That's up to you," Frazier says. "Brass and jazz and funk—put it together and call it jungle music. We play all kinds of jazz. You can tell the difference, though: it's not electrical; it's all brass. That's the main thing."[19] Christie Jordain of the Original Pinettes also has a relativistic view: "You have people in our band who play several instruments and people who can sing. You have people in a regular band that can do brass-band music. In this town, there are no limits. This town is a big old pot of gumbo. Here it's great—it's all love. It's competition, but we still love each other and call each other onto the stage."[20]

Almost without exception, brass-band players I interviewed speak of what they do as "jazz," and many musicians in jazz bands regard what they do as inseparable from brass-band aesthetics. When clarinetist James Evans moved to New Orleans in 2013, he landed in jazz bands led by Leroy Jones and Lucien Barbarin, but his jazz epiphany was Rebirth. "When I first heard the Rebirth Brass band, it was a feeling of homecoming or an awakening— it's very odd, I can't really explain it. I'd been listening to jazz since I was eleven, and I'd always been listening to it unconsciously. I was always aware of this place being the epicenter of what I did, and an origin of what I did." This type of epiphany—a profound feeling of awakening or homecoming—is something we see repeatedly in this book—the moment when the immigrant outsider feels inside, with NOLA the "epicenter," with his or her identity connected to all the genres and crosscurrents. "It was a very special feeling," Evans says. "I wasn't *really* prepared. I was just suddenly—'Oh my goodness.' New Orleans draws people who often feel like they don't fit in anywhere else, and I can definitely relate to that, the freedom and the way that relates to the music."

When I asked how he distinguishes between jazz, brass band, and funk, he expressed disdain for the question. "I'm not much into labels. Jazz means so many different things. It makes sense if you follow one thing to the next. So if you start with King Oliver—well, you start before that—and you follow the lineage, then it makes sense, but if you didn't know they were linked, you wouldn't really think that John Coltrane and the Original Dixieland Jazz Band were necessarily the same style. If you were given that out of context, and you knew nothing about jazz, you wouldn't say they were the same music. When I went to college, I had a good tutor; the first lesson, jazz history: 'Define jazz.' And, of course, you can't. Some people say, 'Well it's got improvising'—well, not always, and there's other music that has improvising; and 'It's got swing'— yeah, but you know, a lot of music swings and it's not really jazz. When I heard the Rebirth, I somehow connected it in my mind to King Oliver particularly, because I suppose that was a bigger band. There was something in the flavor, the feeling, that was the same even though so much is different. People raise their eyebrows when I say that, but I still think it's true. What it is, what you call it, I don't know. Brass-band music is less solo-oriented than jazz, less than other jazz, if you call it jazz."[21]

As with so much NOLA music, one can't construct a simple, linear chart for the history of brass bands; the current brass-band sound is not a culmination of increasingly swingy syncopation that started at Congo Square. In the midst of the current brass renaissance, we tend to forget that brass bands were actually dying by the middle of the twentieth century; younger players started playing gigs in R&B groups, Fats Domino and Ernie K-Doe became rockers, and the brass-band tradition took on an aura of fustiness. The brass-band tradition was in danger of becoming "old people's music," just as Dixieland was "white people's music."

Then, in the early '70s, an unexpected and dramatic fusion occurred. Danny Barker and the Fairview Baptist Church Christian Marching Band, followed by Dejan's Olympia Brass Band, began experimenting with rock, funk, and Mardi Gras Indian material—"Hey Pocky Way," "I Got a Woman," "Mardi Gras in New Orleans." The NOLA brass sound always had plenty of "hotness," but young players in the Fairview group, like Leroy Jones, Lucien Barbarin, and Gregg Stafford, ignited it further, making it attractive to their generation. This sudden jolt of energy was sparked by Barker, a traditionalist (his favored instrument was the "antiquated" banjo) who understood that NOLA tradition is always in the process of becoming something new. For many, Barker is the most important influence on what is happening today. John Boutte exhorts young musicians to steep themselves in Barker's art: "I tell all my young friends: 'You've got to listen to Danny Barker. Learn those tunes, and then you'll know something: 'Save those Bones for Henry Jones,' 'Don't You Feel My Leg?' 'Hard Hearted Hannah,'—his phrasing, his chord progressions: he was the true troubadour. He came from another era; he bridged the gap."[22]

Many musicians regard Barker as the most significant bridge between old and new. Unlike Professor Longhair, who played in obscurity with little idea that he was changing the field, Barker was astutely aware of history and his place in it. According to Michael White, what was "unusual and exceptional" about Barker was that he "had in mind that New Orleans jazz needed a future"; his program to "get local kids into jazz" was not just about the present. And the future needed to come from the street, the poorer neighborhoods, as it always had. As Barker puts it, "As far back as you want to go and the greatest jazz you want to see, New Orleans jazz is street jazz, second-line music, where everybody gets their umbrellas. I don't care if you're ninety years old or three years old, you grab something and hold it up. Everybody likes it. Everybody used to laugh at it once before, but when you saw all them poor black people having fun, you say, 'Let's get some of that too! Shit! Huh? If they're having fun, let us have fun.' So that was the purpose. With the Fairview band, it was a shock to the people to see these young kids playing this music on the street because it has always been old men's music—old jazz men: they'd almost retired."[23]

The identification of brass-band music with youth culture, Barker's legacy, was indeed a "shock to the people," one that has never abated. The musicians who came up under him are poignantly aware of how much they owe him, both personally and aesthetically. "I wouldn't actually be sitting here if it wasn't for him," drummer Shannon Powell says of Barker, who picked Powell up on the street when he was eleven, took him to gigs with the best players in

Danny Barker. Photograph by Bob Benson. Courtesy of the
Hogan Jazz Archive, Tulane University.

the 1970s, and taught him the fundamentals of rhythm as well as how to dress.
"He literally brought me out here. . . . He said, 'You're going to be all right.' He
started breaking me in, taking me on gigs. I was playing with people like Tuts
Washington, Jack Willis—one of the greatest trumpet players to come out of
New Orleans—[and] James Carter. So one time, Jack Willis asked Mr. Barker,
'Man, why you keep hiring this kid? All these grown men looking for work,
why you keep hiring him?' Mr. Barker looked at him and said, 'Guess what?
Somebody give you a break, didn't they?' Just like that. He didn't say nothing
more, and Mr. Jack Willis and me became best friends. He not only taught
him something, he taught me something. This is how you get breaks in life."[24]

For Gregg Stafford, some of the most vivid Barker memories are from the
early days of the Palm Court on Decatur Street, an atmospheric place that has
maintained a sense of timelessness into the twenty-first century. "In the late
'80s, this was one room," Stafford told me after one of his serene Palm Court
Sunday gigs. "On Sunday night, we used to work with Mr. Barker: Danny,
Pud Brown, and I participated in slinging the hammer with Nina [owner of
Palm Court] to knock a hole into the adjacent wall as a wall-breaking event

immediately after we finished the gig on that Sunday night. He was one of the very few individuals that had some foresight in terms of letting young musicians work in his band. He felt that in order to keep the music going, you had to hire younger musicians."[25]

This sense of history is something Barker communicated to his students as much as the music itself; as we see in this book, it's reflected in the way Stafford, Jones, and their colleagues talk about their art as a broadening experience, always looking toward the future. "It was a success," Barker said of the Fairview experiment shortly before his death, "and I'm going to try to continue. Because if you give a kid an instrument, he's not likely to get in trouble. . . . You've got guys like the little Rebirth Band. They go to Japan, Russia—you know, imagine a poor little black kid: they're going over to Sweden, Norway, Finland, they got passports, getting on a plane like they're going to Carrollton or Algiers! Huh? That never happened before. That's what you're doing. You're getting kids who are deprived a chance to see the rest of the world."[26]

"Tuba Fats" Lacen remembers 1974 as the year the band started delivering Barker's "shock to the people," playing funky Mardi Gras tunes as well as new songs like his own "Tuba Fats." Brass bands suddenly became hip again, a startling loop-back in the city's musical history paralleling the new popularity of traditional jazz in the 1990s. Younger groups soon followed, adding new layers of rock and hip hop, a style many in New Orleans believe to be a riff on Mardi Gras Indian "rapping." As we see elsewhere in this book, Michael White, Greg Stafford, and others who were kids in the Fairview era now criticize the newer bands for disrespecting tradition, both the older band style and the rituals of the jazz funeral. We should remember that the jazz funeral and jazz itself were once decried as a degradation of tradition, a disruption of the basic social order. Clearly, we are in a new historical cycle where similar patterns and partisanships are emerging.

One of the most important bands pioneering the new sound was the Dirty Dozen Brass Band. Their breakout hit, "My Feet Can't Fail Me Now," was a radical example of "street" music—pure rhythm without chord changes played at a dizzying tempo. It got dancers out on the floor in clubs where the new brass bands were starting to play, making it clear that this music was not just for marching. According to Phil Frazier, this primitive but irresistible tune was "the Bible" for young brass players seeking to develop a contemporary style in the late '70s; it also became a theme song for groups in other genres, such as the zydeco nouveau band, Rockin' Dopsie and the Zydeco Twisters.

Like so many NOLA bands, the Dirty Dozen emerged spontaneously from the Tremé, playing at softball games, birthday parties, and Halloween parades, getting their name from a pleasure club called Dirty Dozen, at which they

Dirty Dozen Brass Band. Photograph by Harriet Blum.

performed for parties and funerals. Although often on the road, they have
not forgotten their roots and still can play a funeral hymn like "I Shall Not
Be Moved" with goosepimply grandeur. They are proof that, as Matt Sakakeeny argues, there is no "fixed generation gap, with hip hop as a stable line
of demarcation."[27] Now part of the older generation, they have always been
aggressively funky and innovative, and they still draw young crowds.

For young musicians looking for a contemporary sound, the Dirty Dozen
was an irresistible model: Frazier remembers them playing "Blackbird Special" at his cousin's funeral in the late '70s "like it was yesterday. . . . I had never
heard anything like that before in my life."[28] To Victor Goines, the band was
a revelation as well:. "I remember when the Dirty Dozen first hit the scene.
They were smoking, man, and they really had their thing together, and they
had a very good, authentic sound coming out of their brass band."[29] The Dirty
Dozen was to Goines, Frazier, and their generation what Frazier and Rebirth
are to younger players like Evans and the Pinettes—what Evans refers to as
an "awakening."

From a contemporary perspective, the Dirty Dozen may seem "very
authentic," but at the time, it was regarded as anything but. For younger brass
bands, the double-barrel shotgun of Rebirth and Dirty Dozen was the beginning of a new history, setting up a demarcation between past and present: "We
play traditional," says Christie Jordain, drummer for the Original Pinettes,

"but it's a totally different sound than a traditional brass band. We take from the Dirty Dozen and Rebirth brass bands—those were the people who started the funk sound in the brass band, so that's the direction we're going in. When we started, everything we did came from Rebirth; they birthed *us*. You have to understand, we were young, and they changed the game from traditional to funk. They went out on the street and took it to that level and stayed there. They didn't let anybody change their mind. And right now, they are the pioneers of this. They are the ones that every now and then we go back and listen to. And every time you see them, it's always a good show to see. Every time."[30]

By the early '80s, with the Dirty Dozen and Rebirth on the ascendance, the new brass sound was on its way, though resisted by the unceasing chorus of critics who complain about the degeneration of "real New Orleans" and "real jazz." Snare drummer Barry Martyn of Andrew Hall's Society Brass Band remembers Danny Barker in 1985 trying to correct a British trombonist who was loudly denouncing the "kids" for playing "modern music" in Jackson Square: "You don't realize, you guys that come here. The music changes, and these youngsters want to play something that belongs to today. They're playing the traditional tunes, but they're tightening them up."[31]

They became tighter than ever in the '90s as joints like Donna's, Howlin' Wolf, and the Funky Butt Café provided regular venues for indoor brass-band engagements, enabling the emerging bands to develop distinctive styles. Richard Rochester, a former parks ranger who opened the Funky Butt in 1995, regarded his place as representing Danny Barker's legacy. "Richard, I want you to open your own joint," Barker told Rochester in the late '80s: "Make it a nice place and call it the Funky Butt Café."[32] The club served blackened redfish upstairs and brass bands downstairs, the sounds blaring out onto Rampart Street, directly across from what was once Congo Square. Charlie Sims, the former cook on the Southern Crescent Railroad, had even better food in Donna's, and served it for free on Monday nights. The brass bands playing in Donna's, his tiny place three blocks from the Funky Butt, paraded out late at night in second lines. Music fans could move from one club to another, as could the players, a premonition of the club renaissance on Frenchmen Street. The brass-band phenomenon on Rampart Street in the '90s and early 2000s was a high point in New Orleans music history.

The bands have contrived numerous ways to survive. Responding to a changing audience, some have taken on a Jekyll-Hyde duality, playing day gigs for traditionalists under one name and late-night shows for younger people under another. Lumar Leblanc and Derrick Moss were once members of the Young Olympia Brass Band (a descendant of Dejan's Olympia from 1963), but started calling themselves the Soul Rebels for nightclub engagements. "Let

Your Mind Be Free," their signature tune, signals an openness to any genre that works well with a brass-band beat, including reggae, hip hop, and chant-like vocals of their own invention. Just as Rebirth had embraced funk, the Soul Rebels jumped into hip hop, drawing a young crowd and showing how the old and the new could surge ahead together. The band had a regular gig at Donna's during the '90s and early 2000s; then they began holding forth every Thursday night (all night) in Le Bon Temps Roule on Magazine Street to a huge, screaming crowd in a space only slightly less jammed than the Maple Leaf. This charismatic band can mix up anything. I've heard them join Cajun and funk musicians with mind-bending ease. They turn up the voltage on any stage.

The success of the Soul Rebels and bands like them goes beyond local gigs. The brass-band renaissance in New Orleans has reached into a larger national space. Several first-rate groups base their aesthetic on the NOLA renaissance. Typical is the Richmond, Virginia-based No BS Brass Band ("No BS" meaning no drama, just music), a group from 2007 inspired by the Soul Rebels. No BS blends traditional brass-band polyphony and call-response with Mingus, hip hop, and adventurous new songs. They lack the raw power of the Soul Rebels, but they produce a big, gleaming sonority, unerringly in tune (several members are classically trained players). According to saxophonist David Hood, this fullness comes from the use of a concert sousaphone, rounder and darker than what we usually hear on the streets.[33] Like the Soul Rebels, they sound sensational indoors or out. No BS exemplifies Johnny Vidacovich's post-Katrina exhortation to "never let the tradition of the music die because so many beautiful kinds of music have been influenced by it . . . it's been an essential element in music in so many other places."[34]

One reason the brass bands flourish is that elder musicians are more than just musical mentors. They give young players a sense of pride, personhood, and well-being tied directly to their city's heritage. The sense of community and common purpose among young and old is a powerful bond. As Leroy Jones puts it, "There is and has always been a better sense of camaraderie amongst the musicians in New Orleans. For the most part, the older, more experienced musicians, especially within the traditional jazz circles, have always been willing to help and guide the younger ones, as well as being hospitable to musicians from abroad."[35] The tradition invests players with a powerful sense of legacy. Gregg Stafford identifies Danny Barker and other senior players as teachers who "gave us a sense of individual pride. He gave us something to keep and cherish: that you are somebody, that you are important, and these are the reasons to preserve your heritage, as you can pass it on to the next generation. . . . All those guys were like my father. They all had the same pride about themselves." Now Stafford has his own students, who provide him with a similar source of pride—and also an insurance policy against the ups and downs of the music business: "If I get the gig, it's fine, if I don't get it, it's still fine. That's why I went to school and got a degree in education, so I wouldn't have to put up with the unnecessary bullshit. The older musicians used to tell me all the time, 'Gregg, keep your day job. In this city, it's not always how well you play, sometimes it's who you play for and whether they allow you to play.'"[36]

The mentors thus dispensed practical as well as aesthetic wisdom. For Michael White, the father was Doc Paulin, a "great teacher" from the Depression era who "taught a lot of the musical, as well as the spiritual and professional values." Young players learned that music was "a step up," a way to gain self-respect and autonomy. "A lot of people were very proud to be musicians . . . Doc Paulin inherited and passed along that ethic."[37] In the poorer neighborhoods, where residents struggle on a daily basis with racism and violence, that pride can be life-saving. Phil Frazier puts it bluntly: "Better to pick up a musical instrument than pick up a gun. Pick up a horn, and you do all right."[38] This embrace of brass-band tradition as a survival mechanism is something the Katrina doomsayers who said the music would vanish never understood; in the Tremé, the brass bands are a way of life, a *reason* for living.

There are so many functions for brass bands that they are hard to sort out. Some forty social aid and pleasure clubs (there are close to seventy in the city in all) march in four-hour Sunday second-line parades from August to June in a given club's neighborhood. These remarkable organizations don't exist to party, though a casual visitor might think so; they support Mardi Gras Indian tribes and provide burial plots and other important services for members. But parading is a significant part of their agenda. These are often anniversary celebrations. Fans, streamers, umbrellas, baskets, and other accessories matching a given outfit are on ostentatious display. The jazz funeral is sometimes confused with the Sunday parade even though funerals do not occur on Sundays and, in contrast to the colorful costumes of the Sunday second lines, the favored color is black. "The second line is ingrained in the culture," says Ellis Marsalis. "Not a lot of people understand it, and I understand why. They equate the second line with jazz funerals. So a lot of people will come down for them—I remember Danny Barker got upset one time with people saying, 'We got to go to a jazz funeral.' He said, 'Well, what do you want me to do, go kill somebody?' The whole concept of the jazz funeral is peculiar to certain people. Some people don't want nothing to do with that. The second line has developed into a celebratory thing where people, along with the social and pleasure clubs, just get out in the street and do it. There are specific times you can hear a second line, like Super Sunday, when all the Mardi Gras

Lady Jet Setters Social and Pleasure Club. Photograph by
Jack Sullivan.

Indians come out."³⁹ Having someone die is not essential; second lines are for
the living, not just the dead. On the Sunday of a given parade, the organization sends out a route sheet with timings to members, but it's not strictly
necessary; the crowd follows the music wherever it takes them, stopping at
homes and local bars to get a drink, use the bathroom, buy food from vendors
on pickup trucks, or just hang out. The experience is intense, sometimes frenzied, but (given the frequently enormous size of the crowd) oddly comfortable and civilized. It's all fueled by brass-band music, the specific group often
announced just before the parade. It's hard to imagine more happiness and a
more loving sense of community on a city street.

Currently, the city is rocked by the jubilant sounds of the New Wave Brass
Band, the Stooges, the Lil' Rascals, Deja Vu, Tremé, the Baby Boyz, and dozens
of others. Funky innovation is the trend, but some groups, notably Tremé,
New Tuxedo, and Deja Vu, are standard-bearers for the tradition. Breaking
through barriers in a male-dominated form, two all-female Pinettes brass

bands—the Pinettes and the Original Pinettes—have been blasting their way through town in a new wave of popularity after a slow start in the '90s. They have a pop-infused repertory yoked to traditional tunes, emphasizing vocals far more than other brass bands. Angelika Joseph is often the featured vocalist, but the entire group sings. The band has a powerful female aura that is new to brass bands. "The new sound is a recent thing," says trumpet player Veronique Dorsey, "but the original band has existed since 1991, with alumni of St. Mary's Academy. The band director decided to create a brass band to help the parents out with money, and it hasn't stopped since. As far as female brass bands go, we are the only one." And that makes the vibe very different, says drummer Christie Jordain: "We're women; we're different because we bring a different element to the game, a different stage presence. We're really just developing our own style and our own sound. A lot of the guys can't really transfer the streets to the stage. We try to get the crowd involved, we vibe off the crowd vibe. We try to get intimate with the crowd; we let them know that without them, we are nothing. And that's the God-honest truth. If everybody get up and leave now, we're gonna close down."[40]

This is not an off-the-cuff statement; the open-hearted embrace projected by this band is very different from the diffident, look-how-cool-we-are attitude seen in some of the younger male bands. When I asked what it's like being female in the brass world, the members yelled back with one word: "Hard!" "Yes," says Jordain. "It's male dominated. Brass-band music started here in New Orleans, so it's hard because you don't find many of them. We're not trying to be the only one. The age ranges from nineteen to forty, so some of us are married, some have kids, school, full-time jobs, and some do this full-time. I'm an art teacher and play drums at my church. Our saxophone player runs a technology department at St. Mary's Academy. The trombone player works at a dentist's office, and our other trumpet player's still in school. The guys can just get up and go as they choose, but we don't have alternates or replacements; if somebody gets pregnant, they have to go out. We have to work with what we have."

What they have is remarkable. I've heard them in their regular gig at Bullet's Sports Lounge in the Seventh Ward, a tiny joint with a big heart and a happy atmosphere. The drums and sousaphone start the show while Angelika Joseph exhorts people to join the party. At her command, everybody gets up and dances around the cramped tables—it's impossible not to. Singers blend with brass in a sensual current. "We do a lot of chanting and singing," says Jordain. "When we play, it sounds like someone singing; that's what we shoot for."[41] This is what Louis Armstrong shot for as well; the tradition of hornists sounding like singers is still alive and well.

The Pinettes at Bullet's Sports Lounge. Photograph by Brandon Xeureb, Xistence Photography.

Those who are brought up in the brass-band tradition have the second-line vibe in their bloodstream. If they leave town, it stays with them. Jon Batiste says that the "New Orleans ethos" is forever part of him. "You can't take it out of the sound because one thing about the New Orleans sound is that if you come from it, it influences everything. The rhythm, drum, the sound of the tambourine, the snare drums, the bass drum—that's influenced American music so much—and then, the idea of how it influenced each musician that's come out of New Orleans is even more potent, because they've lived in it."[42]

According to Leroy Jones, nothing like the current brass-band renaissance has happened in more than a century: "Brass-band music from New Orleans is not only popular since the '90s, but is more popular than it has ever been since the very latter part of the nineteenth century and beginning of the twentieth. There are so many new brass bands consisting of very young musicians popping up around town until I don't even know the names of half of them! And I think bands like the Hot 8 Brass Band, the Soul Rebels, the Rebirth Brass Band, the Dirty Dozen, the Treme Brass Band, the Original Hurricane Brass Band, and the Young Tuxedo Brass Band continue to uphold the flag of the tradition, the latter incorporating a repertoire more appealing to their peers. Hence the more contemporary brass-band sound, though unmistakably New Orleans."[43]

His one caveat, shared by Lucien Barbarin, is that the youngest members often "have no depth in the repertory"; indeed, sometimes they don't know the standards at all. The flow of new songs from the emergent groups is welcome, but Jones and other seasoned players wonder if the younger players realize how much New Orleans depends on its ancestors. You can't renew a tradition if you don't know it in the first place.

Skeptics like Michael White worry that the very openness and spontaneity that promoted New Orleans music in the first place has a downside: "While evolution and change are in some ways necessary and inevitable, the open-ended, free-spirited nature of the New Orleans tradition has always allowed for so much change that in terms of function, spirit, music, and image, little of the brass bands' original meaning and distinguishing stylistic characteristics remain."[44] The very success of the music in the twenty-first century is problematic, a dilemma that is not unique to New Orleans music: "The popularity is good for the musicians because they get more gigs, but it's bad because the music gets commercialized and watered down; it becomes music for tourists."[45] This concern is echoed by Victor Goines, who believes current bands are trending too far toward an ahistorical commercialism, "taking pop tunes and looking for hits. Of course, there's nothing wrong with that. Look at Duke Ellington. I don't want to be absolute. I don't think it's true of all the brass bands. But it's gotten so commercial that sometimes it lacks the authenticity. It's become an overblown vibe." This argument strikes at the heart of the new brass-band aesthetic. What for some is the most exciting aspect of the new sound—its unwavering intensity—is for others an "overblown vibe," a dynamic range of loud, louder, and loudest. Goines believes "the excitement of playing loud has put to rest the musicianship they brought to the bandstand with their group; I would like to see that not just retained but raised to a higher level. Some brass bands have done tremendous things; others have just capitalized on the popularity of brass bands today. In those early bands, like the Dirty Dozen when they were doing 'Feet Don't Fail Me Now,' the musicianship of Gregory Davis and Kirk Joseph was very high. I would like to see our musicians not give up musicality for the sake of entertainment."[46]

Finding the line between "entertainment" and a higher art is tricky in New Orleans, and many musicians I talk to believe it doesn't exist. The tension has always been there, as the tourist industry is vital for New Orleans's existence, but White believes new challenges exist as well. He cites the obsession with instant gratification in this "age of the self" as antithetical to the discipline and collective improvisation central to brass-band tradition. Traditionalists like White link America's fetish for speed and consumption with a competitive aggressiveness that is the opposite of the more communal New Orleans ethic. Gregg Stafford, who plays trumpet in White's Liberty Jazz Band, puts it starkly: "Music, that means time. You need to sit down and study, learn the songs. They don't want to do that. Anything that takes time, in America now, you can forget it. That's the nature of the society; everything is automation, automatic, quick to make money . . . ; it's a society that breeds selfishness. That's why there is so much anger in the music, and aggressiveness in the music. You've got brass bands coming down the street, singing songs with profanity. What kind of mess is that?" Stafford is heartened by his involve-ment with "the great Young Tuxedo Band," who work "with the last of the real traditional players," but he worries that once the senior players die off, the tradition will become extinct.[47]

An indifference to one's own musical history is dangerous, Stafford believes. A group like the Hot 8 "is so used to playing their style of music on the streets, and the social and pleasure clubs and the second-liners, that's what they're so used to hearing on the streets now—if the old style of New Orleans brass-music were out on the street, they would look at them like they were from another planet; they would run them off the streets: 'What you all play-ing? We don't want to hear that.' That's because people don't know the history of the music; they haven't been educated about the music—out of sight, out of mind."[48] Barry Martyn, who directs the "strictly traditional" Society Brass Band, agrees: "Music has got to move forward. You got Ravel from Mozart somewhere along the line. Brass-band music is the same thing. But last time I went to a funeral, there was a young black band and their hat was on like this [backward], and it said 'kiss me quick' on their T-shirts or some foolish thing, and they had the trumpets in the front and the trombones back of them. I don't know anything about that kind of music, I just don't like that kind of music—but they're New Orleans musicians and I'm not [Martyn came to New Orleans from London], so in a way, what right have I to criticize them? But I don't have to follow in their footsteps—I don't go along with them. I don't *go* to funerals anymore because I can't stand the music." When I asked what he made of Michael White mentoring the Hot 8 Brass Band so they could learn traditional repertory, a project many are heartened by, he said, "Michael's a good guy, but he's beating a dead horse, just like I'm beating a dead horse. You ain't never going to get that. Look, the Eureka Brass Band with Percy Humphrey as the leader: *that* was a brass band—or the Tuxedo Brass Band or the Gibson Brass Band, the three big ones when I came here. If you came to a funeral with your hat on backwards or a white hat instead of black, Percy would just grunt at you [here Martyn makes a rather terrifying guttural sound] and say, 'Go home.'"[49]

Whether these complaints are merely the newest cycle of the older genera-tion showing its impatience with the younger—precisely what Jones and his peers heard from critics when they started up the funky new brass sounds of the '70s—remains to be seen. Those who defend the new bands—and the defenders are by no means only younger musicians—believe this attitude is a puritanical absolutism antithetical to New Orleans tradition. Any wall between "art" and "entertainment" is in the minds of those who erect it and has little to do with the realities of making a living as a musician. The major-ity of musicians I speak with believe the music has always been about mov-ing ahead with the tastes and customs of contemporary audiences, pop tunes included, with brass bands as subject to change as any other form. The Origi-nal Pinettes make no apologies for putting out whatever it takes to please a contemporary audience: "We try to cater to them; we have songs from the tradition, the '70s, the '90s, funk, pop, Cyndi Lauper, whatever it is."[50] They do "Hindustan Blues" with as much verve as Stevie Wonder songs. Shamarr Allen, who got his start with Rebirth and sings lots of pop and hip hop while gigging with traditional bands like Treme, believes eclecticism *is* the tradi-tion: "I grew up listening to rap, rock, country, jazz, folk, everything. I like all music. Even if I hear a punk song I like, I'll use it to my advantage in some way. That's what New Orleans music is."[51]

The prevalence of indoor gigs and recordings has tempted some groups into using keyboards, vibraphones, and other instruments not found in marching bands. This too has prompted dismay from traditionalists, but the brass-band scholar Mick Burns points out that early groups like the Onward and Olympia bands were not averse to using banjos and pianos when they played indoors.[52] For some groups, the move indoors has taken on an energy of its own. Some, like the Forgotten Souls Brass Band, boasting an extra drum set, play inside only, producing a round, walloping sonority. The New Birth, which does the Maple Leaf on Tuesday nights when the Rebirth can't make it, carries the legacy of its namesake forward with new players and new levels of daring.

The quintessential post-Katrina ensemble is the Brass-A-Holics, a brass band that adds so many elements—keyboard, electric guitars, extra percus-sion—that it moves beyond the "extra-added" elements of contemporary brass bands to become something altogether new. Founded in 2010 by Winston Turner (from the Soul Rebels and Pinstripes brass bands), the Brass-A-Holics play brass-band repertory, but a typical set will also offer Bon Jovi, Nirvana, hip hop, swing, Coltrane, classic rock, and unclassifiable compositions of their own. Their energy gets the crowd dancing and screaming—this is a band you cannot sit still for—but they also have a suaveness deriving in part from the enchanting keyboard of Keiko Komaki, one of a growing number of Asian musicians in the city. The blending of genders and races reflects the ethnic diversity of the current scene, and the variety of textures and ensembles— scorching tutti but also delicate solos and brass trios—feels constantly fresh. You think you're in the contemporary world, but then sax player Robin Clabby will sing "It Don't Mean a Thing If It Ain't Got That Swing," with style to spare, and you're transported to an earlier era. When I asked Clabby whether the band was doing something radically new or extending the brass-band tradition, he said, "We definitely play out of the brass-band tradition, but it's got more to do with the way that we play and interact with each other. The music that informs us is that stuff, but all the other stuff we grew up listening to as well—and with this band, that's a pretty big mix. It goes back to Louis Armstrong, but we do 'Wham,' a Royals tune by a sixteen-year-old New Zealand girl, folk songs, heavy metal, funk, anything that catches our fancy—that's the fun of what we do." So does it have any label? "We call it 'go-go brass funk' just to have some kind of tag, but we love the tradition too. What's traditional is the idea that you can react very spontaneously on the spot and everybody listens to each other. You can go through so many stylistic detours and still have something distinct." The variety of textures comes from an ensemble concept where there is no star, the essence of brass-band aesthetics: "Part of it is just capitalizing on how everybody is just so good; we want to give everybody a chance to do what they do." [53]

In one of the oddest and happiest of the new NOLA rituals, cheering locals crowd into claustrophobic bars to hear dense brass sonorities and rocking rhythms meant for outdoor parades. The whole point of the brass-band sound, as opposed to jazz, is that it is heard outdoors, generating a more open sound based on marching instruments. But NOLA is all about establishing traditions, then reconfiguring them for new generations and sensibilities. The indoor brass-band aesthetic is a paradox: music that traditionally dissipates into open air becomes an enclosed, aggressive wall of sound, perhaps the loudest acoustic music anywhere, uncomfortable in its brash intensity yet strangely thrilling.

Chapter Three

FROM ARMSTRONG TO THE NEW TRADITIONALISM: NEW ORLEANS JAZZ IS ALWAYS NOW

In New Orleans, magic is ordinary.
—Todd Duke

Traditional New Orleans jazz has a surprising endurance and a mysterious newness. Like the sonata form of Haydn and Mozart, it retains its integrity even as it branches into innumerable variants to fit the times. In New Orleans, it flourishes as if it were invented yesterday. At Vaughan's Lounge during Mardi Gras season, 2013, I was pulled onto the dance floor by a new local who had moved to NOLA because it was the only place she could hear traditional jazz. "I love trad jazz," she screamed over the music, "and you don't get it in New York." No, you don't, as those who live in New York and love this music can attest. What we were dancing to was indeed traditional, from "Basin Street Blues" to '30s swing, but the Barbecue Swingers were mixing it up with Mardi Gras tunes, pop, hip hop, goofy reefer songs, and much else, as Armstrong did with the sounds of his own several eras.

New Orleans is the only place where traditional jazz is still unapologetically embraced. It is part of the fundamental texture of the place. Because of its openness, both in form and spirit, it can incorporate sounds outside its domain, from Broadway to bebop, without losing its identity. Even when mingled with rock and street funk, as it was during this night at Vaughan's, its essential core is always there: the airy syncopation, tight polyphony, brass-band backbeat, blues harmonies, and soaring melody. When we think of jazz, we usually think of rhythm, the "cult of the displaced accent," as the

Times-Picayune disparagingly called it in 1918, but in New Orleans, whose early history was informed by Creole lyricism, melody is essential to the magic.[1]

That magic has dimmed in many cities, but it hasn't in New Orleans. "People don't respect melody anymore," says trumpeter Wendell Brunious, who left the city for seven years after Katrina, then felt compelled to return. "But they do here. That's why I live in New Orleans."[2] Brunious, one of the great melodists in the city, gets to lay down the line with his trumpet. As drummer Barry Martyn explains it, "With traditional, the first trumpet plays the lead, the solos play when the trumpet takes down, they keep the melody going—just like Michael [White], said, Jelly said, Bunk said, Baby Doll said: 'Always keep the melody in jazz, otherwise you ain't *got* no jazz.'"[3]

The music must swing, but also sing, and with more than one voice at a time. "The essence is polyphony," says singer-pianist Jon Batiste, speaking with quiet awe about his predecessors. "If you listen to early Louis Armstrong or King Oliver, you find that everybody's playing at the same time. How do they keep track?"[4] One way is by not neglecting the melody. "Jazz is more sophisticated than pop," says pianist-composer Jeff Franzel, "but underneath it all should be a thread of 'less is more.' With the players I admire like Sidney Bechet, Louis Armstrong, Lester Young, it's melody—what they do with melody. In my own piano playing, I can go way out, but I come back in. I don't want to lose my listeners. Like a Frank Lloyd Wright: you're not cluttering the space; you're allowing it to breathe."[5] Whether based on blues, Creole tunes, brass-band chorales, or Latin mazurkas, the melody is the heartbeat, so much so that rhythm itself becomes melodic: "One of the most beautiful things about New Orleans rhythm," says drummer Johnny Vidacovich, "is that it does have a melodic rhythm to it with the right cats playing it . . . New Orleans drumming is very melodic. It's wavy, like water."[6] Drummer Shannon Powell also keeps melody front and center: "I'm a self-taught musician, and I hear everything melodically. I stick strictly to the melody of a song. That's how I perform—through melodies."[7] When experiencing the dynamism of Powell's drumming—as we see in this chapter, he is often a fraction of a second ahead of everyone else—melody isn't the first thing we think of, but it's what animates everything.

This essential aspect of New Orleans sensibility goes back to Louis Moreau Gottschalk, whose most important compositions were based on complex slave drumming but whose melodic sense was disarmingly simple, a duplicity summarized by his champion, Hector Berlioz, in 1851: "The charming ease with which he plays simple things seems to belong to a second personality, distinct from that which characterizes his thundering energies."[8] In contemporary parlance, "charming ease" becomes "laid-backness," just as "thundering energies" becomes "really smoking." Musicians are as likely to say that one of these is NOLA's distinctive vibe as the other, but they are really two aspects of the same thing, a duality that sets the place and its music apart. It is essential to remember that New Orleans was a French colonial town, not an Anglo-Saxon one; the French were the descendants of Mediterraneans, not Puritans, and were resolutely committed to the pleasure principle. "If you're from New Orleans," says Delfeayo Marsalis, "cats are going to be grooving and swinging, and having a good time. Equally important is the idea of playing melodies and melodic phrases as opposed to just stringing together a bunch of licks. When you hear a guy from New Orleans, you can always tell."[9] Drummer Earl Palmer believed there is a fundamental happiness in New Orleans jazz: "You find a relaxation in New Orleans drummers that demonstrates his feeling of New Orleans . . . It's a happy feeling about it . . . that you could almost distinguish if you lived long enough and hard enough"; it's something "that you don't feel from other drummers."[10] Pianist Lawrence Sieberth, who plays around the world but lives in New Orleans, says, "There is a laid-backness in the beat that you don't find anywhere else."[11] On the other hand, musicians like Herlin Riley and David Torkanowsky emphasize the volatility and urgency of the music—again, these are aspects they insist you don't find anywhere else.

What unites these qualities is a singular sensuality. Lester Young, who gave music a new sound, a new myth, and a new sense of effortless possibility, bequeathed the myth of "cool," a word he himself coined: the laconic hipster, boozy and smoky, detached and sexy, the equivalent of Bogart and film noir. In contrast to the fat, quavery honk of those who came before him, Young's sonority was lean and sultry. None of these qualities contradicted Young's emotional fervor; in fact, the seeming detachment made his playing more moving and expressive, not less. His influence on NOLA musicians today is incalculable, though his aesthetic goes in and out of fashion. According to jazz singer John Boutte, the 1970s were the nadir: "Everybody had to have an electric guitar. Nobody could hear how sexy Lester Young's sax was anymore."[12]

Exciting as New Orleans's soloists are, it's the ensemble that counts: the cornet line is usually a melody anchored in the harmonies of the piano, "smeared" by the slides of the trombone, embellished by the obbligato of the clarinet or saxophone, and rocked by the second-line syncopations of the drum section. The basic melodic material is memorized in advance, either by "readers" or "fakers," in an ensemble that includes players with dramatically varying levels of musical training, from a great deal to none at all. Jazz is known for rowdiness or "rattiness," but seamlessness is the ideal; brass players strive to sound like singers and vocalists like instrumentalists. Armstrong wanted a trumpet sound that emulated a voice, preferably someone like Caruso. When

Germaine Bazzle was learning to sing, she banished vocal templates, even Ella Fitzgerald and Sarah Vaughan, who were her idols: "For a while I stopped listening to vocalists, and I just listened to instrumentalists. I was a fan of Miles Davis, Stan Kenton, Woody Herman. I was in college at the time, so many of us who were music majors used to sit in our co-op, and we had these tunes on the jukebox. That's how it all got started."[13]

This music has always been communal, its hedonistic energies paradoxically steeped in official practice. Jazz emerged from the French Quarter, the Tremé, and the Marigny, not, as Thomas Fiehrer points out, as a rebellious or "escapist" outlet but a way of life that had its essence in the street: "The colonial regime's active support of dance halls, quadroon balls, religious processions, and public festivities established early on the state's intimate involvement with the public domain. . . . Jazz congealed in response to a peculiarly open public domain—the street as theater."[14] Only later did the decimation of Creole culture and post-Reconstruction racist policies turn jazz into a force of resistance to a segregationist social order.

Jazz began and continues in New Orleans because of the city's singular tradition of parading, playing, singing, and dancing and partying in the streets. For centuries, it has been a jubilant counterpoint to political oppression, flood, disease, and unspeakable humidity. We'll never know precisely what constituted the first jazz; by the time people began caring about the question, those who could bear witness were gone, and recordings came too late to establish origins or tell us what the earliest jazz bands—including those of the cornetist Buddy Bolden—actually sounded like. That doesn't stop people from speculating. Scholars continue a lively, sometimes contentious dispute, offering everything from census data to shifting dance forms in the late nineteenth century to prove that the real jazz start-ups were either African, West Indian, Creole, Afro-Latin, or some combination thereof. The earliest proto-jazz has been variously identified as African ring dances in Congo Square, field hollers, Creole motifs from Paris, Spanish-tinged piano pieces by Gottschalk, ragtime, brass-band parade music, black Indian chants, and the "hot" two-step dances that replaced waltzes and quadrilles. A leap forward from the blaring sonorities of marching bands came with pianos, which brought the music indoors, bequeathing a sophistication and harmonic richness we now take for granted. Aside from the influences, we have early musicians—the Tios, Papa Jack Laine, "Bunk" Johnson, Nick LaRocca, George Baquet, and others—who have not received the star coverage of Armstrong, Bechet, and Morton, but who get cited (sometimes by themselves) as crucial origin figures.

It's astonishing to consider how something that has only been around since the late nineteenth century has already amassed so many names, styles,

Michael White at Preservation Hall. Photograph by Jack Sullivan.

subcultures, and myths. Current scholars, as demonstrated by Lawrence Gushee, have moved away from dogmatic proclamations, a tactical shift since the precise origins are still far from clear: "We have no reason to doubt that by 1905 some bands, whether [Buddy] Bolden's, the Golden Rule or some other, were making music we might consider as an ancestor of jazz." The conditionals—"no reason to doubt," "some," "might"—signify a reluctance to pin down something stubbornly mysterious. The exact origins of ragtime are ambiguous as well: "Just as the origins of jazz become fuzzy once we begin looking at jazz before jazz, so it is with ragtime."[15] One thing certain about jazz, according to musicians I speak to, is that it's American, both in its ethnic layering and its freedom. "Jazz is an American music," says Barry Martyn. "It don't come from Yugoslavia or Australia. It's not the same now as when I came to New Orleans, but it's still exciting, still better than anything they've got in Europe. It's the beat—it's American. If you played a record, eight or nine out of ten, I could tell you if it's an American band."[16] So much about jazz is easier to sense than to identify: Martyn does not attempt to codify what makes the beat American. He just knows—at least eight out of ten times—when it is.

Jazz represents America at its best, the American myth as opposed to the reality. As Cornel West points out, it was the place where America first practiced racial integration personally and artistically—"black music played with

European instruments" and an embodiment of the racial equality America was supposed to practice but so often did not. [17]

Unless one believes Jelly Roll Morton, who claimed to have invented jazz himself, the first jazz players may have had no idea what they were starting up. Part of traditional jazz's charm is its lack of self-consciousness, something that appears to have been present from the beginning. Clarinetist Michael White believes that jazz started as a casual accretion of energy in various NOLA genres that suddenly exploded into something important and uncontainable. When Buddy Bolden and his colleagues "first began to improvise and liven up standard themes and adopt blues vocal effects on wind instruments in the mid-1890s, they became unknowing participants in a musical and social revolution . . . The new 'ratty' style—not called 'jazz' until years later—was a looser, freer, more swinging improvised approach to ragtime, marches, blues, hymns, waltzes, folk songs, and popular music . . . the bouncy danceable tempos and sheer passion in the new, mainly instrumental new style were too exciting to relegate to any one area, ethnic group or social level."[18]

As White points out, early jazz was not confined to one ethnic group, but was a "crazy quilt" of ethnicities unthinkable in the rest of America. It was never for an elite. Everyone was included, all skin colors and economic classes, the Big Easy's "relatively warm and easy intermingling of races," as Tennessee Williams puts it in the stage directions to *A Streetcar Named Desire*. Williams is careful to qualify his statement with "relatively," but the most cursory look at archives and photos of early NOLA jazz bands reveals black and white players alike, and research by recent scholars has uncovered a startling variety of early players: African American, Latino, Afro-Latin, Afro-French, Sicilian, Mexican, Albanian, Romanian, and much else—all converging in a new style of dance music uniting peoples and neighborhoods that racist laws were designed to segregate.[19] In his Harvard lectures, Wynton Marsalis describes jazz as a "music of freedom" consisting of "low-down refinement, Voodoo-ized religion, Creole-ized Africanism, Italian passion, Spanish fire, and American insouciance."[20]

New Orleans is often called a "new Atlantis," in the words of author John Swenson, or a "Constantinople." The Crescent City's position on the Mississippi, the hub of commerce, and its proximity to Central America and the Caribbean, guaranteed that it would keep pumping an inexhaustible flow of work songs, spirituals, blues, island rhythms, and vernacular music from across the Americas, all converging into something called jazz in the early twentieth century. "The special thing about New Orleans," says Jon Batiste, "is that it was a blend of people who settled there because it was a port city. You had the English colonization, the French colonization; you have this blending there based on their style of takeover, and then you have people coming in from the Caribbean and the African influence and the Spanish influence and Congo Square. And then you have all of this music, and you think when all that blends together, what do you play at a social gathering? What music is going to happen? You don't play Spanish music for the Spanish people, then Irish music for the Irish people. What music is going to happen, what do they dance to? I think that at the turn of the century, all this has marinated and spent its time developing in this port city, this little bubble, and it explodes, and you have these people produced who are genius musicians of this culture, representing it and taking it across the world, and at the same time, the recorded medium of an album and vinyl records come into play, and now people can hear it everywhere, and that sound is something. Their life wasn't like that; it's only in New Orleans at this point. So they hear it, and they're like, 'Wow! This is amazing! This speaks to us.' So it's really an interesting phenomenon: it's perfect place, perfect time."[21]

The constant invasion of new people, always a threat to established musicians, is a long-term advantage that insures the music stays fresh. "We have a greater amalgamation of folks," says John Boutte. "In jazz, having the same thing all the time leads to musical weakness. We always have a fresh gene pool, always new people coming in. It is totally unlike the rest of America."[22]

A living embodiment of jazz from its beginnings to now is the Tuxedo Jazz Band, which celebrated its centenary in 2010. Drummer Bob French, who stepped down in 2011, was only the fourth leader of the ensemble. Tuxedo got its name from a Storyville club where it first began playing in 1910. Like so many NOLA bands, it is a family affair and has included enough important musicians to constitute a small history of New Orleans jazz, including Louis Armstrong, who began playing with the brass-band version of the group when its founder, "Papa" Celestin (so named by Armstrong), was unavailable for a gig in 1915. (Tuxedo claims to have taught Armstrong to read music, but early biographers deny this.) As Bruce Raeburn eloquently puts it, Tuxedo has not only "transcended the stereotypes [of pimps, brothels, and Dixieland antics], but has survived for more than a century, a feat that has never been equaled in jazz history, working its way from the black tenderloin into the houses and hearts of the city's affluent, white social elite in less than a decade . . . the Original Tuxedo Jazz Band became a means of promoting mutuality and reconciliation that subverted the dehumanizing effects of racism and lasted for generations. Such is the power of New Orleans jazz, when performed from the heart."[23]

With Tuxedo, heart is dispensed with laconic restraint. Celebratory numbers like "Bourbon Street Parade" and "Hey, What's the Matter with Me?"

combine thumping cross-rhythms with sly subtlety. The band holds back just a bit, creating a rising crescendo that blows the audience away in the final chorus. The former leader, Bob French, had an eloquently grainy voice; his nephew and successor, Gerald, also a drummer, is a booming bass. They have a very different sound, yet the vibe remains the same, a mischievous laid-backness that affects everyone, allowing players to be most fully themselves: When Kermit Ruffins sits in, his skats are happier and looser than ever; when John Boutte appears (sometimes in his pajamas during the Donna's era), his cantilena is smoother; when Yolanda Windsay sings the blues, her voice has an extra richness; when Henry Butler thunders through "Bogalusa Strut," a jazz joint becomes a concert hall.

Since 1995, I have been bringing Rider University students to Tuxedo's regular gig on Monday nights, when a huge repertory of traditional pieces—"The Second Line," "Muskrat Ramble," "St. James Infirmary," "At Last," "Bourbon Street Parade," as well as out-of-town numbers like "A-Train" and "Mack the Knife"—are performed with wit and panache. No one has been playing jazz longer, yet an influx of new players keeps everything fresh. Bob French played with Fats Domino as a young man and always carried forward the Fats ethic of racial inclusiveness, as does Gerald. Their shows bring in a multiracial array of players: bassist Richard Moten; pianists David Torkanowsky, Fred Sanders, Mari Wantanabe, and Lawrence Sieberth; singers Tricia "Sista Teedy" Boutte, Juanita Brooks, Ellen Smith, and Davell Crawford; trombonists Craig Klein, Lucien Barbarin, and Freddie Lonzo; sax player Eric Traub; trumpeters Wendell Brunious and "Kid Chocolate" Brown. Others wander in from the street for the privilege and fun of playing with Tuxedo, notably Trombone Shorty (before his rise to stardom) and Kermit Ruffins. One need not be a star; the band invites musicians in from around the world, requiring only that they ask permission in advance. Every year, the Frenches have allowed singers in my Westminster Choir College class to sit in—the thrill of their lives, several have told me. "Don't hit too many of those high notes," Bob French used to tell the sopranos. "You might break the wine glasses." The year before Katrina, a young woman I'd never seen sat in at Tuxedo's Donna's gig and sang jazz standards with a voice so precise and powerful that I nearly fell off the bar stool. She told me at the break that she had flown in from London and was a Covent Garden opera singer. When I asked why, she said, "Because I've always wanted to do this."

French established a tradition of deadpan humor that was almost as entertaining as the music itself. One night, when Boutte arrived earlier than usual, French told the audience, "John Boutte got out of the coffin early tonight." There was something wonderfully mischievous about French's every gesture,

Tuxedo Jazz Band at Irvin Mayfield's Jazz Playhouse, Danielle Marchand singing.
Photograph by Jack Sullivan.

yet he had a strong sense of propriety; when tourists crashed in the door
from Bourbon Street, drinks in hand, he would snap, "That's ghetto behavior,"
shooting them a glance of singular malevolence from the bandstand, and they
would lurch right back out. After Katrina nearly washed away Donna's, he
wore a red T-shirt that said "Trailer Trash," referring to his FEMA trailer, and
assured everyone that the music (despite what the press was saying) was not
going away.

The band's fondness for cutting up and juxtaposing even the most serious
repertory with jokes (usually about sex and alcohol) is a basic characteristic
of traditional jazz. The performances are often right on the edge of mimicry
and self-parody—especially when Carnival season begins to roll in—without quite going over the edge. The final cadence in "St. James Infirmary," for
example, is often held for a ludicrously long time, bringing the Grim Reaper
down a few notches even as the song retains its dark majesty. (As Ambrose
Bierce puts it in "The Devil's Dictionary": "A jest in the death chamber con-
quers by surprise.") Tuxedo does it more seamlessly than most simply because
they have been doing it longer. One shouldn't forget that Louis Armstrong, an
irrepressible jokester, is part of their history. Armstrong was criticized for this

raucous sense of fun, often harshly, but in this, as with so many other things, his spirit has prevailed.

In 2007, the band moved their gig to Frenchmen Street, the new jazz mecca, then to the Royal Sonesta Hotel, where the Monday night continued under Gerald, who has sustained both the laughs and the variety show tradition, inviting a colorful array of musicians to sit in, including the Chapman sisters. Jazz is back on Bourbon Street, with many forgotten songs revived thanks to Gerald's meticulous research in the Hogan Jazz Archive. Tuxedo serves up what the audience wants—as long as it falls into the wide net of traditional jazz. This has always been a secret to the band's amazing longevity, as Raeburn affirms: "All the various musicians who were affiliated with the Tuxedo knew the importance of combining art with entertainment and never drew false distinctions based on ideas of purity or authenticity. They played what the people who paid for their services wanted to hear." [24] As Bob French always said at the end of a show, "If you enjoyed yourself, tell your friends; if you didn't, don't tell nobody." Fans always want to hear the outrageously bawdy "Keyhole Blues" ("His key was way too small; his key don't fit in my lock no more"), and the sultry Ellen Smith is there to belt it out; they always want to hear Mardi Gras music; and the band's "Hey Pocky A-Way" makes Carnival come alive any time of year. To hear Tuxedo perform live (their recordings sound a bit wan) is to experience the continuing saga of America's greatest cultural invention.

Tuxedo is sometimes called the Tuxedo Brass Band (a situation further confused by a group called the Young Tuxedo Brass Band, formed in 1938), and the Rebirth Brass Band was called the Rebirth Jazz Band at its inception in the early 1980s. The loose usage of terms like "jazz," "swing," and "brass band" indicates once again how little NOLA musicians care about defining and separating genres. Historians like to say jazz developed from brass bands, but which is which is a question of degree and the needs of the moment; in the early twentieth century, marching-band players began doing dance-band gigs at night, and ten-member bands slimmed into trios and quartets, which were the first jazz ensembles. The demand for dance music—in cabarets, picnics, saloons, lawn parties, and much else—was constant, as it continues to be. Today, the differences between jazz and brass band often seem arbitrary. In theory, jazz ensembles have sit-down instruments, such as pianos and basses, and marching brass bands do not—it's inside versus outside playing, a brash outdoor sound versus a more mellow sonority—but brass bands often use keyboard instruments when they come in from the streets and play in the bars, and jazz bands have so many brass players sitting in by the end of the night that they sound like souped-up brass bands.

Gregg Stafford. Photograph by Brandon Xeureb, Xistence Photography.

Many jazz players come from brass bands, the gateway to jazz. "Most were brass-band musicians," Gregg Stafford says of today's jazz players, "because brass bands are always the breeding grounds for traditional jazz. They go through the brass bands into the cabaret settings, then the quintets and sextets and seven piece bands. So they were very open-minded about allowing young musicians to come in—the Onward Brass Band, the Young Tuxedo Brass Band, Harold Dejan and the Olympia Brass Band—all those guys worked around town, Bourbon Street and other venues. So once you start working with them, you develop a relationship: 'Come around to the [Preservation] Hall, I'm working there tomorrow night, or come over to Heritage Hall and listen to the music.' Bourbon Street was a place where you could really go and hear musicians play because they still had bands on the street."[25]

The street is important, but black churches, according to many, are the real inaugurator of the jazz and R&B revolution, a primal source for emotional fervor, exuberant showmanship, and melodic techniques associated with the blues. During a recent gig at Rock 'n' Bowl (yes, they do both there), Kermit Ruffins speculated that "sometime in the nineteenth century, a cat went into a church with a trumpet and came out into a second line. Hymns in church became something else in the streets." Ruffins is not an ethnomusicologist— indeed, he is not musically trained at all—but his theory makes sense. The church and the second line, the gospel singers and the partiers, the high school marching bands and the soloists with careers, are the beginning and end of the same Big Easy parade.[26]

Charmaine Neville, Shannon Powell, Walter "Wolfman" Washington, Ernie K-Doe, and many others cite churches as their initial inspiration. For Michael White and Gregg Stafford, the experience is deeply ingrained, and much of their repertory is gospel. There is a fascinating doubleness, for New Orleans is a French Catholic town infused with black Protestant music. John Boutte is a Creole who was raised Catholic, "and they weren't really known for jammin." But he was also inundated by Protestant gospel: "The strumming guitars or Gregorian chants of my Catholic upbringing have shaped my sound. But listening to the sanctified service at the church behind my mother's home or playing piano for Baptist and Pentecostal choirs in the army definitely taught me to emote and let loose." The rowdy gospel music Boutte picked up on his own, combined with a French-Catholic sensibility, gives even his funkiest "letting loose" music-making a surprising refinement and structure, reinforced by his training in classical music at Xavier College. Trumpeter Leroy Jones has a similar background. He was brought up Catholic, studied classical, and got his musical grounding in black gospel at the Fairview Baptist Church: "Like John, I was raised within Catholicism, attending parochial schools, even on to one year's attendance at a Catholic university, Loyola. From my experience as a young boy, having an opportunity to also attend religious services at the Fairview Baptist Church, the music during the praise and worship surely had a profound influence on my development musically and spiritually in a way that did not occur attending mass at St. Leo the Great. At Fairview and other Baptist church services, the gospel music and singing got me grounded into an understanding of soulfulness and the inflection of the blues. It's quite possible that without having been exposed to it, my musical expression would differ from what it is today."

Unlike some of his colleagues, Jones does not believe this direct exposure is necessary, but it certainly doesn't hurt: "There are musicians from other parts of the world who have access to recordings, even video. If they are gifted and have had a variety of reference points or influences and are able to retain the information, their vibe is usually very similar to other players. Still, there is something very special about good black gospel music."[27]

Shouters and gospel singers were important mentors and childhood influences for NOLA musicians across genres. Some of the more charismatic examples include Reverend Utah Smith, who carried his electric guitar, attached to a long cord, through the church out into the street, combining indoor and outdoor performance, and Archie Brownlee, vocalist for the Five Blind Boys of Mississippi, who stretched his singing lines into bent notes, and is credited by Ira Tucker of the Dixie Hummingbirds with starting "that scream you hear all the soul singers do."[28] New Orleans jazz was always about the crowd, particularly young people hungry for new styles of dance music. The crowd still makes it happen, a dynamic gathering of musicians and fans, of those who might at any moment pop up on the stage to sit in—much like churchgoers suddenly coming up to the altar to be saved—as well as devotees of the band, of locals as well as tourists who venture beyond Bourbon Street.

The latter are perhaps more informed than ever, thanks to the internet. As pianist Tom McDermott points out, the "tourist demand for music" is essential for the city's continual survival as a jazz mecca. "A lot of my playing is done for tourists. The biggest jazz audience is out-of-towners." Although the music comes out of local neighborhoods and always has, it is sustained more by outsiders than by locals, who often "don't have a clue" about their own traditions, as McDermott "perhaps too harshly" puts it. [29] The crowd will never be the same as the mobs for pop stars, a reality the musicians know and accept. "You don't need huge crowds like rock 'n' roll," says bassist Richard Moten. "You just need enough to keep it going."[30]

According to pianist Lars Edegran, those who keep it going are young and old alike: "People expect traditional jazz when they come to New Orleans. They don't want to hear New York jazz. Thirty years ago, mostly old people came to Preservation Hall. Now there are lots of young people as well. People are more open to tradition now; they really respond well to traditional jazz. They don't regard it as 'old people's music.'"[31] Paul Longstreth, whose showy, cheerleading persona is a contrast to Edegran's gravitas, agrees: "The traditional music *is* going on. Even young people, if given the opportunity to listen, say, 'Hey, that's the kind of jazz I like.'"[32] According to Eric Bloom, who plays everything from contemporary funk to gigs at Preservation Hall, hipsters are attracted to trad: "It's now a hipster type of thing. They want to experience it, learn about it, and dance to it. It's not necessarily something they will listen to all day, but they'll come to your gigs."[33] Since its inception, jazz has been championed by young people who think of themselves as both discerning and cutting-edge, so the hipster phenomenon is in line with history. Anyone who doubts its reality need only check out the crowd at trad gigs on Frenchmen Street by artists like Meschiya Lake and Aurora Nealand.

So popular is traditional jazz that modernists play it, sometimes because they love it, sometimes because they want to stay employed. "Even the modern players do traditional because they think there's money in it," says Barry Martyn. "That doesn't mean you have to be old-fashioned. I play traditional jazz, but it's not old-fashioned. We play any songs that are requested of us."[34]

This promiscuity horrifies the more staunch traditionalists. Clarinetist Tom Fischer, who performs mainly traditional jazz because there "isn't as much call" for the modernism he once practiced, is surrounded by grumpy purists: "The scene is quite healthy, but there are some diehard traditionalists who say it's really bad right now, players I work with who would have nothing to do with the kind of music I just played on that first set tonight. They would say it's way too modern." This "modern" repertory consisted of songs like "Yes, Sir, That's My Baby" and "Walking with the King," played in the Palm Court, which only allows traditional jazz.[35]

Far from sounding old-fashioned, traditional jazz usually sounds new because no one plays the same songs the same way. As Katja Toivola explains, the songs are reinvented, not played to formula: "They don't play them in a repertory way because that's already been done. People put their own stamp on the music, but it's not contrived, which is why I don't enjoy some of the more traditional Dixieland bands as much as the more authentic New Orleans bands. Often I find what they do corny. It's been done already. 'Why are you doing it again? Do something that *you* do.'"[36]

The Shotgun Jazz Band, featuring the smoldering blues vocals of Marla Dixon, is a good example of this reinvention. They play standards with absolute fidelity to the tradition but with their own youthful vibe: "Traditional jazz is a real thing with young people," says Dixon. "People are playing the traditional tunes, but in a more modern style. It's my first love of music, and I love this style. I see young people coming here and saying, 'Wow, that's kind of interesting,' and trying to learn it and get their head around it, and a lot of people from out of town are coming here to try to find this music, and they're discovering that, 'Oh, I'm happy to do this.'" The challenge is to insure that the essence of the music is not lost in the effort to make it new: "They listen to old records and talk with old folks and try and get back to an older sensibility. I don't know if they're getting it or not, but they're trying."

Dixon's band is definitely getting it, keeping alive both the letter and the spirit, evidenced by their use of a jazz banjo rather than a five-string instrument. Banjoist John Dixon regrets that, with notable exceptions—such as Don Vappie, Joseph Faison, Chris Edmonds, John Parker—the jazz banjo is not thriving. It's not dead, but it's "on hold. There are more banjoists in town, but a lot of them are playing five-string stuff. As far as traditional jazz banjo, I haven't seen a whole lot more in town."[37] It is striking how purist this stance is—how close to the attitude of "authentic" period instrumentalists in classical music—given that Shotgun is an out-of-town group. It flies in the face of the worry by indigenous musicians that the new arrivals don't care about the tradition.

Veteran cornetist Jack Fine, who founded the Jazz Vipers in 1998 but is from Brooklyn, believes clubs need to do more to promote the kind of music that Shotgun plays at the Spotted Cat. Like many senior musicians, Fine has a childlike enthusiasm coupled with a palpable anxiety about the tradition vanishing: "A lot of people who run clubs on Frenchmen Street don't seem to realize that that's what people come down to New Orleans for: they want to hear New Orleans music. The more successful clubs know that. I have to try and get them to do more. We mustn't lose the tradition. Those of us who respect the tradition must uphold it." When I spoke with Fine in 2014, he was having too many health problems to continue performing, a source of profound frustration. "When I come out to a place like this [Vaughan's] and have a few drinks, I want to jump in and do one song, just one song."[38]

Finding Fine next to me at Vaughan's—totally randomly—is the kind of thing that happens often in New Orleans. When I told guitarist Todd Duke that in New York I can hear the Vienna Philharmonic at Carnegie Hall at 8 p.m., then jazz at 11 at Birdland down the street, then more jazz further downtown, Duke gently scoffed, reminding me that these are compartmentalized experiences. In New Orleans, the music is a continual flow from the streets. With a little planning and luck, you can see the same artist two or three times in one night, both on the stage and at the bar. Duke pointed to the door: "You see that tuba player coming in the bar from the street [the tubist for the Soul Rebels]? That doesn't happen anywhere else. In New Orleans, magic is ordinary."

Magic is ordinary all the time—not just on weekends, Mardi Gras, and Jazz Fest, when New Orleanians draw in tourists to recoup their perpetually plummeting fortunes. Unexpected things happen frequently, both to fans and musicians. The first time that John Boutte heard drummer Earl Palmer was during a gig in Storyville on Bourbon Street. "I was working with the director Taylor Hackford, and Sam Cooke's brother was supposed to play, but he forgot his drumsticks—he was a little tipsy, right?—and Earl was in the audience and sat in, so how lucky am I? The great Earl Palmer said, 'I can do that for you, brother.' I said, 'Sure.'"[39]

The special intimacy of jazz often exists in inverse proportion to what brings in crowds and money. Carnival and Jazz Fest are essential for the city, but one of the most satisfying experiences is an off night at a place like the Palm Court, where musicians give their all to a small, rapt audience. After one of these serene evenings, Jason Marsalis, an avatar of the new, told me that the strength of New Orleans jazz comes from the old. New Orleans "is a community where players participate with each other and exchange gigs. You've heard me in three different bands this week, right?" New York, on the other hand, is "always wanting to grab the next new thing" at the expense of "core musical values." New York "always moves on. In New Orleans, the traditions keep going. Part of it is that certain things—Mardi Gras, Jazz Fest—happen every year. In New York, so many new things happen all the time. They move on. There's good and bad: I think both are needed." When his brother Wynton moved there, he said, "people said he was retro because he cared about the Armstrong tradition." New York jazz players, Marsalis says, do their own thing, with little sense of a home community. "New York never really had its own music. Very few musicians are really from there. Let's look at the history: Charlie Parker—Kansas City; Miles Davis—St. Louis; Thelonious Monk—Rocky Mount, North Carolina; John Coltrane—North Carolina (raised in Philadelphia); Wayne Shorter—Newark. You get the idea. Because New York was a business epicenter, musicians moved there. That's why the music always changes, for better and worse."[40]

One can always hear good jazz in New York; it's one of the city's defining pleasures. But each experience is a separate one, and it is hard to find a continuous thread. Something that always "grabs for the next new thing" risks defaulting to a bleak and random universe. The next new thing quickly becomes the previous old thing, as *New York Times* jazz critic Ben Ratliff implies when he writes that there is currently "no center in jazz, no steady voice in the back of the head."[41] Without a center, there is little urgency or stake in anything. Something that always changes never changes.

In his own playing, Jason Marsalis blends the old and the new, with the former providing a constant heartbeat, a basis for development and change. He plays the straight-ahead jazz pioneered by his father, Ellis, while tapping into traditions of Mardi Gras Indian, Brazilian, and Afro-Cuban (especially in the versatile band, Los Hombres Calientes, which he co-founded). Whether rocking audiences onto the dance floor with explosive drumming or seducing them with quiet overtones from his vibraphone band, he projects an authority both fiery and cerebral. He is classically trained (like Parker and Coltrane, a Stravinsky aficionado), yet steeped in second-line aesthetics. The Jason Marsalis Vibes Quartet, which combines classical coolness with NOLA soul, exemplifies how a New Orleans tradition is passed on to a new generation within a family. Jason's father, Ellis, believes "the skills learned in second lines and musical training must continue to be passed on to those who are willing to move beyond the mediocre stuff" if the art is to be advanced and made relevant to new eras: "My younger son has his own group where he plays vibes. He has what you call a twenty-first-century trad band."[42] Ellis speaks with casual pride about his accomplished children: Delfeayo, founder of the Uptown Jazz Orchestra, who has his own twenty-first-century trad band; Wynton, who has the big one in New York; and Branford, who is increasingly

Ellis Marsalis. Photograph by Erika Goldring / Getty Images.

a fixture of the symphony orchestra scene. All have moved way "beyond the mediocre stuff" and have taken the second-line aesthetic with them.

In New Orleans, the new is not the "next big thing" displacing everything else, but another spice thrown into the gumbo pot; a vital center, the roux of the gumbo, is always there, not only because of New Orleans traditions like Super Sunday and Mardi Gras, but because the same musicians migrate from band to band, doing the core repertory while inventing new material, continually reinventing themselves as they welcome new players who sit in. As Bruce Raeburn puts it, each musician "works with multiple bands playing a spectrum of repertories, which makes their music broad and deep."[43] Musicians come together for neighborhood rehearsals with what Dr. John calls "skull arrangements," an internal core of material worked out orally and verbally with colleagues. This combination of breadth and depth makes music in New Orleans both grounded and airborne. Loyalty to tradition coexists with freedom: "You have the liberty to do what you want and embellish the harmonies to the point where the melody is still recognizable," says Leroy Jones, "but you have the freedom to just play. We're not trying to copy Jelly Roll Morton or James Johnson or Duke or whatever: just be yourself."[44]

Katja Toivola believes that "New Orleans is about musicians, not bands."[45] With notable exceptions (Tuxedo, Liberty, Preservation Hall), the bands come and go, often swiftly, but the musicians keep improvising with new ensembles,

Leon "Kid Chocolate" Brown at Donna's. Photograph by Jack Sullivan.

taking their talent to new levels. I remember hearing a new trad band in Donna's called the Players in 2003. Among other songs, they played "Dippermouth Blues" with remarkable fidelity to Joe Oliver's 1923 Creole Jazz Band recording, but the uncanny togetherness of the ensemble combined with the individuality of the solos made it sound new. The Players broke up a few years later, but segued into other bands. Leon "Kid Chocolate" Brown, for example, formed his own group; Mark Braud became leader of the Preservation Hall Jazz Band after the sudden death of John Brunious. Musicians always seem to find new ensembles, often juggling several at once.

This is not to say that New Orleans is one happy jazz family without rivalries or tensions. Music is a business, jazz has always had to fight for its survival in a corporate-pop environment, and bands compete for a limited number of gigs. Yet the very smallness of the scene enforces a kind of camaraderie, with hostilities lying just beneath the surface and for the most part staying there. (Several musicians I interviewed delivered scathing—and often hilarious—denunciations of certain colleagues, only to back away from them three sentences later or tell me after the interview not to print, as one put it, "anything unkind that I said.") New Orleans players are so dependent on each other for gigs that insults are deeply unwise. Tom McDermott says that when he is tempted to say something negative about another player, the best thing is to "let it go, go, go." Victor Goines, a New Orleans native who has mastered the scene in New York and Chicago, believes "every city has its cliques, New Orleans included. I just think you can't afford to be that cliquish in New Orleans because you will alienate yourself a lot. There are obviously certain people who work together and other people who don't work together, just like New York. You have a much smaller, concentrated area of musicians in New Orleans as opposed to New York, where the body of musicians is huge. The divisions of cliques are much more obvious here than in New Orleans. There was the Zinc bar or Bradley's or Sweet Basil, now it's the Iridium, the Vanguard or Smalls—so there are cliques of musicians who go to different places for different reasons: it might be economic, the type of music being played, the group, or just the people coming through on a given day—Roy Haynes or Ellis Marsalis. When you get to the larger cities, the divisions are going to become more obvious as opposed to smaller cities, where everyone has to pull upon anyone else to make a living, especially when you are a talented drummer like Jason Marsalis.

"Everybody is asking for you to be part of them because we all want to play with someone who's better than us, so for the musicians in New Orleans to play with Jason is to play with a better musician each and every time, so often he's getting those calls whereas other musicians may not."[46]

Wanting to play with someone "who's better than us" is indeed a strong impulse in New Orleans. Many players have told me they will go out of their way to gig with Marsalis or others they revere in order to improve their game. This is an important aspect of the city's communal vibe, the constant search for mentors and sources of inspiration. It's reflected in the humility of the players—many of whom would much rather talk about colleagues they admire than about themselves—a quality that makes conversations with them almost as pleasurable as their music-making.

The unerring focus on the next gig produces a certain unpretentiousness and informality. Barry Martyn almost did not make it out of the city the day Katrina hit because he had an afternoon gig and didn't want to pass it up, prompting Samuel Charters to remark: "In New Orleans, jazz musicians take any kind of job just to keep things turning over, and their casual attitude toward what they might be asked to play has lent its own laid-back character to traditional New Orleans jazz sound."[47]

In the actual behavior of musicians, always in need of gigs, there is a resistance to purism, yet many hold it up as a kind of Holy Grail, an unattainable ideal corrupted by money or faddism, and constantly in need of defending. When I told trumpeter Charlie Miller that I heard contemporary brass bands in Preservation Hall after Katrina, he was dismayed, saying, "Oh God, are they really doing that?" He thought it "sad" that Preservation, the capital of traditional ensemble jazz, might not be the dependable citadel of tradition it once was. If Preservation isn't preserving, who is? Pianist Tom McDermott is open to new sounds (he has, for example, brought the Brazilian Choro into his repertory), but also believes there is "a real distinction" between traditional New Orleans jazz and other types of music, one the city ignores at its peril.[48] Michael White, the most historically circumscribed of the traditionalists, has a sober analysis based as much on economics as aesthetics. The disappearance of the middle class from street culture has taken with it a knowledge of jazz tradition and practice, so that "the few who do enter the jazz field know very little about the history or stylistic basis of 'the New Orleans thing,' which at times they may 'fake' when financial opportunity arises."[49] This ignorance could have lasting consequences. White warned me just after Katrina that once those who currently play traditional jazz are gone, an entire oral history will pass away.[50] White admits that many musicians perform traditional songs, but "it is a question of style, not repertory. Kermit [Ruffins] plays the repertory, but the electronic instruments in his band are not really traditional." The same is true of young bands like the Brass-A-Holics, even though White admires their musicianship. "Now there's a lot of great music here, and a lot of creative music going on, but not really coming out of the traditional style, so that's what my concern is. I would like to see that style continue."

White believes it is possible "to create something new in the tradition that uses the principles of traditional music," and has written many compositions since Katrina—"Sunday Morning," for example, which movingly evokes Sunday morning parades (not the same as Sunday second lines).[51] He has also experimented with idioms and instruments not part of his previous repertory. After an all-gospel show, he told me he had been jamming "with a band from Senegal and the Ivory Coast. The main guy played the balafon and the djembe drum and sang; his name is Seguenon Kone, and he lives here, actually. I wanted to get closer to the roots of West African music and to learn to use instruments like the balafon. It was nice." This experimentation with pre-jazz African influences reminds us that African music was historically associated with the modernist avant-garde of Gauguin, Picasso, and Stravinsky; indeed, White refers to his work with these musicians as "bordering on avant-garde" and has recently sat in with "the legend of avant-garde music," Perry Robinson. White says, "Stuff is starting to happen. I think I'm more open and more receptive to hearing different styles on the horn. I've even started to play some modern jazz standards. Not with the usual bebop lines, but with whatever I'm hearing, whatever is coming out." He even admits to playing Coltrane, but usually when "no one's paying attention."[52]

Evan Christopher, another prominent clarinetist, supports "keeping the intentions of the music in there, in the spirit originally intended," but recognizes that in his case, this "intention is based much more on crossover elements." Christopher believes it is imperative "to update the appeal." He and his band "play a couple of warhorses" in scrupulously traditional style but also songs (particularly Latin material) from the fringes of the repertory. Because Christopher is a trained academic who knows jazz history, he is able to make very conscious choices about how to refine or expand the tradition.[53]

The traditionalist with the greatest ambition and name recognition is someone who does not live in New Orleans, Wynton Marsalis. He started, like his father, as a modernist before becoming a passionate advocate for traditional jazz. Marsalis has not lived in New Orleans for some thirty years, but as artistic director of Jazz at Lincoln Center, he represents the New Orleans tradition in the largest city in the United States. He experienced his trad epiphany after playing with the Olympia Brass Band in the mid-'90s, an experience that made him realize the importance of his hometown tradition. Since then, he has promoted it with a militancy that has provoked lively, often acrimonious controversy. He has been accused of a stifling neo-classicism and of retarding the progress of jazz (those are the kinder comments), but he has not backed down in his advocacy of music that promotes New Orleans polyphony, call-response, and, most important, the grandeur of the blues. He wants jazz to be modeled on the legacy of giants—Armstrong, Oliver, Morton, Ellington, Parker, Coltrane, Coleman—who are either squarely in the New Orleans tradition or what he regards as the offshoots of it, and he finds much of contemporary jazz and pop to be shallow. He dismisses "progressive" forms such as "world music" as neither progressive nor worldly but parodies and rip-offs of other cultures. Music can only "be innovated this way," he says, "when people of different ethnic origins live together and develop experiences together, as the people of New Orleans did in the early days of jazz."[54] He is no fan of hip hop, which he regards as regressive and misogynist: "After the Civil War, white folks were offered minstrel shows that offered 'real coons from the real plantation,' and to me that's like rappers today, with their talk of keeping it real, giving themselves a minstrel name, boasting about how they can degrade their women."[55]

One can dismiss Marsalis's diatribes as angry nostalgia, the usual fogey critique of young people—except that he unleashed his most provocative statements when he himself was young. Like his brother Jason, he is troubled by a marketplace where so much is based on trends of the moment rather than core musical values, and he has used his position at Lincoln Center to promote that core. By the mid-2000s, Marsalis's supporters were saying he had "tempered" his "purist" views, and several scholars and associates have told me he has "mellowed." To be sure, he has been programming a broader spectrum of artists at Lincoln Center and has been appearing at benefits with pop stars, but he still maintains that jazz is rooted in African American experience and still deplores a "cheap populism" that is responsible for not putting the best music in front of people. "There's a cynicism in it and the best of our music has never had that. It's always been optimistic in the belief that with a little bit of education, something that is of a high level of quality can be embraced, and I think Jazz at Lincoln Center has proven that."[56]

By the early twenty-first century, Marsalis's critics were announcing that few took him seriously any longer, that his star was waning and about to fall. Some linked his fortunes with jazz itself, lamenting (yet again) that jazz was dying.

None of this has come to pass. Marsalis is still a sought-after player, educator, and lecturer. Most important, he presides over Jazz at Lincoln Center. Marsalis wants the organization to be an "international symbol of jazz" shaped by "many different people's tastes," a way to give jazz the status it deserves and to ensure it lasts.[57] The Rose Jazz Center sits atop an overgrown shopping mall in the Time Warner building. The major venues, the Rose and Allen Rooms, are glitzy, multi-genre New York establishments presenting classical and opera as well as jazz. I wish they were more intimate, but Marsalis makes jazz happen at Lincoln Center on an impressive scale (over 100 concerts a year), a significant achievement in a once-great jazz city where venues are dwindling. With his inauguration of jazz courses, pubic school curricula, master classes, and young people's concerts, Marsalis promotes jazz as an essential American experience rather than merely a series of concerts. In May 2017, he led a second-line parade at Columbus Circle to promote solidarity in the face of Trump-era budget cuts to the arts.

In the smallest venue, Dizzy's Club Coca Cola, a New Yorker can get a taste of a New Orleans jazz bar (even though the gumbo is woefully under-spiced). This is an atmospheric place with a terrific view of the city just behind the bandstand. The shows often feature New Orleans artists. It's where I first heard Jon Batiste, and where Ellis Marsalis celebrated his eightieth birthday in 2014 with a moving concert backed up by top New Orleans players, including Derek Douget, Herlin Riley, and Jason Stewart, a quartet made in heaven. Dizzy's also has late-night open mic gigs on Thursdays and Saturdays, New York's best-kept jazz secret. As in the Big Easy, these happenings deliver wonderful surprises: New York is full of talented jazz musicians and not enough venues to go around.

Marsalis's recordings do not always present New Orleans jazz. He has written a number of symphonic "crossover" works that exist in their own

Wynton Marsalis. Photograph by Rob Waymen.

realm. In his straightforward jazz compositions and performances, he seems most completely himself. "Spring Yaounde" is a languid specimen of Creole lyricism; "The Death of Jazz," a funeral march, is a deadpan rejoinder to the "jazz is dead" crowd; and "Sometimes I Feel Like a Motherless Child" has a moving simplicity and melancholy, capturing the essence of spirituals in a concert setting.

The live experience is something else again. The first time I heard Marsalis play was at the Spoleto USA festival in Charleston in the '80s, where he produced colors and nuances that expanded my knowledge of what the trumpet could do. He was fiery and combative between numbers, blasting the genteel, white audience for supporting racism and white privilege. When I sat down with him at Birdland twenty years later in 2004, the night he received the Musician of the Year award from Musical America, he was in a relaxed mood, clearly happy about an honor that normally goes to classical artists. He was also strikingly serene and humble. His fierce public persona when battling James Collier and other jazz critics is one thing, his personal manner another. He spoke about the importance of education, of making sure jazz gets into young people's souls and sensibilities. When I told him my ten-year-old son was taking trombone lessons from a young musician who was studying jazz, he only wanted to talk about that. "Nothing is more important," he said. "We've got to pass it on to our children."[58]

The Marsalis wars raise anew the question of what jazz tradition really is. To Marsalis, it is the blues, a rural form transplanted to the city, one he believes is the emotional core of jazz. Others concentrate on stylistic elements. Michael White believes, as we have seen, that the tradition is *about* style, not repertory. To David Torkanowsky, however, "tradition is an attitude, not a style." A "traditional" band can stay within the style but produce a commercial caricature, whereas a multi-genre band like the Brass-A-Holics can "respect the tradition." To limit oneself to a single style is to "eschew anything not in the 1920s or '30s," something "very cool" but equally limiting. Torkanowsky makes a strong distinction between traditional jazz and Dixieland, which he believes to be an inauthentic form with a racially offensive brand: "We don't call it that here because of the connotation of 'Dixie,' but we call it 'traditional.'"[59] Many have a similarly dismissive view of "Dixieland," but not Barry Martyn: "There is an argument about that. I call what I play 'Dixieland.' Kid Thomas called his band the 'Thomas Dixieland Band.' And then later someone came up with the idea that it should be called 'The Algiers Stompers,' and people called it that. George Lewis would never use the 'Dixieland' label because his management told him Dixieland was white music, but I don't think that's right; I think the absolute opposite. When I come here [in 1961], *all* the bands were called Dixieland bands. Some may tell you differently, but I have longevity going for me—I do have that."[60] Even after "Dixieland" became politically incorrect, some, like Doc Paulin, continued to regard it fondly, as Jason Berry reminds us: "Long after 'Dixieland' became freighted with negative racial and cultural meanings for African Americans, [Doc Paulin] maintained a drum emblazoned 'Doc Paulin's Dixieland Jazz Band.' I suspect it was a business decision; other people liked the term."[61]

No matter how one defines the tradition, many believe it can only be passed down on the street. Fred Johnson says, "You can't be soulful in your art if you haven't been baptized on the street."[62] According to Les Getrex, who played guitar for Fats Domino, "People learn it in the streets before they do in school—if in school at all. It goes from the streets to the schools to the parades. You see your elders playing in the street when you're a kid and say, 'I want to do that.'"[63] "It's the history and the culture." Says Original Pinettes member Christie Jordain: "Being that jazz started up here, when you're young that's what you grow up on. You see the second line passing in front of your house; you're hearing bands and parades. My family were musicians, but even when you got to elementary school, it was expected you pick up an instrument."[64] Chris Edmunds, who plays guitar and six string banjo with the New

Orleans Moonshiners, says the inspiration from the street is part of a broad cultural reality that includes food, speech patterns, and much else: "I learned this music on the street; it's passed down generation to generation. It's not like New York or Chicago or Kansas City. Music is ingrained in us here, it's part of life. New Orleans is different—we have our own way of talking, cooking, celebrating, and making music. The music has always been here. It's not something you learn in school. You can't teach New Orleans jazz in school; it's not institutionalized." When I point out that jazz is taught in many schools, including the University of New Orleans, Loyola, Tulane, and Xavier, he is undeterred: "That's not jazz, that's bebop."[65]

New Orleans is actually full of musicians who have formal musical educations (Germaine Bazzle, Delfeayo Marsalis, Leroy Jones, Katja Toivola, Charlie Miller, Michael White, to name a few, many with graduate degrees.) Education is critical in sustaining jazz, as it is for any art form. Bassist Roland Guerin told me the reason so many young people are actively involved in the scene is that jazz is taught extensively in New Orleans schools, at all genres and levels. "It's traditional to learn it in schools in New Orleans, whether you are from there. Then you can take it somewhere else."[66] UNO, Loyola, and other jazz schools train students to make it in the jazz world outside New Orleans, and defenders of the system argue it makes sense to teach modern jazz since traditional music exists only scantily outside New Orleans. This is not to say traditional jazz is not part of the curriculum. Evan Christopher, Don Vappie, and other traditionalists teach trad jazz, though they may be a minority. A balance is provided in the curriculum championed by Ellis Marsalis, which incorporates both traditional and modern, with his quintet as the vehicle. "Jazz is an evolutionary process that can be notated," he insists.[67]

Nevertheless, the "I-learned-it-on-the-street" myth is so potent that those who are schooled are quick to point out they have moved beyond their schooling. Tom McDermott, who has years of classical training, says, "Schools just show you how to listen and transcribe solos and to play with other musicians. Ultimately, you learn on your own."[68] Ellis Marsalis states that musical education is essential if the music is to move beyond the fundamentals, but even more important is firsthand exposure to second lines. For him, it's an arc, moving from the neighborhood to the school and back again: "You have to be born in New Orleans, then decide to go beyond the mediocre stuff that everybody knows—develop some skills on the instrument, learn more about music in general, and then bring with that the whole of the New Orleans experience."[69] The newer bands boast a combination of street experience and school training. Robin Clabby, singer and saxophonist for the Brass-A-Holics, says the group is a mix of Kermit-like street players and trained musicians:

Kermit Ruffins at Rock 'n' Bowl. Photograph by Jack Sullivan.

"We have guys who came up on their ear and guys who came up reading and writing, but at some point you really have to be able to do both. We have guys who grew up with no traditions, but everybody at this point has a natural ear for it and then also knows the language."[70]

Musicians who don't read music often rely on those who can, so a band might consist of "readers" and "fakers"—to the benefit of everyone. The "fakers" are forthright. "Do I read music?" asks Walter "Wolfman" Washington, "No. I don't know how to read nothing. They put some dots in front of me, I say, 'No.' Now if they write the chord changes—say, 'Play this chord or that chord,' I know how to do that. But to read dots, no. I tried. Don't think I didn't try.... When I play solos, that just what I be thinking and hearing in my mind. I do the band arrangement. See, my tenor player writes; he can read. So what I do, I just tell them what I hear and they write it down."[71]

The quintessential street player is Kermit Ruffins, making music for his fans and passing what he learned on the street to others. He embodies New Orleans music history in a precise way, playing for tips in Jackson Square as a kid, helping launch the Rebirth Brass Band in high school, and finally moving on to his own career as an avatar of swing. John Blanchard, owner of Rock 'n' Bowl, says that "for Kermit, it's not about being better than anybody else; he has a childlike charisma. He's very innocent." [72] This is true in every aspect of his art. One of my students told me he was struck by the way "Kermit just comes in the door with the people" when he shows up for a gig. There are no handlers or entourages, none of the pretentious trappings of celebrity. The open-hearted, "childlike" persona is palpable. Once Ruffins starts up, his connection with the audience is so strong it becomes a two-way pull. With his long, teaser cadences, it appears he doesn't want to relinquish the microphone, but that's because no one wants him to. He's there to have a good time, and he shows it overtly, toasting the crowd with a celebratory bottle of beer, though he is perfectly happy with colleagues who adopt a more abstemious demeanor: "The cat who looks serious while he's playing is having just as much fun as the cat who cuts up and drinks beer on the stage; it's the way you're brought up."

I first heard Ruffins when he was a teenager, playing funky contemporary material with the Rebirth Brass Band in New Orleans and New York (where he has always felt comfortable); in the '90s, he played modern jazz at the Funky Butt Café, drawing modest but enthusiastic crowds, which he has painstakingly nourished. "Kermit starts out with Rebirth," says Bruce Raeburn. "He's a raging experimentalist, and then when he gets into his twenties, he reflects on the tradition and changes pathways." [73] His ensemble, the Barbecue Swingers, is a reference to Armstrong's '30s style and to his fondness for cooking barbecue for his fans. With Armstrong as his model, he began polishing his vocals and practicing his scatting: "I knew that if I was going to be like him, I had to work on my singing," he told me. His vocal style is now as distinctive as his trumpeting; you know less than a minute into any Ruffins song that it's his happy, growly voice. His version of "It's a Wonderful World" takes Armstrong's sultriness to a more languid level, a sleepy ecstasy that risks somnolence. His signature tune, "Skokiaan," blazes in the opposite direction toward an African incandescence that threatens to take the roof off the Blue Nile, the Frenchmen Street bar where he began playing every Friday night as his twenty-year gig at Vaughan's wound down. His willingness to blend modern material with a traditional sound, especially late at night, is typical of a certain type of NOLA traditionalist who knows how to lure young people by incorporating contemporary sounds. Victor Goines, a more formal artist, is generous in his assessment, as are many who are not in Ruffins's camp: "He is a really good entertainer. He has managed to develop his audience. He is a different kind of trumpet player than Terence Blanchard, Nicholas Payton, Irvin Mayfield, or Wynton, but he has developed his own thing, his own following; he's done really well in it, and he's taken it to the next level where he's fortunate enough to be in *Treme* and to travel the world. He's been able to incorporate a lot of what New Orleans means to him in his music."[74]

Leroy Jones represents another type of musician, the one who begins with a street-band aesthetic, then moves on to a more classical sound, the legacy of opera and Creole song. Jones has a buttery sonority in both his trumpet and voice, as if they were two aspects of the same instrument. It is a legato style achieved through arduous study and practice. One can hear fifty gigs, whether traditional or modern, and never hear an inelegant phrase or choppy line. According to Jones, "Every accomplished trumpeter has his or her own personal sound or tone, be it coarse, brassy, silky, or elegant. I reckon I've always desired to have a smooth, controlled tone, no matter what register I play in. I want my notes to flow as smoothly as if I was an accomplished violinist. Perhaps I think of my trumpet sound being more like that of a flugelhorn, warm, yet it still projects."

When I first heard Jones in the '90s at Preservation Hall, I was struck by his brilliant projection; now he sounds warmer and more intimate, but the bolder colors emerge whenever needed. The search for a "personal sound" makes New Orleans musicians wildly idiosyncratic compared to the relatively generic players in other places. Jones does not dismiss the importance of innate talent ("being blessed," he calls it), but believes that whatever he has achieved has been through painstaking practice and preparation. "When I first started playing the horn, my tone was definitely not elegant. Through a combination of practicing diligently, learning how to use my air, in conjunction with lip compression, as well as being quite blessed early on, I have developed my own unique sound."

Jones sees himself as part of a tightly interlocking network of New Orleans traditions, and he has an expansive sense of how he fits into musical history: "The traditions or realities that make the city so special for music are a combination of different, yet related components. The jazz funeral, the black Indians, New Orleans brass bands, Jazz Fest, French Quarter Festival, Carnival, social aid and pleasure clubs, second lines, school marching bands and music programs, rhythm and blues, the Louisiana Philharmonic, Southern Baptist gospel music, and New Orleans being the birth place of jazz are key ingredients that make the city so special for music. It's like a good gumbo."

Jones is basically upbeat about the current scene: "Those traditions or realities continue to be nourished in this present day by the interest from outsiders, musicians from other parts of the United States, even more so from abroad: Europe, Japan, and other foreign countries. More importantly, those traditions have continued to be passed on locally, from one generation to the

Leroy Jones. Photograph by Katja Toivola.

next. Generally speaking, more and more non-musicians, simply music lovers, have been making their pilgrimage to New Orleans to absorb, experience and contribute to the city's unique culture." In passing his legacy to younger players, he takes advantage of modern networking: "I'm fortunate to have accumulated a bit of a following from young aspiring trumpeters, also other instrumentalists. Social networking has provided me with an opportunity to discover many of the younger musicians who are inspired by me and look up to me as their mentor. In recent years I've given a trumpet lesson or two, from beginners to advanced players seeking music degrees."

Jones's mentors are diverse, beginning (not surprisingly) with Armstrong, whose records he heard as a child and whom he impersonated as a teenager during a Sugar Bowl halftime show the year after Armstrong's death: "Louis Armstrong is my foremost mentor, along with my first trumpet teachers, Sister Mary Hilary, Lawrence Winchester, Dalton Rousseau, Terry Gabriel, and Ernest Cagnolatti. Along the road to developing into the trumpeter and musician I am today, I've been influenced by others like Clifford Brown, Lee Morgan, Freddie Hubbard, Jack Willis, Thomas Jefferson, Miles Davis, and Clark Terry." As is implied by this list, Jones is hard to pin down. His roots are traditional, but he plays all kinds of jazz, refusing to be pigeonholed: "You take your pick. The musical genres I play within are relative."[75]

Most NOLA musicians enjoyed a similarly wide spectrum of mentors, ensuring variety in their repertory. "We are all standing on the shoulders of the giants who came before us," says Jon Cleary, who got to New Orleans in 1981, too late to gig with Professor Longhair, but in time for James Booker, whom he joined as a sideman. "In my early career here I was playing with the old boys who invented this stuff: Snooks Eaglin, Johnny Adams, James Booker, Earl King, people like that, so I was lucky: I got to learn from the first guys to do it."[76] Singer Yolanda Windsay studied in Baton Rouge with Alvin Batiste, Benny Carter, Max Roach, Frank Foster, Clark Terry, and Nat Adderley: "I mean, they had some heavy hitters. I remember those days so well."[77] John Boutte had jazz, classical, and gospel mentors, but the decisive catalyst was Stevie Wonder: "It was like meeting with the Dali Lama. He was a kind, knowing spirit. I knew it was real then: no more fake stuff."[78]

The "take your pick" relativity cited by Leroy Jones is something one hears frequently. Nicholas Payton even regards "jazz" as a false term and believes the labels to be business inventions: "I don't make the distinctions. And I don't think the musicians make those distinctions. Those were categories placed on the music by promoters and marketers."[79] No one cares how you label yourself as long as you have a real connection to the city. "If someone comes in off the street and doesn't know 'Walkin' to New Orleans,'" says Chris Edmunds, "it's a dead giveaway."[80] Lucien Barbarin says that traditional jazz endures because of its flexibility and openness to newness: "Yes, we play traditional, but we enhance it to keep it fresh for young people. We allow in some hip hop, we don't just redo '40s and '50s music."[81] Openness to the new is surely the hallmark of any great city, and this quality has always characterized New Orleans. According to trumpeter Lionel Ferbos, who played at the Palm Court until his death in 2014 at age 103, bands were always eclectic. Unless the group had a job calling only for Dixieland, it would be asked to play a variety of music, including rock and Latin.[82] As Bruce Raeburn says, the "purism" of academics has little to do with what NOLA musicians, who "want to constantly experiment," actually do for a living.[83] Eric Bloom states that "in order to play traditional jazz well, you have to know it all, including bop, and if you can play jazz, you can play funk, which grows out of jazz. It's all one." And there is the usual financial imperative: "If you limit yourself to one type of music, you can only make a meager living. It's better to play all styles. One day I play a bebop gig, the next a trad gig. The point is to sound like yourself in all of them and to be appropriate within the style." To Bloom, this behavior is simply "natural. I'm a normal jazz trumpet player."[84] The day I talked with Bloom, he was getting ready for a funktronica gig with Gravity at Tipitina's, but he also spoke eagerly about his favorite trad ensemble, the Preservation Hall Jazz Band, with whom he plays regularly.

This eclecticism has enabled jazz to survive even the worst times. The greatest threat, rock 'n' roll, was handled in typical NOLA fashion, through assimilation. "If you can't beat them, join them" has been the operative New Orleans cliché since the slaves imported Voodoo into Catholicism. In the early '60s, rock swept into the city and threatened to consume its music, as it did everywhere else. Eliot Hoffman, Preservation Hall's lawyer (who describes himself as "one of Sidney Bechet's less promising students") writes that the late '50s was the low point for New Orleans jazz: "The radio and record stores in those days only wanted to know about artists like Chubby Checker, Frankie Avalon, and Elvis Presley. The practitioners of New Orleans jazz were working wherever they could, but most of the time as cab drivers, stevedores, and field hands. Some of them got together only once in a while to remember King Oliver, Fate Marable, Bunk Johnson, and marching bands like Eureka and Onward." (A more immediate geographical threat was the crassly commercialized "jazz" that had begun redefining Bourbon Street.) A momentary panic set in among the jazz community, who in 1961 retreated to Preservation Hall where they could practice their art on a nightly basis. [85] This, however, turned out to be a false alarm; relatively quickly, rock was subsumed by local funk and R&B bands, which retained their traditions even as they turned up the electricity and tempo to suit the new fad. Far from being the enemy of jazz, rock 'n' roll and rhythm and blues became a boon for jazz players who chose to transition between genres, especially in sessions at Cosimo Matassa's studio on Rampart Street. Even seeming outliers like zydeco found it easy to stoke up their accordions with faster percussion, creating a new sound called "zydeco nouveau." (Indeed, as we see elsewhere in this book, some scholars view zydeco as a precursor of rock.) Rock was also subsumed by brass bands, a natural phenomenon since young bands pick up popular music of the day off the streets and from the radio. As Leroy Jones explains, the second line provides a way of folding rock and pop into traditional New Orleans structures, providing a "fusion of musical idioms together with the old style. So then they're attracting the young people who love it, they're playing some of the popular hits that are on the radio and some of the hits that are on CDs from the popular artists of today ... And it's acoustic, and it still has the elements of New Orleans jazz, New Orleans music."[86] Today, jazz singers, brass bands, and zydeco groups play Beatles, Elvis, and Rolling Stone numbers as part of their repertory.

The way to ensure that a tradition remains alive is to write new material for it. As Joseph Irrera of *Offbeat* magazine points out, "the possibilities of new songs in traditional style are still endless."[87] The new millennium has seen a promising uptick in fresh composition, much of it reflecting the increasing coming together of genres. Among many are Wynton Marsalis's "School Boy," a childhood reminiscence that is touchingly personal; Kermit Ruffins's "New Orleans (My Home Town)," a hot rhythm and blues tune that smokes in more ways than one ("I'm gonna smoke my mojo in New Orleans, my home town"); Shamarr Allen's "Can You Feel?" a blues song that switches gears when "the trumpet plays that rock 'n' roll"; and Michael White's "Algeria," an intoxicating mingling of French and Arabic motifs.

One of the most surprising ventures into newness comes from an unlikely source. In 2013, the Preservation Hall Jazz Band began performing a raft of new songs, an attempt, according to producer Jim James (of My Morning Jacket), to remain true to New Orleans tradition while infusing it with "a sound that might appeal to listeners of contemporary soul, hip hop or rock."[88] Bruce Raeburn believes this project is "perfectly consistent with how New Orleans musicians have conducted themselves in the past, embracing eclecticism and experimentation and seeking to attract the widest audiences possible to their music. These are issues being raised by musicians who are affiliated with the Hall, and they talk about tradition because at the Hall it is a really important thing even though they are reworking it pretty drastically under what Benjy's been doing—all for the best as far as I'm concerned."[89] Raeburn refers here to Ben Jaffe, whose mission since he took over running Preservation Hall after his father, Allan, died in 1987 has been to attract a younger crowd: "The more I recognized Preservation Hall's role in keeping New Orleans's music traditions alive, the more I realized the way those traditions were being represented would have to change. When I joined the Preservation Hall Band, it was rare that you'd find anyone in our audience under sixty years old. It was a very mature audience."[90]

It isn't so mature any more. The audience is mixed, both in terms of age and ethnicity. When the band plays at the McKittrick in New York, lines as long as those for the Hall stretch down the block. The night I went, the hotel was crammed almost entirely with young people, cheering and dancing while listening intently to the music, much as audiences do in New Orleans. It's anybody's guess whether these new songs will make it into the repertory, but the audience's response to them was full-throttle, and they got an education in traditional style. Songs like "Come With Me" and "Dear Lord" had jazz and gospel chord structures. "Halfway Right, Halfway Wrong" added a rock beat; "The Darker It Gets," featuring Ben Jaffe's elegant banjo, was a rag-inflected love song, the kind of thing once called Dixieland. The most evocative was "I Think I Love You," featuring the dusky crooning of octogenarian clarinetist Charlie Gabriel. The most exotic modulations were in "August Nights," caressed by mysterious mutes.

"Yellow Moon," a samba co-written by Jaffe and Gabriel, provided the Spanish tinge. Not all the songs were new; when Mark Braud, nephew of Wendell Brunious, led the band in "Bourbon Street Parade" and "Little Liza," his trumpet blazing through the hotel, the effect was seamless, tying everything together. The spontaneous call-response from the audience was reminiscent of what happens at Preservation Hall every night. "The material is constantly developing," Braud told me, "and we're having fun creating it. We're doing some writing right now."[91]

As leader of the band, Braud evinces the loose, unaffected serenity of NOLA trumpeters. The reputation of New Orleans jazz for this kind of "laid-backness" produces odd distortions. The term is regularly confused with a kind of sleepiness, and people who hear it live for the first time are often taken aback by the music's visceral power. Emigré James Evans quickly found that "everyone has a different beat; all my friends here are obsessing about how that can be. Everyone is physically relaxed, so they are not straining against themselves. That's partly because of the weather and the culture that reflects the weather, the whole attitude, so that every bit goes into the music. In England, they talk about the music being very relaxed, and then they play music that sounds like they were going to sleep. Then I got here, and that's not how it is at all! The whole thing is, it's physically relaxed, but it's also full on." When Evans plays with the explosive Shannon Powell, "he's ahead of me, and I'm playing behind the beat, but he still sounds laid-back."[92] Pianist David Torkanowsky says that musicians are constantly "pushing against the humidity with formidable resistance to get the spirit up. There is an urgency at the music's core."[93]

There is also a mysterious tension. Everyone is in sync, but with a subtle discontinuity. Jon Batiste believes that sync "is not necessarily about the same time. Sync is more about what feels good, which sometimes can mean one person being a little ahead, another a little behind, and the tensions between this person pulling and that one pulling creates this medium that makes the listener have this euphoric reaction. In New York, the environment is not conducive to that; the environment is more conducive to being very precise because the venues are that way. There's a beauty in that as well." Batiste often goes underground, where precision is not the point. "We try to make that energy happen when we go down in the subways."[94]

Some players move the beat forward. Jon Cleary likes "guys who push; Jelly Bean is a great example. Then I can lag behind a little bit if I need to. That's what makes funk work."[95] "Everybody likes to feel driven," says Wendell Brunious. "That's why Shannon Powell gets so much work here."[96] The phenomenon is not the same as syncopation but larger, going back to brass band and earlier—to Africa, many believe. "They call it 'playing on top of the beat,'" says Richard Moten. "Drummers and bass players that play on top of the beat—just a little bit ahead but always in time: kind of a push but never rushed. It's not exactly the same as syncopation, it's something else."[97] John Boutte agrees: "It's not the same as syncopation; it's being a little ahead of the beat or behind the beat. You're still within the meter, but you're just a hair ahead. They call it the backbeat, but it's really in front of the beat."[98] To some extent, the special beat comes from the spatial dimension of parades. "The beat is from street bands and Mardi Gras Indian parades," says John Gros. "Each voice is an independent part, like a Bach fugue. These are not unison lines; there is a lot of give and take with the line, plus, because it's a parade, the players are constantly moving. The downbeat in front is different from that of the guy in the back. This carried over to Fats, the Meters, and is true even today. It makes us unique. The beat is more precise in the Caribbean and other places the music originally came from. I won't say it's mechanical, but it's not the same."[99]

The effect is twofold: the music is more laid-back even as it has greater tension; the listener feels pumped up but mellow. In Shannon Powell's view, the tension exists not just because of the African or parade vibe but because "everybody is so different in New Orleans, and no one is willing to give that up."[100] And everybody sees it a different way. Evans believes it comes mainly from Powell and other drummers: "The drums tend to lead here, whereas in other parts of the world and the US, the bass tends to lead." Boutte believes it can come from other sources, including the brass or the voice: "We have so many great drummers: Shannon Powell, Smokey Johnson, Jason Marsalis, Earl Palmer, June Gardner, Idris Muhammad, Brian Blade, the guys from Preservation Hall, those old cats. In the African origins of the music, drums are very important. Some people say drums were the first instruments. I beg to differ. The voice was. So take that, drummers! One thing Louis Armstrong was fabulous at was controlling the rhythm section just with his phrasing. That's something I've learned with my band when I want them to push it up or pull it back, using my voice almost like the reins on a horse.'"[101] Katja Toivola describes it as African, in opposition to the Dixieland tradition, "a kind of friction or tension, but a good tension; that's the real African roots coming out that the Dixieland people tried to polish off. These were white people who were playing the repertory but trying to make it 'correct.' They looked down on the 'raggedy' black bands: their attitude was 'we're going to show you how this is supposed to be.' In that process they lost the very essence of the music."[102]

Others see the phenomenon in personal rather than racial terms. Clarinetist Tom Fischer believes it is "more the individual player in any style of jazz.

There are people who play modern jazz who are really laid-back and play on the back end of the beat, and other people who are really on top of the beat. Chet Baker and Dexter Gordon and those guys were laid way back, their sense of a down beat was always a second behind the drummer's, and other players like Dizzy Gillespie were always right on top of the beat."[103] David Torkanowsky simply says, "There is a wonderful tension that comes from agreeing to disagree," a sentiment echoed by Victor Goines, who believes the beat is like life, "full of tensions, but also full of releases. The pulls of different things are what bring us together and appreciate when things are actually in sync. So the drummer who plays on top of the beat and the bass player who plays behind the beat can actually seem like they are opposing each other, but it's like the husband and wife who are against each other: ultimately they've got to come together just a little bit of the time to work together, then they can go back to going against each other. That pull, constantly going back and forth, does something. It does something. So when I play with singers like Germaine Bazzle, she wants the drummer to be on top of me; everything in her body motion says, 'Come on, come on with me.' She wants you to be on top of the beat with her. The best thing you can do if you want to do that gig with her, not only that night but the next night, is to get on top of the beat with her."[104]

Whatever it is, it is not an occasional phenomenon but something eerily constant, always happening, with "every beat, really," says Evans. "So much goes on with the beat here. And it's not one thing: everybody does it differently. There is a strange interaction I've become really aware of where if I'm playing behind the beat, and the drums are expecting me to play behind the beat, then they're playing ahead of my beat, so we're both doing what each other is expecting and at some point psychically we have to come to a middle where we are consistently to the right side of each other where we're both expected—which is impossible but seems to happen, nonetheless."

Is it unique to New Orleans? "It's certainly more pronounced," says Evans. Often it doesn't exist at all in other places: when Lawrence Sieberth was transcribing and directing the music for an HBO movie about Bessie Smith, he "tried to get the LA players to not exactly synchronize," but found it difficult, not only because "the Delta blues vibe is not the same as the New Orleans vibe," but because in New Orleans the vibe itself "is more important than the correct note." Sieberth prefers "to get in the space between swing and the straight eighth note, which comes more naturally to New Orleans players.[105] In that space exists a mysterious freedom. "Here there is more liberty played with where you are," says Evans. "The drums are sometimes a long way ahead of the bass, which would never happen in New York. There, it's all up on top of the beat, pushing, which is great, but it's a different thing. Here there are huge gaps; in the front line, there is quite a sizable fraction of a second behind the beat, maybe more than that; some people are almost nearer to the next beat they're so far behind the beat, and somehow there's an understanding that's what's going on; they're not slowing down, they're just slightly later each time. Actually, someone like Leroy Jones, whom I've very much observed, is behind the beat and still manages to sound like he's pushing it, like he's pushing the time forward. That's because he's so relentless. But he just happens to be a fraction after the drums." Evans pauses, trying to sort it out and put the phenomenon into words before laughing in bewilderment. "It's very resistant to scientific analysis."[106]

What enables Leroy Jones to "push time forward," according to Jones himself, is the steadfastness of the rhythm section. His trumpet can be a fraction of a second behind or in front only if the basic pulse is steady: "Everybody has to be in the pocket," he says, with grave insistence. "If it stays there, the soloist or singer or horn man has the liberty to play with the time, to play behind the beat. Dexter Gordon and Ben Webster and all those cats were famous for that, but they had excellent rhythm sections; when the tempo was kicked off, it stayed right there. It didn't go faster, it didn't go slower, and it allowed them when doing solos to manipulate the tempo; they could slide behind if they wanted and then come back. But you can't do it if a cat is rushing. If you listen to funk, with James Brown, that groove was so solid. It ain't moving, it's right there, what they call 'in the pocket.' It's 'swinging' if it's jazz, 'in the pocket' if it's funk. And I think it's all one and the same. It needs to be in the pocket, *period*, so you can do your thing, you can play better."[107]

In New Orleans, there is a beat before the beat, a silence charged with meaning, that repeals physical time. James Evans describes working with Shannon Powell this way: "There is just that moment when you hit something, and you're about to hit it, you know it's coming, and then there seems to be this moment that's either infinite or infinitely small in length. *Then* he hits it. There's some indefinable quality about the time just before the actual hit." At its most sublime, this is what New Orleans jazz gives us: a moment of infinity.

Chapter Four

IMPROVISATION: THE TRUTH IS NOW

I never know what's going to happen next.
—Keith Frazier

In New Orleans, there is rarely a song without improvisation. People play and sing music in parades, on porches, in churches, at barbecues, in the streets and bars, creating new sounds day and night. Jamming is as basic as eating or sleeping. Dancing in the streets is part of it, "just as much an improvised thing as the actual soloing that's going on within the structure of the band music," says Leroy Jones.[1] Musicians are compelled to break out of predictable patterns because so many sit in, and they all learn from one another. By the last set, with new people on the stage and lots of alcohol freeing everyone up, the ensemble is trying new things, "surrendering to the moment" in the best sense. Sitting in goes back to the beginnings of improvisation in jazz neighborhoods, and players still trust people off the street to contribute to the ensemble: "We let anybody come up and play," says Les Getrex, "Just yesterday, a boy from Chicago got up here."[2]

It's not just players coming together to improvise, but ensembles joining with other bands. I once saw the Soul Rebels Brass Band come on the stage with a Cajun group from Lafayette, their horns blasting chords over elaborate fiddle tunes, creating sounds I'd never heard. This communitarian spirit, based on African tribal ritual, has defined New Orleans music since the first call-response of the slaves and the first African dances in Congo Square. This is so even though Jelly Roll Morton, King Oliver, and other early jazz stars invoked rituals of combat and usurpation, and even though improvisation is a release from that community, indeed, from time itself. A productive paradox—flamboyant solo virtuosity joined with self-effacing communalism—has always defined the city's musical tradition. In the current scene, improvisation is global. The Hosting Improvising Performers Festival, for example, brings together musical improvisers from around the world to jam with New Orleans musicians. Prominent out-of-towners, including Fabrizio Puglisi and Steve Lehman, play with established NOLA players and with each other in a series of musical happenings.

Musicians are constantly mixing things up spontaneously. Pianist Henry Butler begins his sets with elaborate preludes, "which could start anywhere, might get atonal or funky or go wherever I choose. If I had to just play a blues as a blues, play jazz just like jazz, maybe I'd do something else for a living."[3] The non-tonal crunches and clusters doing battle with tonal material makes a Butler performance unique. Often the wildest notions are the most productive. "Every now and then I get a crazy idea," John Boutte told me. "Recently, I had the band play a polka in the middle of the show, and I got up and started dancing with people in the audience. Did you ever see Lawrence Welk do that? He goes out and starts dancing with the old ladies. I just said, 'Do a polka,' and the guys in the band are so versatile, they started playing a polka, man. Another instance—just before a show, I pulled out a Little Willie John tune called 'Walk Slow,' basically a blues with a bridge, very beautiful, and we had a piano right there, so I gave them the format, and they'd never played it before, and the audience loved it. In fact, I got three emails saying, 'Did you record that tune?' And that was the very first time we did it. We have certain set tunes, but a lot of stuff happens in the moment."[4]

In New Orleans, improvisation is like breathing. "Every time I sit down at the piano, I improvise," says Allen Toussaint, "because I don't have rigid rules. I just play from the heart."[5] For some, a lack of improvisational talent is incomprehensible. "Not knowing how to improvise—there's something wrong with that," says Charmaine Neville. "Wherever you go in the world and people play, musicians in this city know how to sit in with them and improvise. But other people from other places . . . I remember in New York somebody said to me, 'Oh, you can't sit in with us . . . we have everything exactly how.' So somebody else in the band says, 'Come up and do this song.' So I got up there and I improvised, because I didn't know their arrangement. And the other guy was like, 'Oh my God.' I said, 'Yeah, baby, I'm from New Orleans.'"[6]

Improvisation in New Orleans is very different from what I often hear in New York, where one soloist plays improvised chromatic patterns, then another, as the audience listens silently, applauding politely only after each has his or her turn; in New York, a song is often an object to be deconstructed and, in many cases, decimated. Some jazz histories tell us improvisation did not really happen until soloists became stars and melody retreated to the

Panorama Jazz Band (left to right): Charlie Halloran, trombone; Scott Brian, drums; Aurora Nealand, alto saxophone; Steve Glenn, sousaphone; Matt Bell, banjo; Ben Schenck, clarinet; Matt Schreiber, accordion. Photograph by Greg Miles.

background. In this view, jazz is an art of iconoclasm and individualism, where ensemble is a kind of necessary nuisance. In New Orleans, as we see elsewhere in this book, the kind of improvisation that leaves behind melody, dancers, and the rest of the band is an aberration. Buddy Bolden, Sidney Bechet, King Oliver, Kid Ory, Freddie Keppard, and other early jazz stars inaugurated a new kind of solo virtuoso, but the communitarian core of the form remained unshakable.

"New Orleans music is based on ensemble improvisation," says Aurora Nealand. "Our ears are geared toward improvisational ensemble playing more than a lot of other places." Like everyone, Nealand improvises differently depending on the genre: "It's different for different settings. I think about gestures and texture a lot. That's the place I'm coming from, seeing things in a programmatic fashion inside my mind. When I play free improvisation gigs, I think about texture and color. In traditional music—geez, I don't know, I just try to make beautiful melodies. I'm better at the textures!"[7] One hears this a great deal. Improvising complex scales and textures would appear harder, but "making beautiful melodies" is the greater challenge. Whatever the style, from Sidney Bechet to free jazz to Jacques Brel, Nealand improvises with an unobtrusive virtuosity that can suddenly explode, looking downward with dour concentration through expositional passages, then throwing her head back with abandon to launch an ecstatic crescendo.

In New Orleans, improvisation is dialogical, a witty and passionate conversation. For pianist Meghan Swartz, it is as natural as speaking: "I think of it the same way I think about having a conversation. With improvising, you don't necessarily know what someone's going to ask you, but you kind of know how to put the words and phrases together, so even if it might be somewhat spontaneous, still it's in the context of what you're playing, so it's not random. Do you premeditate things before you say them when you're talking to someone? Kind of sometimes, sometimes not."[8] Donald Harrison also believes improvisation to be "the same as talking, a way of conversing with other musicians in a language that's harder than the English language, the language of jazz or rhythm and blues or funk." His vision is expansive, almost theological, an embrace of "the salvation of musical language." Harrison wants to capture "the essence of the blues, African rhythm, European harmony, and African harmony; jazz has embraced the music of the world."[9] This broad view cuts across genres. When I asked members of the Stooges Brass Band during a wildly improvised uptown second line what style they were playing, they answered, "We play everything. We gotta give them the world. There are lots of legends out here—we give them the world."[10]

From the beginning, New Orleans jazz has been a "conversation," in the words of clarinetist Tom Sancton, a different thing from the showy virtuosity often associated with the idiom. Sancton is the extreme example of a player who values chamber music intimacy over solo flash: "We listen to each other. I listen to Gregg [Stafford} and see what he's doing and fill in the gaps and make it fit together. That's the old ensemble style of collective improvisation." The sensibility may be laid-back, but the texture is complex. "It's not just about a solo accompanied by chords. Everybody has a voice—an equal voice, and they weave a tapestry of music together." There are plenty of solos in trad jazz, but these, Sancton believes, are not the point nor were they meant to be. "It's impossible to go back, but jazz was conceived as a communal unity. When Armstrong started doing flashy riffs and solos, he broke the game apart. He was miles ahead of anybody else." Too often since the inauguration of swing, players have used the solo convention as an excuse: "People get lazy. The trumpet player wants to rest his chops and let the piano player do a solo. You pace yourself more easily that way. If you listen to the old Sam Morgan band or King Oliver recordings, there are few solos." Sancton plays solos himself, exquisite ones; when I point this out, he shrugs: "Yes, but I don't really like doing them."[11] This is the paradox—many of us are drawn into New

Orleans jazz because of the brilliant solos of a Wendell Brunious or an Evan Christopher, but the more we listen, the more we realize that such solos aren't the point. As John Boutte points out, the best bands achieve good ensemble because everyone is a professional, often a leader, willing to subsume their personalities for a larger cause: "I'm lucky because everybody in my band is a bandleader, so they know not to give me shit. Because they don't like shit when they're running the band. We have mutual respect. We don't have any whiners. Nobody says, 'Oh I didn't get enough time to play.' They'll keep their mouths shut until after the show, which is really nice. *Then* they might bitch."[12]

This give-and-take between soloistic freedom and ensemble discipline has always characterized New Orleans music. As Joachim Berendt points out, "the possibilities of free and unlimited improvised solo playing are particularly enlarged when the soloist knows what the musicians playing with him are doing . . . Even the early jazz musicians—King Oliver, Jelly Roll Morton, Clarence Williams, Louis Armstrong—arrived through improvisation at set, repeatable turns of ensemble playing." To illustrate how this paradox "can be fertilized to an unimaginable extent," Berendt quotes seemingly irreconcilable statements from early masters: "Jelly Roll Morton told his musicians, 'You please me if you'd just play those little black dots that I put down there. If you play them, you'll please me. You don't have to make a lot of noise and ad lib. All I want you to do is play what's written. That's all I ask.' And despite this, clarinetist Omer Simeon—long a member of Morton's bands—and guitarist Johnny St. Cyr said, 'Reason his records are so full of tricks and changes is the liberty he gave his men . . . He was always open for suggestions.' This is the tension which has to be dealt with in art—and one cannot do much theorizing about it."[13]

Rather than theorizing, the players I talk with use everyday analogies. Conversation is the most persistent one, but there are others, some of which are quite imaginative. It is fascinating to hear musicians speak about improvisation, to articulate what it means to them, because so much of it is deeply personal and subconscious, and therefore not easily amenable to language even though it *is* a language. Trumpeter Eric Bloom tries to be "comical and loose. I play clean, thoughtful, and bluesy. I can hear anything around me and add it at any point. It's very conversational and deliberate at the same time. Someone will say something, and it will affect what you say, and then you'll say it later on. It's like being a kid in a candy store. You can't buy it all!"[14] Jeff Franzel, who plays every conceivable style of music, learned how to improvise while watching and listening to bands in the French Quarter during the '70s: "We lived in Houston, and my father would bring me in to New Orleans where I heard the Preservation Hall Jazz Band all the time, along with Ellis

Marsalis and other great musicians. I also grew up listening to Louis Armstrong—these were my influences. Improvising is like my playground. It's my language. Whatever I'm feeling, it comes through, and if you tell me what you're feeling, I can convey that through the language of music, the vocabulary of melody, chords, rhythm, it all comes through, like a dialogue. It's very natural for me."[15]

Musicians speak of improvisation using metaphors like playgrounds and candy stores, suggesting something childlike and fundamental. The young trumpeter Chadrick Honore is one of many NOLA musicians who improvised as a child: "Improvising is like drawing a picture, whatever you draw in your mind or whatever you illustrate from how you feel. I was improvising before I even knew how to read music. I started playing when I was about six; I didn't read music until I was thirteen. I was professionally playing in Japan at twelve, before I was even reading music. I play trumpet, but I can pick up a saxophone, drums, piano, anything. That was my childhood; I didn't do sports. I was the bad-ass child with all the instruments playing, going around the house beating on everything. The technical side helped me learn what I was playing so I could explain it. I could tell people, 'I play A, B, G flat, a minor seventh.' Some people improvise technically, some people improvise how they feel. I improvise how I feel. I can't play what I just played because I improvise how I feel. If I record it, I can remember it, and maybe play it again, but technically I'm a different person. I've learned my horn over a long period of time; it helps me illustrate what I have in my head better."[16] When Honore plays with the Rebirth Brass Band, he is ostensibly a trumpeter, but he picks up a tuba or saxophone when it moves him: "It fucks them up every time."

This is one reason a band like Rebirth is as fun to watch as to hear. Phil Frazier believes that the group has maintained an edge in the burgeoning brass-band world because they push improvisation further than others: "We're spontaneous, we're raw. I never know what's going to happen next. If it sounds good, I say, I love that crazy thing, and if it sounds bad, I love it. We do lots of improvising."

The band has been playing the same Tuesday performance since the early '90s, a remarkably consistent gig. Stability is essential for the kind of group improvisation practiced in New Orleans, something that wouldn't happen as much if the band were continually staying in hotels and living out of suitcases. The players are bonded to each other as though they are a single organism. Musicians who choose to stay in the city as hometown players, touring to make money but returning for regular gigs, make a distinction between themselves and those who are consistently on the road.

With nine players and one of the most solid ensembles in the business, Rebirth is a showcase for communitarian improvisation: solos rip in and out, interacting with each other against a dense wall of sound that comes at you like a big train. It's physically dizzying, but the texture is tightly woven. Phil Frazier says the trick is finding the balance between organization and spirit, planning and spontaneity. "We play more spontaneous music than most bands do. We're organized but unorganized. Know what I'm saying? Keep the spirit going so you don't really know what you're going to do next."[17] The tension between organization and anarchy is so daunting that Keith believes it's wise to "stay sober" on the stage. Otherwise, "things can get sloppy. Because it's always busy, there's a lot going on. We do a lot of improvisation—we might change the head of a song right on the spot. Sometimes it just happens. I don't know how the horn players do it. We're playing, someone is talking a solo, no one knows what's coming next, and the horn players are just talking, and they just come in on a riff together. And Philip gives a lot of signals from the bass horn. It's never written down; we never know what songs we're going to play— it just happens. The music is just different things we hear—there's different age groups in the band, people listen at different stuff. People might want to come in and do, for instance, a Curtis Mayfield song. They come in and give Philip the bass part, and the horn players figure it out. Although everyone in the band can read charts, we don't like to do it; people feel it more without."[18]

Many jazz books state that New Orleans improvisation is more "embellishment" than real improvisation.[19] This may have been true a century ago, but as Keith Frazier's description of Rebirth's process shows, it has little to do with the contemporary scene, where embellishment is the least of it and instantaneous creation happens on a regular basis. When Keith Frazier says "no one knows what's coming next," he is referring to the musicians as well as the audience; the horn players "figure it out" as they play. Again, conversation is the metaphor; the horns are "just talking," a discourse that, at least in this band, is "never written down." Eclecticism is the order of the day, both with material and "different age groups in the band" who bring in "different things we hear" for new improvisational possibilities.

What happens in the moment is partly a function of the audience, an important part of improvisation since the energy a crowd gives a band can substantially change its playing. What a brass band plays in a church is very different from what it blasts in a bar at 2 a.m.; the tasteful versions of standards that Leroy Jones plays in Preservation Hall are very different from the edgier variations—at once darker and more ecstatic—he plays uptown. In New Orleans, everyone is part of the "performance." Art Neville believes that, without a strong connection to the fans, the band lacks power and spontaneity, what he calls "the Force": "The people are who you're playing for, you ain't playin' for yourself . . . we got a lot of bad dudes but in different groups—it ain't gonna happen like that. Unless you've got the force, you're just another bar band; you've gotta know how to pull it together."[20]

New Orleans has traditional jazz at its center, but it also has an important modernist history. The 1960s inaugurated a move to create "a music that was spontaneous improvisation," in the words of saxophonist Earl Turbinton. The Jazz Workshop was a brief, brave plunge into modernism that organized itself by thinking about what was happening with traditional jazz and R&B. When black boppers like Turbinton, Ellis Marsalis, Alvin Batiste, and Nat Perrilliat began playing in the city in 1961, they were feeling as threatened by rock 'n' roll as traditionalists were, and they used Preservation Hall as a model for how to establish tiny citadels for their art, places that were largely drug- and alcohol-free, where people were high only on the music. Again, the city found a way to parallel, if not unite, the old with the new. According to Turbinton, "Alcohol and drugs permeated the whole atmosphere. It was not good for young people." There was a need to "create some new New Orleans music to inspire younger musicians."

The other analogue for the Workshop was the newly emerging style of R&B. Perrilliat and others teamed up with Allen Toussaint to create a sound reflecting the energies of the '60s. The modern jazz crowd believed bebop could be an analogue to the new funk. Turbinton and his colleagues appreciated traditional jazz, but believed it was out of tune with the times, much as Toussaint believed the smoothed-out style of early rock was out of tune for the '60s. Later in the decade, as the civil rights and black power movements began sweeping the country, Turbinton felt this was truer than ever. "I could appreciate traditional," he recalled, but its ethos was "inharmonious to the late '60s." New Orleans needed a music to embody a time during which "we were moving as black people and Americans more attuned to a harmony in the mid- and late '60s, celebrating music, celebrating life in a way that was nonexistent before . . . something new and exciting."[21]

This statement might seem odd given how extensively marchers in the civil rights movement intoned traditional gospel and blues songs as the repertory of protest, but by the late '60s, Coltrane and Parker were in favor with the black power movement. Armstrong was out, the boppers were in. I remember from in my own involvement with SNCC, SSOC, and other groups that black organizers were especially smitten with Coltrane, whose smoldering, fearless style embodied the militancy of the moment. A pioneer of advanced harmony and metaphysical interiority, Coltrane considered himself a classical rather than a popular artist, and was thus bound to appeal to Ellis Marsalis and his colleagues. Steeped in the restless aesthetics of Miles Davis and Thelonious Monk, whose bands gave him his start, Coltrane was a bold improviser who invented a new style about every six months, moving through dizzying chord experiments, leaping glissando patterns, abstracted spirituals, and remote Eastern modes toward a final, atonal blast into *Interstellar Space*, the aptly titled late album released just before his sudden death of liver cancer. At his height, as in the 1964 *A Love Supreme*, he achieved a grandeur only hinted at by his mentors. Through all this, his sound on both tenor and soprano sax remained intact: a hard, vibrato-free hunk of steel. This too went down well in New Orleans, a town where the cultivation of an individual sound is highly prized.

In the Workshop, located on Decatur Street, musicians began playing together in the morning so they could rehearse and "tune into each other." At night, they would gig until 2 a.m., playing Ornette Coleman, Miles Davis, the "freer elements" in late Coltrane, as well as "Stella by Starlight," "All the Things You Are," "Giant Steps," and "Moment's Notice." Blues and jazz standards were not neglected, and some musicians from the time remember Workshop modernism being imbued with a blues sensibility that was different from New York and the West coast.[22] As Jason Patterson, the talent booker at Snug Harbor, puts it, Turbinton "took Coltrane's approach and made it personal."[23] This legacy has endured. Ellis Marsalis's rich, blues-inflected improvisations at Snug Harbor are different from the cooler modernism practiced in other places. David Torkanowsky's playing is bracingly free yet evokes the ancestors in very arpeggio. Wendell Brunious's modern gigs are often blues spiced with altered chords. Richard Moten, whose bass improvisations are so airborne they sound both boppy and traditional, believes enough time has passed that one tradition is really as modern or antiquated as the other: "Remember, bop has been around sixty years; it's traditional too."[24]

Improvisation is associated in the popular imagination with something ungraspable and spontaneous, but Leroy Jones, Les Getrex, and many others confirm the testament of Chadrick Honore: the ability to improvise is part of childhood, a social activity as central as sports or learning to speak. In New Orleans, regular community musical gatherings are an intrinsic part of family experience, and the ability to improvise is a useful skill. Recent scholars are eager to emphasize this utilitarian factor and remove the veil of mystery and spontaneity. Still, to deny the mystery altogether and reduce it to socioeconomic factors is to miss something essential. With a master like Professor Longhair, whose improvisations are described by Eddie Bo and others as coming from another planet, there *is* something mysterious. It's a talent partly innate, not simply a sociological phenomenon. James Evans, for example,

Jason Marsalis, with singer Erina Perlstein. Photograph by Jack Sullivan.

was a classically trained clarinetist in Wales long before he migrated to New Orleans. He comes from a culture where jazz was scant. "I was a terrible clarinet player," he says. "It wasn't until somebody said, 'You can improvise,' that it made any sense at all. That's when it became feasible that I might actually be all right." Since he came to New Orleans in 2013, his ability to improvise has been continuously nourished, but it was there from the beginning.[25]

For many of the newer bands, improvising is central not only to what one does with a song, but to the song itself. When I asked Robin Clabby of the Brass-A-Holics how much they improvise, he said, "Tons, tons. We can't even do a set list. We tried it once or twice, but what's really important is the feel of the night. Our music grows out of us improvising together. We don't actually rehearse in a room very often; we do it in front of people. With new tunes, we just pull them up as we go; somebody will have an idea and we'll just work it out on stage."[26]

Ultimately, improvisation is about surprise. "I try to make moments that are unexpected," say Jason Marsalis. "On drums, I like to play solos that have space—core melodies with short, memorable rhythms. People don't expect it, and when they hear it, they're stunned. With vibes, too, I'm interested in creating different moments, each a separate tune. The more you study, the more you realize what is possible." This is why a Jason Marsalis performance, whether of a standard or a new composition, sounds like no other, with brilliant short phrases and lightning thoughts—a sense of constant adventure. Yet the core of it all is a second-line continuity that makes improvisation possible. The improvised phrase is conceived, executed, and over in a second, existing only in that second, yet nurtured and given form by a powerful tradition. [27]

The tradition is all about letting go, using history to escape from history, getting into a space outside time. New Orleans thrusts its players into the moment, where they need to be. As trumpeter Nicholas Payton says, "You have to let go of everything you've seen and heard to experience the truth. A lie is anything that has nothing to do with now. Truth is now."[28]

Chapter Five

STOMPING AND STUDYING: THE TWO CULTURES OF JAZZ

> The rhythms are coming from the bottom, from the earth.
> That's why people dance; you can hardly sit still with New
> Orleans music because the rhythm is so infectious.
> —Herlin Riley

In the late 1960s, Dizzy Gillespie told *Time* magazine that the difference between the new boppers and the old Armstrong sound was that "we study," whereas "all [Armstrong] did was play strictly from the soul." The "all" says it all. From the beginning, New Orleans music has been unapologetically soulful. It is a sound that moves and interpenetrates, gathering its energies and inspiration from the crowd, especially from dancers. Ridiculed by Gillespie, Miles Davis, and other modernists for his ebullient loyalty to his audience, Armstrong dismissed bop on the grounds that it "doesn't come from the heart" and is "all just flash."[1] Condescension toward Armstrong continues in many jazz circles, but Satchmo's devotion to New Orleans lyricism served him and his city well. Certainly he has had the last word: in the twenty-first century, Snug Harbor and a few other clubs continue to host modernists, but their sit-down studiousness is an anomaly in the rowdy Big Easy, where Armstrong's open-heartedness is triumphant.

Danny Barker called modern jazz "starving music" for good reason. Unlike jazz in New York and Paris—and classical music everywhere—New Orleans was never consumed by a purist avant-garde. In the northeast, audiences were delighted when Miles Davis and his colleagues literally turned their backs on them—programmed alienation at its hippest—but New Orleans music lovers found such coolness peculiar at best. As we will see in this chapter, New

Orleans found a way to integrate bop into its culture, making it part of its tradition, but the melding has not been easy.

Since the '60s, post-Coltranian abstraction has dominated New York and other northeast jazz scenes, but in New Orleans, the idea of abandoning the music that gave paraders and dancers their defining energy was never taken seriously. Even when playing with bop ensembles in Chicago and New York, New Orleans artists like Lester Young retained the soulful lyricism fundamental to the city. Renowned for his subtlety, capable of producing chromatic modulations as daring as any bopper, Young nevertheless focused on dancers rather than the inert "modern jazz" crowd; he preferred working with colleagues who knew the songs rather than technicians who just "played the changes."[2] Imported from out of town, bop and its descendants established a vital presence in the Crescent City, but modernism was always a subculture. There is scant demand for modernists, despite the existence of wonderful artists: "There are a lot of modern jazz players, but little market," says pianist Tom McDermott. "They get overshadowed." McDermott believes that the city still flourishes as a great jazz center because of "the culture of second lines." Not only New Orleanians but tourists have come to expect "music that is functional," a sound that people can dance, parade, marry, barbecue, and party to. This in turn "generates musicians' demand" and keeps the gigs coming.[3]

New Orleans musicians care more about having a good time than technical perfection, a priority tied to the funky informality of the city. According to Jon Batiste, it's easier to let loose in the Big Easy than in the Big Apple because "there's less of a consequence—who's watching, what the stage is, what that stage represents historically. Across the street [from Juilliard, where this interview took place] we have Alice Tully Hall, the Met, Carnegie Hall just down the street, then Town Hall, then Jazz at Lincoln Center at Time Warner. There's this cosmopolitan pressure. When you're in New Orleans, there's the Frenchmen Street strip, and the mindset is to come there and be part of something, whereas here, the mindset is less about being part of something than witnessing it at its highest level. There are lots of critics. If you mess up, how many people are going to say, 'We're just having a good time?'"[4]

Those with the most formidable technique are often the most vehement on the subject. "My whole feeling is that music should be expressing something," says clarinetist Tom Fischer, a master of his instrument both in modern and traditional styles. "A lot of players leave me cold. I'd much rather do something a little wrong but *say* something than be perfect all the time. There are friends of mine in New York who are good players; they play beautiful notes, and it's all very pretty, but it doesn't move me, you know? They can do things

Katja Toivola. Photograph by Katja Liebing.

I can't do, but still—there's no emotion. It's all too neat, clean, and tidy. Maybe that's why I like being here in New Orleans. There's nothing neat or clean or tidy about this place, physically or mentally or musically."[5]

Another musician who is unimpressed by tidiness is trombonist Katja Toivola. She hears a great deal of jazz that is mechanically perfect and chromatically intricate but not emotionally compelling: "I go and try to be open-minded, and I want to like this, and the people are playing so well, and it just makes no f-in' sense to me. It's like 'alloole alloole alloole' [she makes noises like chromatic glissandos]—good grief. And the thing is, most of those people *all sound the same and you can't tell one from the other.* I think it's because they all go to those schools, and they all go through the same methods; they're almost like robots. You read these interviews, and they talk about how this is so 'spiritual,' and then you listen to the record and you're in disbelief about the way they talk about the music and then it comes out the way it does. From the verbal description, you'd think it was something spectacular."[6] Trumpeter Wendell Brunious makes similar noises to describe what he regards as soulless jazz: "Badoobadoooobadoobadoo, Badoobadoooobadoobadoo, Badoobaoooobadoobadoo—it just gets to be like, what? What's next? It's kind of what they know. It's kind of unfortunate." Brunious plays out of town a great deal—I've heard him do killer performances with Dr. John in New York—but he prefers to be in New Orleans: "New Orleans music is always going to have feeling and the blues. That's what we do here."[7]

An abhorrence of robotic precision, where "people all sound the same," is something that unites NOLA musicians across genres. John Gros, who presided over the Papa Grows Funk gig at the Maple Leaf for thirty years, puts it succinctly: "Precision is not the most important thing. Whether it feels good is what matters."[8] Trumpeter Irvin Mayfield says it's "really about the passion for what we do. That's what this place is a testament to: a bunch of people doing what they're passionate about."[9]

That New Orleans is a city more of stompers than studiers, where "feel-good music" is the standard, relates in part to its colonialist past. New Orleans would not be the uniquely sensual city it is without its French origins. As jazz pianist Henry Butler, exiled to New York by Katrina, told me in 2010, Mardi Gras, jazz funerals, second lines, and other rituals were not the source of New Orleans's staying power, "just manifestations. It goes back to the beginnings, to the French. It's a looseness, lots of drinking and love." In Butler's view, the city was lucky; the Spanish, who came next, projected a similar spirit, not as loose as the French but far removed from the frosty Puritanism of other New World colonies. New Orleanians inhabited Spain's elegant gardens and elaborate balconies—the Spanish look of the "French Quarter"—but remained stubbornly loyal to French customs. Does Butler find any of this Franco-Spanish hedonism in New York? "New York understands it intellectually, but it's imported."[10]

The idea of a cerebral, "imported" New Orleans in jazz cities like New York is key to understanding why the Big Easy is so separate from the rest of America. As John Boutte puts it, "Music is more organic in New Orleans, and the people are more out there. We didn't have the Puritans—we had the French and the Spanish. We've always had a non-Puritan approach to life. Yes, there were hard-core Catholics, but they still drank, people still knew how to live—we didn't have restrictions."[11] Danny Barker remembers the Lyric, the Pit, and the Orpheum, major vaudeville venues where risqué love ballades were saved from censorship by double entendres: "If it wasn't too rash or too bombastic, people would accept it. Burlesque shows done nothing but that type of material . . . The sanctimonious states were strict on them kind of laws, but they have people in the world that wants to hear that type of material, to laugh at themselves and laugh at the world. That's why you have clowns on the stage, people playing drunkard's parts, fallen women falling by the wayside—that's life. . . . Today they're very sanctimonious, but the French people were outspoken with that. . . . The United States is always trying to hide what the rap singers are singing—well, they would go to a night club and they would hear that, the same type of thing—shock treatment."[12]

So what's the difference between Henry Butler, who is now "imported" himself, and John Boutte, who remains in New Orleans? At a Boutte show like his regular gig at d.b.a., large numbers of fans and tourists, young and old, dance in front of the stage or move to the music from one bar to the other in d.b.a.'s two rectangular rooms. d.b.a. is a large, rambling venue, but the concert is focused, partly because Boutte is such a personable artist and partly because the crowd is attentive, glued to what's happening on stage even when they are dancing, carousing, and drinking, which they do to gratifying excess.

Henry Butler's performances used to be like this. In places like Joe's Cozy Corner and the Funky Butt Café, he rocked the audience into ecstasy, powered further by a continual string of surprise musicians coming from Rampart Street or Claiborne Avenue to sit in. In New York, things are different. Butler livens up places like the Jazz Standard and Lincoln Center's Damrosch Park, but does so against the grain of the culture. In August 2013, I heard him with a superb group of New York players in a band called the Hot Nine (now an established ensemble). It was their Lincoln Center debut, and they were stoked. The repertory was traditional—Jelly Roll Morton, Fats Waller, Bessie Smith, plus incendiary medleys of Butler's own devising. Butler's fingers surged from one end of the keyboard to the other with steely arpeggios and thunderous chords. His playing was improvisational and organic, as always, whereas that of his colleagues was technically beyond reproach, but for the most part "imported." (The exception was Herlin Riley, whose drumming, as ever, brought New Orleans to New York.) For Butler, the music came from the heart, whereas for his colleagues it was something carefully studied and beautifully rendered—not a bad thing, but not the same thing. It was a classic instance of stompers versus studiers. Trumpeter Steve Bernstein, leader of the band, was charmingly blunt: "I'm a Jew from New York—I play this music from the outside, unlike Henry. He plays it from the inside." This concert was as good as an import gets, but it lacked spontaneity, and because there was no dancing, it lacked the total NOLA experience.

Herlin Riley believes the essential New Orleans vibe comes from the power and prevalence of the second line bass drum: "All music starts with rhythm, and rhythm defines whatever style you are playing. So if you deal with New

Professor Longhair. Courtesy of the Abner Milner
Collection, Hogan Jazz Archive, Tulane University.

Orleans music, the rhythm that's prevalent comes from the bass drum, from the bottom up, as opposed to bebop, where it is from the top down. The cymbals are the most prevalent part of the drum set. But in New Orleans music, it's the bass drum that's prevalent—the bass and the snare drum. The rhythms are coming from the bottom, from the earth. That's why people dance; you can hardly sit still with New Orleans music because the rhythm is so infectious."[13] As we see throughout this book, the idea of music seeping up from the earth, articulated by musicians as different as Dr. John and Michael White, comes from an animistic conviction that New Orleans's ancestors are part of the vibe, summoning music from deep down below. It's an "infectious" disease, as Riley asserts, one everyone in love with this music has contracted, and its main symptom is an inability to sit still once the music starts.

In New Orleans, there is no contradiction between being serious about the music and letting loose. This is a paradox that other cultures do not comprehend. YouTube videos of live New Orleans music are full of snarky "comments" about people partying when they should be listening. But to NOLA players, an inert audience is as unsatisfactory as a crowd that talks over their music. Professor Longhair complained about both: "If they can't get a drink or be out with a girlfriend, they just as soon not go in. That's not really being interested in the music. He just wants to go someplace." When people do go in, Professor Longhair, who was a dancer himself, wanted them to get on their feet. The absence of dancers was a downer, and he preferred Tipitina's (established in his honor) to other places because everyone danced, so much so that other venues depressed him: "[They] make me feel real down.... Some people sit just like that. You be working and working, you building up sweat.... You trying to stamp their feet or anything, clap their hands or applaud right there. They sit there. The only way you can beat that is if you don't pay them people no mind." To avoid being "distracted" by a depressing audience, Fess (as the Professor was called) would "always watch my keyboard or the mens on the bandstand."

What's poignant about the Professor's lament is the fantasy that he could stamp *their* feet, clap *their* hands, so the energy wouldn't die. He saw performer and audience as part of the same entity.[14] This view has not changed. Nothing really matters, says Keith "Wolf" Anderson, "as long as they're dancing, as long as they move. That's the only thing . . . if they're sitting down we're not too happy. We're still able to play, but you know, we're not too happy. We're not too happy." Anderson is clear that a dancing audience enhances the band's playing: "Yes, it does, for the better . . . because we feed off their energy . . . we're doing something and we know they like it, it makes us wanna do better and better."[15] For Kermit Ruffins as well, "the audience kind of makes the gig," especially second-liners: "When you have people dancing like that, it's easier to play. The gig is real short . . . it's like nothing compared to people sitting down. . . . Even the musicians are real bored if people are just sitting there." For the irrepressible Ruffins, the sit-downers don't entirely spoil the performance; the band is still "gonna play their butts off," in a "more intimate" situation where they are playing for each other rather than the audience. The latter is the norm in modern jazz, whereas for New Orleans musicians, it is an occasional necessity. "Do Whatcha Wanna," which Ruffins calls "my only hit," defines not only an attitude but physical movement: "When we said 'do whatcha wanna,' we was talking about actual dance steps too. That's the only thing that was in my head when I started singing that. . . . Was somebody dancing?" If the audience is predominately black, the question is moot. "In the Tremé neighborhood, or anywhere in the black neighborhoods, the music is definitely gonna be a lot hotter just because they're dancing, and they're yelling, and they're hyping the band up, and they know the guys personally, so . . . 'If you don't play my number' . . . and all that kind of stuff, just makes it real exciting, whereas in a white bar . . . the band doesn't tend to show off as much, it's more of a 'just a gig' type of thing."[16]

In New Orleans, a dead crowd is simply not acceptable. Bands pull audiences up on the stage, where they become a fundamental part of the show's choreography. Ensembles as formal as the Tuxedo Jazz Band and the Palm Court Strutters, who wear suits and comport themselves with elegance, expect their audiences to dance and will often drag inhibited tourists onto the dance floor. The T-shirt/sneakers musicians like Shamarr Allen and the Rebirth Brass Band resort to technology: Allen dances into the crowd with his cell phone aloft, calling out his phone number so people can connect with him. It gets them going every time—and the number is real.

Wynton Marsalis believes that the decline of dancing in jazz culture is "definitely a loss. When you see people dancing to music you have a combination of two art forms at one time. So, just on that level, it's more complex. Plus, as a musician, you can get inspired by looking at people dancing. Then there is the whole sensuousness and the romance of slow drag tunes, just the type of feeling that that music has in it. It's different, and getting away from it was definitely a loss."

Marsalis believes that a fetish for mechanical speed was part of the problem: "The whole conception of playing something sensual on your horn, of having people dance to it and fall in love to the sound of instrumental music, wasn't a conception of our era [the '70s]. So we've had to use the experiences that we've had to figure out where it went wrong. Why is it that we didn't ritualistically learn these things? How did these rituals break down?"[17]

They never broke down in the Big Easy. "In New Orleans," Gregg Stafford told me, "people were always looking to dancing. They love to dance. Not that people in other parts of the United States don't like to dance, but that's why you had so many rhythm and blues songs coming out in New Orleans, because we had all these social and pleasure clubs giving dances, and they had all these other clubs that were just clubs. They were having dances every week; we had bars on every corner when I was growing up, music coming out of every last one of them. When I was seven until I was fifteen, I lived next door to a dance hall called the People's Defense League Hall, and every weekend there were receptions and dances."[18]

Today, the music is hotter, the tempos wilder, the crowds younger. As musician-writer Samuel Charters points out, "The harder tempos and the new sophistication of the rhythm have given the bands a younger audience that reacts the way young fans react to music everywhere—they dance to it."[19] That energy has only gotten more kinetic since Charters (who has observed the scene since the '50s) made this observation in 2006. The ever-faster rhythms from groups like Dumpstaphunk, the Brass-A-Holics, and Hot 8 may have compromised the rhythmic subtlety of older songs and ballads, but have also created a new dynamism. Some, like singer-educator Banu Gibson, believe tempos are now so fast that they need a correction. The first thing she does in her New Orleans Traditional Jazz Camp is to get the students out of the speed of contemporary culture and into a dance vibe, using NOLA's notorious humidity as a check: "People forget that it used to be dance music, and that if you can't dance to it, you're playing the wrong tempo. A lot of these guys have never second-lined, so we start by marching them around the French Quarter in the heat . . . within a couple blocks you're hitting the natural tempo that you need for that New Orleans feel."[20]

Dance music does not have to be simple. "You can play a lot of notes," says Nicholas Payton. "You can play in multiple rhythms—Louis Armstrong was doing a lot of that, too, playing five over four and using rhythmic displacements. But when you start to take the music out of the environment and it becomes an intellectual pursuit, it's problematic. And that's why it leaves a lot of people cold. I'm a musician and I don't want to hear it . . . I want to reach the people, and I attribute that to my upbringing in New Orleans, playing in second-line bands and playing for people who danced. And the biggest difference between musicians now and musicians back in the day is that they played for people who danced. To me, even if it's free form or out of time, that dance sensibility should be implied. Even if there's going to be a meter change in every bar, that feeling and passion should be there."[21] The dance groove is a sensibility, not a specific beat or level of complexity.

Zydeco and Cajun music, both historically tied to dancing, have an increasing presence in New Orleans. These related forms come from southwest Louisiana, but have established a beachhead in twenty-first-century New Orleans. They were conceived as exclusively dance music in rural communities, but the happy twang of Cajun and the dynamism of zydeco proved irresistible to larger audiences once RCA Victor began recording them. As we have seen in the introduction, the Sunday afternoon Cajun dance feat is still one of the most reliable parts of Tipitina's calendar, and the Thursday night zydeco events at Rock 'n' Bowl bring in impressive bands from the bayou. The moment the band starts, the pumping accordions and percussive washboards fire people out onto the dance floor. When the tempo slows down for a waltz, the dancers swirl out in arabesque patterns. Cajun players, who keep alive a tradition that started in the early 1800s, tend to be fierce traditionalists, but "zydeco nouveau" groups like Rockin' Dopsie and the Zydeco Twisters and Nathan and the Zydeco Cha Chas mix traditional washboard-accordion tropes with funk and pop.[22]

A dance dynamic often extends to the relationship between player and instrument. Trombone Shorty and Shamarr Allen dance on the stage, swinging, twirling, and caressing their instruments as if they were partners. Clarinetist James Evans describes the style of his colleague Shannon Powell as a near- carnal interaction with the drum set. "I was playing in a second line with Shannon, and we came in here [the Palm Court] and he turned his drum on its side and he was playing it, and he had his whole body around it—it had become part of him. It was like a dance as much as it was somebody playing an instrument." This experience can only happen live: "You just don't get it on record. You can't. You can't relate it. And when you actually hear it, it blows you away."[23]

Many musicians say that if you can't dance to it, it isn't New Orleans music. John Boutte points out that dancing has always been part of the culture: "As far back as the 1700s, aristocrats complained about 'Negro noise' in New Orleans. One of them wrote that black folks were loud, common, 'disturbing whole neighborhoods,' dancing in the fucking streets. We haven't changed much." Boutte believes that jazz is intrinsically sexy and exists for dancers and lovers; it should be music "you can court with. Can you dance to bop? Fuck that. If somebody tries to dance to bop, give him his medication." [24]

When Charlie Parker asserted that bop was "no love-child of jazz" but instead "something entirely separate and apart," he was anticipating what Boutte and many NOLA traditionalists interviewed for this book say from the New Orleans side. They take the original boppers at their word.[25] According to Boutte, bop rises and wanes continually in New Orleans, but is "never going to go anywhere." It's "still a scene," and always will be, offering talented, sometimes "genius" players, but it ends up being "what the fuck?" Bop requires great dexterity and proficiency, but "it's like modern times, like highway I-10. I get tired of all those chromatic runs. I want to hear a simple fucking melody."[26]

I remember members of Percy Humphrey's Preservation Hall Jazz Band telling me in the '80s that "we don't play any of that damn bebop." This statement and others like it brought to mind the jazz wars in the '60s, when Coltrane and his colleagues were either canonized as Great Jazz Artists or denounced, in Ralph Ellison's words, for "fucking up the blues." Danny Barker was one of the bluntest: "Today [1995, during one of his final interviews], you go on a job, and they see a banjo, and everybody tries to get as far as they can from you. I watch them, how they give you a false-ass smile, but they don't like it. Everybody wants to be modern. But a real jazz band had a banjo—a good banjo, a good bass player, and a good drummer. They can't beat that. That's why the music was so great . . . Some of these people now don't know nothin' about it and never will get it. They didn't know nothin' about swing until Louis Armstrong started swingin' an instrument. Now everybody's Dizzy Gillespie this, Buck Clayton this, Roy Eldridge that—them people couldn't play shit if it wasn't for Louis."[27] This kind of talk never quite dies down: Wendell Brunious told me in 2015 that his colleagues at the New Orleans Center for Creative Arts (NOCCA) only cared about "flash"—an exact echo of Armstrong's objection to bop.

These denunciations of bop always struck me as odd since Brunious and many of his traditionalist colleagues actually play it—the patterns, the harmonies, the songs—and do so beautifully. I recall numerous Tuxedo Jazz Band gigs in the '90s that interspersed traditional New Orleans jazz with bebop numbers, which puzzled me because I thought the whole point of Tuxedo was its traditionalism. As I've since learned, the partiers and the boppers are not mutually exclusive—at least not in NOLA. Barry Martyn explains that the distinction between modern and traditional is not always observed in New Orleans: "There is not much of a differentiation down here, which is a good thing. Someone like Leroy Jones, a good musician, can do either, but someone like Michael White, who is also good, isn't interested in the modern stuff."[28] Jones dismisses the idea that bop isn't danceable: "People like to say that's not dance music, but it was, because in the joints people would dance. With bebop, the pulse was there; there was extensive improvisation over those chords, but people were dancing because the music was swinging. It was like small big bands, but the soloist was predominant; it grooved and made you want to get up and do something."[29]

Indeed, when Jones and his colleagues launch from trad into a bop number, people do not stop dancing. Jones was once part of a bop dance scene himself, as his partner Katja Toivola explains: "There was a little bebop scene in the mid-to-late '70s and early '80s. People like Ed Frank, Leroy Jones, and Wendell Brunious had those gigs back then. They played in joints like Joe's—a bandstand, some tables, and a little dance floor-where people would come and dance. It wasn't New Orleans music; it was a bebop gig. Basically, bebop is soulful, small-band swing. It was dance music back in its day. To me, bebop is Charlie Parker, Clifford Brown, Lee Morgan. That's danceable, that's swinging." It's more danceable in New Orleans than other places because it's transformed by second-line syncopation into "a combination of bebop and brass band. It sounds weird, but it isn't at all when you think about it. Whatever the great New Orleans drummers play, they are always implying the New Orleans feeling, which is the brass-band roots. Even when somebody like Bob French played straight-ahead swing, the accent on the bass drum, the accent on the snare, always had that brass-band funk. That's a unique New Orleans thing. If you listen to the old brass bands—Eureka, the Young Tuxedo Brass Band on the old recordings—the essence of the music is the same. They didn't have the bop element. That's with those who play authentic New Orleans jazz today. With someone like Herlin Riley, you can see those two elements come together. If you listen to Gerald French now, he does the same thing. So does Shannon Powell, Jerry Barbarin Anderson—that's New Orleans drumming, and it's all in there. The drummers, piano players, guitar players all sound New Orleans regardless of what they do."[30] Vernel Fournier with Ahmad Jamal is another example of a New Orleans modernist drummer with a second-line vibe; Ed Blackwell with Ornette Coleman is yet another. Even New Orleans musicians who end up in New York never let go of the New Orleans vibe, nor could they if they wanted to: "I'm always the same," says Herlin Riley, who plays with Wynton Marsalis. "The experience is always the same; the vibration is always the same. It's just a different genre of music in New York."[31]

Another element that made the war between traditional and bop less incendiary in New Orleans was the eruption of rock 'n' roll. Trad jazz, promoted by the management of a 1939 publication called *Jazzmen*, always had the upper hand. As Samuel Charters points out, the larger national battle was "only resolved by the unexpected appearance on the scene of rock 'n' roll in the mid-'50s, which overnight swept the jazz field and made the jazz predicament largely irrelevant."

In New Orleans, however, the traditionalists dominated the music scene, and much of the underpinning of what they were attempting to achieve with their 'revival' had been articulated a generation before in *Jazzmen*."[32]

David Torkanowsky also believes bop to be traditional. "Traditional is not a style, but a philosophy. There used to be a band around here called the Storyville Jazz Band. Ellis Marsalis was in it, and they played traditional forms absolutely true to the way they were intended. It can have bebop in it. It means to swing and to pay homage to the ancestors. But then it's cool to play, and you can play what you feel, and if it's 'bopsyland,' as the old cats called Storyville, it was still an incredible band."[33] Bebop has thus been absorbed into the New Orleans vibe, the "modern" layered onto the traditional, a defining feature of the culture, one that resembles European cities more than American. The result is a color and variety that keeps everyone happy. Toivola believes that the anti-bop crowd is really resistant to hard bop, post-bop, and other forms of modern jazz, not classic bebop, which fits neatly into a traditional show: "A gig might start with a two-beat New Orleans street beat, then when the soloist starts, they switch to straight-ahead swing, and it makes perfect sense; it fits like a glove. This is not Benny Goodman swing but straight-ahead, more like bebop before Tony Williams." Since this is New Orleans, where players resist genre classification, it's not surprising that bebop has become internalized. "There's not really a bop scene here now, but most New Orleans jazz musicians don't box things like that—they just play. So the bop scene is in

Leroy's playing or Wendell's playing, or Lucien's playing. No one really has an interest in doing an all-bop gig. In the true New Orleans bands, the repertory is very wide; it's completely normal to play 'Panama Rag" from 1912, then 'At Last', then 'Now is the Time', and from that to 'All of Me'. It all makes sense; everything is played in the New Orleans vein, but with the style and the songs themselves, there is quite a spectrum. The people take it like, 'Why not?'"[34] New Orleans musicians make bop sound like New Orleans, as Herlin Riley explains: "An identifiable trait of all New Orleans drummers is that we incorporate the bass drum into our playing, so even when we play bebop, you may hear the big four—ka-dump, ka-dump, kadump–bang! It may be very subtle, but you can hear it, like an unknown, unspoken characteristic of almost all New Orleans drummers, those who come from there, who are part of the culture, from the second lines and jazz funerals and all those things: we have internalized that vibe so much until it's a part of who we are, being from that area and that culture. In our playing, we instinctively incorporate New Orleans."[35]

There is still modern jazz in New Orleans, including up-to-the-minute free jazz, but those who practice the latter often feel underappreciated. According to Larry Sieberth, who performs and composes his own brand of avant-jazz, including Middle Eastern idioms (sometimes teaming up with the haunting singer, Amit Chatterjee), "The contemporary music scene gets pushed under the more traditional view of what New Orleans music is supposed to be like—the 'Down By the Riverside' trad kind of thing. That's always been a problem in my experience. I used to play a lot in Europe, and all they wanted to hear was 'Down By the Riverside' and 'When the Saints Go Marching In.' They would never think of bringing in anything contemporary. When you say, 'New Orleans music', they really want to hear black musicians—Louis Armstrong; they have presuppositions of what New Orleans music is supposed to sound like."[36]

The odd thing about this lament is that when I spoke to Sieberth, he was playing a gig with the Tuxedo Jazz Band, as traditional as one can get, with mostly black musicians, and with a leader, Gerald French, who complains about how young players are only taught bop and contemporary to the exclusion of tradition. This kind of ironic juxtaposition happens all the time. Traditionalists are perpetually afraid their art is dying, though the constancy of their gigs and increasing numbers of young people in both bands and audience tell a different story—as if fighting to keep the tradition alive against hopeless odds is itself part of the tradition. And modernists have always felt marginalized, as they often were. Sieberth is experimenting with what he calls "jazztronica," a mélange of acoustic and electronic sound, undaunted by what he considers the long odds of success. And his playing in "trad kind of things," though thoroughly idiomatic, allows for his personal brand of modernism to creep in, spiked as it is with the accidentals and chromatic touches the more inventive trad pianists have always brought to the table. When the saints go marching in with Sieberth's piano, their march has a slightly modern step, which makes us want all the more "to be in that number."

For some, mixing bop up with tradition is an explicit aesthetic. "I was influenced by George Shearing, Oscar Peterson, Art Tatum," recalled pianist Eddie Bo, whose rocking piano is spiced with bop harmonies. "They were *players*." His mission was to "mix the two up"—the boppers with "the funky flavor of the city." He attributes this innovation to education: "If I hadn't gone to study [at the Grunewald School of Music], I would have just played what I heard around. I found out there were other things, other melodic lines laying out there, and I thought maybe I could make them blend in." Bo is a studier, but also a stomper who writes everything for dancers. The sophistication of his chords by no means crowds out the partiers, whom he views as fundamental: "Kids in all generations like dance. They set the stage for music. If you watch the rhythmic patterns of their bodies, you can just about feel what the rhythm pattern should be. You can fall away from it, and they'll fall in line with any variation you make on a pattern. I always try to write around the patterns of their bodies."[37] Bo always got people dancing, whether playing with the Platters or the Wild Magnolias. His passing in 2009 robbed New Orleans of one of its most soulful and original artists.

In most towns outside the Big Easy, the partiers and studiers remain segregated. Perhaps I've been unlucky, but I've rarely seen dancing at a bop or postbop gig in New York, Chicago, Las Vegas, or any place besides New Orleans. People sit down and behave themselves like they're supposed to. When NOLA partiers invade the studiers, they have to be careful. When I asked the Rebirth Brass Band what they anticipated when they played at the Blue Note, Keith Frazier said, "There won't be no cussin'—no cussin' and no 'Buck Naked Sex' [trumpeter Kabuki's outrageously scatological new song]. But there were limits to what they would put up with. When one of their assistants advised them, "You can't go in jeans, you can't go in T-shirts," Frazier was dismayed: "You crazy? No jeans? No T-shirts? Shit, we're in trouble, guys." But he vowed to "liven the place up. It won't be like a church."[38] The band has been around long enough to know that when they venture to the heartland—or even New York—they have to repress themselves a bit while retaining enough NOLA spirit to give the crowd what they think is an "authentic" experience. Phil Frazier says that in a buttoned-down place like the Blue Note or Maxine's, "we have to behave ourselves, but people understand, 'That's Rebirth!' We cut

Trombone Shorty at Snug Harbor. Photograph by Jack Sullivan.

loose a little bit, give them a taste of it, tradition and funk at the same time. Yes, people sit down in a place like Maxine's, but I say, 'We're playing here tonight, so take off your shirt, take off your shirt, why don't you take *this*!'"[39] The end of Frazier's sentence is as aggressive as his sousaphone.

The stompers can ignite the studiers. That's their mission. I remember Trombone Shorty playing a show in 2010 in Snug Harbor, a place known for sit-down decorum. This was the period just before Shorty's rise to international stardom. His big eyes blazing, he told me before the show, "We're going to make this place rock," and that's what he did.[40] Perpetually in motion, leaping and dancing, waving trombone and trumpet, bounding from stage to balcony as he exhorted the audience to scream in call-response, he transformed Snug Harbor into a crazy party. People leapt up from their tiny tables and danced to Troy's horn lines, which rocketed up to the rafters or reigned down from them seconds later—a kind of solo antiphony. It didn't seem like Snug Harbor, and the managers were visibly discomfited (though not the young waiters, who were having a blast). A set at Snug Harbor only lasts an hour, but the out-of-context intensity made the evening seem blissfully longer.

The same thing can happen anywhere. Donald Harrison and Henry Butler recently played a long set of post-bop at New York's Iridium club; clearly, the band thought this was what a sophisticated New York crowd would want to hear. Near the end of the evening, Butler finally said, "Let's get direct," bursting into a joyful medley of traditional jazz and Mardi Gras Indian music. The audience, dutifully solemn and studious throughout the evening, suddenly broke into cheers, applause, and screaming. A library turned into a party. For better or worse, jazz is now both.

Chapter Six

MARDI GRAS INDIANS GET FUNKY

That frenzied beat is around all the time, even when they're not playing it
because it's in the fabric, it's in the mortar, it seeps up out of the streets.
—Allen Toussaint

Every year on Mardi Gras Day, Super Sunday, and St. Joseph's Day, working-class African Americans dress up in elaborate American Indian costumes and parade through the city, chanting, pounding percussion, and invoking secret codes and rituals. Each neighborhood "tribe" has a Big Chief, a Queen, a Scout, a Second Chief, a Flag Boy, a Wild Man, and other personae representing celebration and political resistance. It's a family affair, with paraders aged nine to ninety jamming the streets and jamming music. The Wild Man, wearing formidable horns, is a bodyguard who protects the Chief: best not to mess with him. The Scout, parading ahead of the tribe, directs the celebrants through the neighborhoods. Children march with their elders, hoping to become bad enough to be future Wild Men. Don't be deceived by their age: "If you mess with the bull," the refrain goes, "you will get the horn."

All year, the Indians sew fantastical costumes, each representing a specific tribe and built for the person wearing it, depicting deserts, sand flowers, eagles, sea shells, fish leaping from waves, some three or more years in the making, weighing as much as 125 pounds. Every Sunday throughout the year, the Indians practice for the next Mardi Gras, and on Mardi Gras Day, beginning at 8 a.m. they parade in their neighborhoods rather than in the larger Mardi Gras scene in the French Quarter, Canal Street, and St. Charles Avenue. The tribes have little to do with the conventional Mardi Gras krewes; they are underground societies, though far more visible now than ever before. They are very sure that they have the better Mardi Gras.

Mardi Gras Indians. © Mark Hertzberg.

Behind the costumed paraders are the ubiquitous second-liners, a rowdy personification of the neighborhoods that support the tribes. The visual spectacle is Indian, but the music is African, a mélange of percussion, chant, and, most recently, brass band. It is raw, impassioned, hypnotically repetitive, and complex in its rhythmic crisscrossings. One must see the Indians on the street, chanting and banging in multicolored splendor, to get the full ecstatic charge. The clubs don't deliver the experience, and recordings don't come close.

No one knows when the Mardi Gras Indian phenomenon began, which is surely part of its charm and mystique. Dr. John, the most celebrated Indian executant, comments on this phenomenon in his enigmatic song, "Who Knows?" ("Who knows how the head of two tribes ended up side by side?") The first recorded instance of New Orleans black people "masking" as American Indians was Creole Wild West, a tribe founded by plasterer Becate Batiste, who was inspired in the late nineteenth century by Buffalo Bill Cody's Wild West Show, but the tradition goes back much further. African Americans have always felt a profound empathy with Native Americans, also a dispossessed people, who hid and interbred with them during the slavery era.

Tourists who don't choose to venture into the neighborhoods can catch a bit of all this if they are at the right place at the right time. In the months leading up to Carnival, Mardi Gras Indian tribes parade into the bars to dance and sing, a colorful and jubilant happening, but masking and parading are a way of life, something that happens all year, not a diversion. "It *is* my life," says Big Queen Littdell Banister. "All the holidays we celebrate go a long way, but all the money and all the time go to Mardi Gras Indians. We are really Mardi Gras Indians, not sometimes, all the time." The exclusivity is part of the allure: "It's very important to the black community because we keep it alive. It's the tradition here and nowhere else." Even in New Orleans, it retains a certain fabulous obscurity, but to practitioners, the importance is clear. "Most people from here don't even know what it's about or why we do it," says Banister. "They think we do it because we want to be Indians. How it got started was because of the slave running away from the slave owner. They started running to the Indian reservation, and the slave owner would not go in there and get them. It's not about the Caribbean, it's not about Africa, it's about the Indians helping the slaves when they ran away from the slave owners."[1]

Enslaved people finding ways to unite, using music as a bond and Carnival as a means of escaping one's oppressed identity—that's what a great deal of New Orleans music is about. Mardi Gras is misrule, a turning of the tables where those who are put down rise up and become someone else, where the body and spirit become liberated, even if only for a day—after which the crescendo toward the next frenzy begins almost immediately. Charmaine Neville puts it starkly: "The two things the slave owners hated was Indians and slaves. We were never treated as people. We were treated as property and trash. You were never treated like something that was a real person, a real man or a real woman. So when Mardi Gras came you could be somebody else. And to be an Indian and black! The Indians were the ones who took us in and treated us like real people, so we pay homage every single year to that. What they did for us is something that we'll never forget . . . So it's an honor." Like the rest of her musical family, Neville's art is deeply entangled with Indian tradition. Her great uncle was Chief Jolly; she has been Queen of the Wild Tchoupitoulas and a K-Doe Baby Doll. Besides honor and homage, the Indian tradition is about beauty—the visual and musical splendor of feathers and percussion streaming through the neighborhoods. In the past, as Neville reminds us, "the Indians actually would fight. Now the fighting is about who's the prettiest, which is better . . . And everybody's beautiful. Everybody."[2]

Indians today insist that black tribes and their customs stem from drumming in Congo Square, and that they are thus the oldest progenitors of the African music on which jazz is based. Big Chief Donald Harrison contends that "it all goes back to Congo Square, where Africans were allowed to drum, chant, and dance. Everything is an offshoot of that. It continues in the culture of New Orleans."[3] The arguments about what constituted the "first jazz"— the jazz before jazz—take on a special fascination with Indian music, partly

The Meters. Photograph by Jack Sullivan.

because the phenomenon is so singular and partly because the case for the
Indians is so compelling. Some scholars see this mysterious art as the crucial
"link" to a huge array of vernacular music. "For the student of contemporary popular music and its African-American underpinnings," writes John
Sinclair, "Wild Indian music provides the 'missing link' which connected
the West African perambulating chants, the 'ring shouts' and 'sankeys' of the
slaves on the eastern seaboard, the brass-band marches of the post-Civil War
period, the piano ragtime of Missouri, the earliest Mississippi blues, and the
musical remnants of European court dances brought over by the French and
Spanish to the first strains of American jazz as played by King Buddy Bolden
and his 'ratty' New Orleans ensemble at dances, 'outings,' picnics and parades
starting around 1894–95."[4]

That's a lot of linking, but Sinclair is an authoritative scholar, and every
musician I've talked to, in whatever tradition, affirms that the Indian vibe
is part of their musical DNA. The basic sound—the pounding percussion,
open intervals, complex polyrhythms—is unchanging, no matter what contemporary continuo has been added. "Most of New Orleans music is the
Mardi Gras Indians and the second lines,"[5] says Jon Batiste. Even when invisible, the Indians are present inside nearly all styles, a basic part of the groove.
The most important continuity, as Allen Toussaint points out, is unrelenting
percussion: "It's full of percussiveness: percussion, percussion, percussion!" A

group like the Meters, Toussaint's studio band—whose rhythmic electricity has rocked the world since 1969—relies on the Indian tradition: "If you get a chance to catch the Meters, catch them. They are a rare commodity. I don't care what instrument they're playing, they're all playing percussion. Sparks are popping everywhere. And in much of the music of New Orleans, everybody's playing some sort of percussion because that Indian drive to a frenzy is in us."[6] Big Chief Donald Harrison also believes it comes from drums, "the key component. Miles Davis used to say, 'If you get a different drummer, you have a different band.'"[7]

Funk musician John Gros, leader of Papa Grows Funk, a spectacular Monday-night Maple Leaf gig from 2000 to 2013, also believes the Indians are the foundation: "It all comes out of that. Thanks to the Indians, New Orleans music is something that does not exist anywhere else in the world." For Gros, whose training was in classical French horn, the Indian spectacle on Mardi Gras Day was his epiphany: "I'd heard the music, but seeing the Big Chiefs, the songs and stories, on Mardi Gras Day, that's when I got what the whole culture was about. As an outsider in the culture, you were welcomed as an insider in the music." Gros's influences are a typical configuration: Big Chief Monk Boudreaux ("a great mentor and a great teacher of life"), Allen Toussaint, Dr. John, George Porter Jr., Art Neville, Fats Domino (whom he credits with inventing rock 'n' roll), and especially Norwood "Geechi" Johnson, bass drummer for the Wild Magnolias: "No one infected us like Geechi did. His voice is the heart that pumps the blood through New Orleans music."[8]

Besides the Indians, Gros's main influence was Armstrong, who brought the tradition to the world. Gros believes that he and his colleagues represent far more than just "funk," a loose term at best; he is there "to uphold this legendary historic tradition. Louis Armstrong changed the world with his trumpet and singing . . . That's a lot to live up to, to walk in those shoes and feel that lineage."[9] Like many musicians covered in this book, Gros experiences lineage as a palpable entity, living in every phrase and inflection.

The basic style of the Indians is even more unvarying than other forms. As Big Chief Tyrone Casby of the Mohawk Hunters from Algiers explains, children learn songs they continue singing through their lives, which they pass on to their own families: "It's like Christmas. Christmas carols don't change. Within the song, you still have the call and response that can be related to a situation, an issue at hand, or maybe a costume, or a sewing pattern or something. Lyrics might be changing, but the style itself is still the same."[10] The specificity of the lyrics—sewing patterns, ancestral battles, legendary Big Chiefs—makes them fabulously odd for the uninitiated, as does the Choctaw-Creole-patois language, often consisting of made-up words. "The elements that existed before are still there," says Toussaint. "And the whole vernacular—'Tooti Ma,' 'Two-way Pocky-way'—those phrases have meanings unrelated to the mass, the progressive world. Whenever I'm questioned about what goes into that salad, or gumbo as I prefer to call it, the Mardi Gras Indians are very strong—and the street brass band, of course, and Professor Longhair—but the Mardi Gras Indian music is played for another reason than trying to make a hit record or get on the charts. That music is done for the purpose of driving them into a frenzy. It's actually geared toward Mardi Gras. They have meetings all year round getting ready, and it's done for that reason, so it has a kind of honesty that you don't get with music that's trying to keep up with the pulse of the day. It has nothing to do with 'What's the trend now?' or 'Is Michael Jackson hot?'—though I love Michael Jackson."[11]

Pianist Larry Sieberth believes that "the Mardi Gras Indian thing was originally about the tambourine rhythms. Over the years they've become funkified. From what I understand, the rhythm was the bamboula, and that was probably the derivative of some African rhythm that passed through the islands and ran into New Orleans." These were the intricate rhythms picked up by Gottschalk, Delius, and other classical figures in the larger history of New Orleans (as we see in chapter one). "The more primitive the culture," says Sieberth, "the more complex the rhythms."[12] My first exposure to the "funkified" Indian vibe was the Dixie Cups' hit rendition of "Iko Iko," a version prefigured by "Sugar Boy" Crawford's 1954 "Jock-A-Mo" (also called "Iko, Iko"). "Sugar Boy," grandfather of the blues-gospel singer Davell Crawford, explained that it came "from two Indian chants that I put music to. 'Iko Iko' was like a victory chant that the Indians would shout. 'Jock-A-Mo' was a chant that was called when the Indians went into battle."[13]

More aggressive versions by the Neville Brothers, Gerald French, Kermit Ruffins, and other artists today make the Dixie Cups hit seem charmingly innocent, almost childlike, but it was the beginning of a Wild Indian revolution in American popular music. To this day, the "Hey Now! Hey Now!" call-response incites audiences into an Indian frenzy.

In turning Indian songs like "Big Chief," "Indian Red," and "Iko Iko" into hits associated with NOLA popular culture, funk bands united with the tribes, much as brass bands would a decade later, a parallel loopback that could only happen in New Orleans. When Big Chief Bo Dollis, guitarist Snooks Eaglin, and pianist Wille Tee recorded "Handa Wanda" in 1970—the first Mardi Gras Indian single—the Indians stepped into the larger culture with electric guitars, synthesizers, and the rest of the accoutrement of rhythm and blues, and they have occupied it ever since. As Bruce Raeburn explains: "The Meters as a rhythm section, and Willie Tee as a kind of session leader for Bo Dollis and

Big Chief Robert Silvers. © Mark Hertzberg.

the Wild Magnolias doing 'Handa Wanda' in 1970—that's a turning point for the Indians."[14] Since the original Indian sound was fusion to begin with—the joining of African and Native American traditions—the layering in of another idiom seemed natural, especially since second-line syncopation was always part of the Indian vibe. Suddenly the chants, tambourines, cymbals, snares, and beer bottles of Indian music mixed with guitars and brass. Indian music became multidimensional; a song like Dr. John's "Tootie Ma" is spiked with Bo Dollis's gravelly vocals and Michael Ward's relentless congas as Davell Crawford's piano sets up a lyrical counterpoint. Raeburn points out that Indian music is as intertwined with jazz as with funk: "With Donald Harrison, Mardi Gras Indian music works its way into his repertory, so you can't consider Harrison without the Indians. Herlin Riley drums on Indian rhythms to find structure for Wynton [Marsalis]."[15]

Everything about Indian music is associated with neighborhoods, including funk. The imperious Robert Silvers, Big Chief of the Wild Tchoupitoulas, a downtown tribe, told me that when the Indians who are "into music" perform with a funk band, it "takes on a different style," but the fusion is "natural": "We worked with the Meters and the Neville Brothers, which is an uptown sound."[16] The Nevilles were exposed to Indian music from childhood, and it was only a question of time before they returned the favor. According to Art Neville, growing up with the Indians playing in the neighborhood was "what it was all about: Mardi Gras all year long!" They were influenced by an array of styles—Sam Cooke, Riders of the Purple Sage, even Gene Autry—but the Indians were a constant in their bloodstream.[17]

Gospel music is also an important link to Indian tradition in the neighborhoods. John Boutte, Shannon Powell, Kermit Ruffins, and others speak of their good fortune growing up in neighborhoods where Indian and black church music were both around: "The church was first," says Powell. "The Indians that I saw on the streets, that was a whole other different kind of rhythm but the same sort of technique—the way you hold it and all—but different tempos" [by clapping his hands, he demonstrates the styles, first singing "Two-way Pocky-way" and then going into "This Little Light of Mine"]. It's "the same style," he says. "It's all connected."[18]

The history of Indian culture in the modern world is as full of cross rhythms as the music itself, with odd side stories that disrupt any semblance of linearity. One of the most influential practitioners of Indian-inspired funk was Professor Longhair, but it's hard to place him in an orderly "evolution" because he is such a singular figure. His style, from piano playing to whistling, was so compelling to so many that it constitutes a tradition of its own, a third rail no one wants to get off. According to those under his spell, his creativity and virtuosity were unrivaled. He "influenced everybody here," said pianist-composer Eddie Bo. "Can't you hear him in everybody? Everybody! You listen to Allen [Toussaint], you hear *all* the Professor. He could do more with two fingers than we could do with all of them. I first heard him at Caledonia. I was too young to get in, but I could listen outside: I heard a thump. I never knew what it was. It sounded like a bass drum; he was hitting the meter with his foot. I was influenced by Fats, but more by the Professor because he was so unorthodox. He was just laying it out like he heard it. I don't think he was from here. He was from another planet—he didn't come from this Earth. He was as great as anybody. And I mean the arts, back to the symphonic players. He was bad. He was as bad as any of those people. He didn't know what he was playing, but he was playing what comes from his heart . . . He was a dangerous man—he was dangerous."[19] Other New Orleans pianists—Dr. John, Marcia Ball, Henry Butler, Allen Toussaint, Tom McDermott, David Torkanowsky, Larry Sieberth, Davell Crawford—all fell under the Professor's "bad" influence. As Bo implies, there was a symphonic breadth to his playing, a sustained counterpoint in both rhythm and melody. Dr. John, who calls Professor Longhair "the high priest of it all," credits him with inventing funk and rock both. It's a hard statement to prove, but hearing the Professor's "Big Chief" or "Tipitina," one almost believes it. Professor Longhair was to the late twentieth century what Jelly Roll Morton was to the early, a decisive part of musical history.

The renowned banjoist and bandleader Danny Barker was also a significant figure in Indian history (as he was in brass-band music), but in an invisible way. He was actually there earlier than the funk crowd, but his contribution was aborted by a sudden change in the recording industry: "I was the first one to record Indian music. I pressed songs like 'Chocko Mo Feendo Hey,' 'My Indian Red,' 'Corrine Died on the Battlefield'—two records, four sides—I made 1,500 of each record on 78s." Then suddenly came the "disaster" of 45s replacing 78s: "I sent the records down, but records had changed to 45s; you couldn't put them on a jukebox. I was going to flood the city with them tunes, get a record company started. I gave most of them away to some little cat who had a food stand, used to sell records. I should have kept them, but I had nowhere to store them. Then all of a sudden there was a big Indian thing. They didn't pay the Indians no mind before, and nobody was masking because of the roughnecks—you wouldn't put on an Indian suit on Mardi Gras Day, because they would come pluck all your feathers out your hat, them bad cats on the corner. You're supposed to be a chief, Crazy Horse or something, let's see how crazy you are."[20] Here is another reminder of the singular vision of Danny Barker. Bruce Raeburn fills in Barker's account: "Danny's records of Mardi Gras Indian music were two 78s done circa 1954 (you will see 1947 on Wikipedia, but I think that may be too early) on the King Zulu label: 'My Indian Red,' 'Tootie Ma Is a Big Fine Thing,' 'Corrine Died on the Battlefield,' and 'Chocko Mo Feendo Hey.' They were pre-funk—some swing, some march."[21] Who knows how Indian music history might have been affected had the change to 45s come a few months later than it did?

Katrina helped the Indians attain yet another level of visibility: the HBO show, *Treme*, ostensibly a hurricane-recovery piece, turned out to be a surprisingly eloquent and detailed depiction of Indian practices, both visually and aurally. Nothing remotely like it had appeared in major media before. The show made it clear that Indian music is closely entwined with jazz, brass band, and racial politics. "There's nothing like being in New Orleans for four years," the actor Clarke Peters told me. "I learned more about the Mardi Gras Indians than an anthropologist. It was a great experience." The charisma and tragic dignity of Peters's performance as *Treme*'s Big Chief capture something essential and noble about Indian culture.[22]

Funk, the music that put the Indians on the map of popular culture, is an elusive genre. It is hard to define, and some of its major practitioners believe the term to be somewhat bogus. It arose to fulfill the need for new rhythms in songs for a young generation, much as jazz did. Allen Toussaint, who was in on the ground floor, remembers it as a new direction rather than a distinct genre, a surge of rhythmic changes that swept away the steady rock 'n' roll beat of Fats Domino and David Bartholomew, replacing it with syncopations from the Indians and from Latin music: "Many, many years ago, people like David Bartholomew and Fats Domino put us on the map. That music was a whole other dododo dododo . . . che cha cha cha che cha cha cha . . . our time came along and we added so many other things . . . it's not Fats Domino any more, it's not Smiley Lewis, or Guitar Slim even."

It was difficult to move out of the shadow of Fats Domino, a towering figure who links back to jazz, influenced as he was by Armstrong, and forward to rock 'n' roll. The city's preeminent rhythm and blues artist, he had an astonishingly wide fan base, from the poor blacks in his Lower Ninth Ward neighborhood to blue-collar workers all over the United States. Bartholomew was formidable as well. He was on the bandstand when R&B smoothed out into rock 'n' roll, and his wry commentary is invaluable: "In the early days, the white kids didn't understand [R&B]. It was just what it says. If you sang blues, you sang with a harsh background. You talk about all the hard times you had: your woman done left you, you're going back home, all those sorts of things. The crossover meant that we would sweeten the lead . . . we wouldn't make it exactly that harsh. They're doing it in hard rock now—they're doing everything now—but in the crossover, we went over real light, our leads became like pop music; we had the same rhythm and blues background, but what they were singing was pop. We would soften the background too. They were smoothing out a little to get away from that harsh rhythm and blues sound. In those days, the white kids, they didn't even know how to dance. They can dance now, but they didn't know how to dance in those days. They would do anything just to say that they were with it. You understand? I was on the bandstand, so I know, playing and looking: it was a goddamn shame; they didn't know what the hell they were doing. But after they kept on trying, they got their shit together."[23]

After the transition from R&B to rock, the next step was to disrupt what Bartholomew regards as the "smoothing" effect of rock. What Toussaint calls the "push-pull" of the early '60s was a more complex, samba-infused sound brought to the table by Toussaint and his contemporaries, especially Ernie K-Doe, Irma Thomas, Aaron Neville, and John Boudreaux. Toussaint was the binding force, acting as pianist, producer, arranger, vocalist, and cheerleader. He and his colleagues felt "a calling" to do something new. "We ventured away from don don don don don don right away . . . The way our songs were constructed called for other things." There was "no more walking bass" from the '40s or predictable rock beat from the '50s; it was "a different feel." Toussaint calls it the "the Ooo Poo Pah Do era," the label coming from a Jessie Hill song for which he felt an initial distaste. Toussaint describes it as "a whole group of people unrestricted by what had been going on; we wrote down new parts for new musicians—the older ones wouldn't know it." The new music did not eschew jazz. Saxophonist Nat Perrilliat, a veteran jazz musician who played everything from bop to Professor Longhair, helped Toussaint get first-rate jazz musicians, including Melvin Lastie on trumpet. Jazz was part of funk from the beginning, and Toussaint insisted that the band have "good jazz players," and thus he "hired what we needed," creating something that was "not a genre," but "a different direction, though unplanned; we needed something new for the new songs, not old patterns. We knew the difference in rhumbas, sambas, boleros—I don't know how we knew." According to Robert Palmer, "no one actually recalls hearing Latin music, but they knew it."[24] Since early New Orleans jazz had a "Spanish tinge," the new funk, like so much New Orleans music, was actually picking up something old and recreating it for a new generation.

Whatever one makes of funk, nearly everyone agrees that James Brown, who is not from New Orleans, was one of its most important progenitors, and members of Brown's band are often regarded by New Orleans players as equally important. An example is North Carolina saxophonist Maceo Parker, who played with Brown, and has an all-embracing ambiance that one could easily mistake for a New Orleans jazzer. Clarinetist James Evans was struck by Parker saying on the radio he was going to play 5 percent jazz and 95 percent funk: "To me, he was communicating an attitude that said he 'wasn't going to show off his chops, he was just going to be as funky as he could.' But then again, that's good jazz for me. When I see Maceo live, I think, 'There's just something about him that has the same ethos as Louis Armstrong or Lester Young or someone like that who's just connected with people and playing the groove, and just projecting his personality—a really warm and very big, avuncular presence.' Like this guy's seen life, and he knows what he's saying is valid."[25]

Another outside group admired by NOLA funksters is the Rolling Stones, whose legacy is regularly honored at major venues like Tipitina's. Some of the most sensational Neville Brothers gigs came when they covered with the Stones. For Art Neville, their dynamic ensemble was a revelation: "What they do is serious; they are businessmen, they take care of business. It's not about how much better I can play than this cat or another dude, they play *together* on stage to the point where they just devastate the audience. When they hit that stage, they knew what it was to make that thing work. That's power . . . they got the right cats. Nobody would know if they don't get along."[26] This was a poignant lesson given the efflorescence and dissipation of the Nevilles in their various manifestations as the Meters, the Neville Brothers, the Funky Meters, and the Wild Tchoupitoulas. The implacableness of the Stones—what

Neville calls "the force"—is something that eluded the Nevilles, as it does most bands. The story of the Neville Brothers shows again that the culture of New Orleans simply does not fit with the prevailing corporate ethos. Funk is much closer to the Indians, historically and aesthetically, than to a pop group like the Stones, and NOLA's greatest funk bands, though often popular, fail to achieve full celebrity. The frustrated annotator for a 1988 "History of the Neville Brothers" recording contrasted the blazing energy of the Nevilles with the "McDonald's culture of mall-land America," complaining that "if there were any justice in the world . . . and talent were of paramount importance, the Neville Brothers would long ago have been rubbing shoulders with the trendy fashion plates clogging the top of the pop charts. They've certainly tried everything, from big-name producers to opening tours for the Rolling Stones . . . but their success individually and collectively has largely been limited to local and regional hits."[27] New Orleans music remains stubbornly local and neighborhood-driven, especially music linked to the Indians. When I heard the Nevilles in New York during the period when this annotation was written, they had a polite but tepid reception, but at Tipitina's they played to an adoring, standing-room crowd that knew the repertory and danced with them through the night. Since Katrina, with more NOLA groups than ever playing in New York, audiences have become more acculturated to the music and the shows have gotten livelier, but the bands still do their most exciting gigs in New Orleans.

As Toussaint points out, funk is not really a genre. If anyone should know what it is, it would be George Porter Jr., since he played with James Brown at the Apollo Theater in the early '60s as a roadie, but to him it is a concocted word: "What the Meters were doing in the '60s was called R&B at the time—straight-up R&B. Now I'm talking about our first three albums only [*The Meters*, *Look-Ka Py Py*, and *Struttin'*]. Those three albums are now considered funk—and even considered the beginning of funk." By 2014, the "jam band" genre—Galactic, Dumpstaphunk, and others—had brought funk up to date, but Porter doesn't think much of that label either: "I've had a problem with that 'jam band' term for a while, too. I mean, where did that come from? It's just another term to classify our music. . . . Funk music evolved from musicians who played jazz *and* R&B. Myself, I played jazz, bebop and a little bit of every music that could be played, growing up. I even played country songs like 'Home on the Range' and 'Red River Valley' when I was learning the acoustic guitar as a kid. Those labels aren't for musicians." Indeed, they aren't, as we have seen repeatedly in this book.

As Porter points out—and demonstrated through his own career—funk is part of a stream that takes in R&B, jazz, and other forms, including hip hop, which has absorbed funk samples as part of its basic identity. Still, *something* was different about funk, even if it was just a new synthesis: "When the Meters' musical style surfaced in 1967, that music made a loud, broad statement across the entire music community in all directions . . . I think it was the syncopation. So many of our songs were not 'on the 1.' It seems like everyone else on the planet was playing downbeat stuff . . . 1,2,3,4—1,2,3,4. And we were playing 'and 1 and 2 and 3 and 4—and 1 and 2 and 3 and 4.' We were playing 'off the one.' We weren't pronouncing 1. Our first notes were usually *before* 1."[28]

This is the "push-pull" cited by Toussaint, its roots in Latin and Indian syncopation. As Ivan Neville points out, it can turn up in many types of music and is ultimately undefinable: "That's why there is no Grammy category for it, no iTunes category."[29]

After funk, the next Indian fusion occurred in the '90s with the new brass bands. As we see in chapter two, this phenomenon began with the Dirty Dozen and the early days of Rebirth. According to Bruce Raeburn, a visual element was added, "a logical working out of the convergences in the '70s," when Indians began showing up at brass-band funerals "with their own instruments such as cowbells and tambourines. The '90s added funerals for the deceased in both worlds."[30] My first inkling of this was the passing of Danny Barker, where brass bands and Indians converged in a jazz funeral that had more sprawl and spectacle than any I'd experienced. Today, funerals incorporate the two traditions as a matter of course; the deceased not only go out in style, but in two styles.

New songs continue to enliven the Indian repertory, bringing up to date what Dr. John's lyric calls "a brand-new culture." Indian music even finds its way into avant-garde bands like Galactic, whose jazz-hip hop song "Second and Dryades" loops drumming sounds and samples Chief Boudreaux. Lines of mentorship are complex and unpredictable. Henry Butler, for example, was taught by Alvin Batiste, who got Butler to a single but unforgettable piano lesson with Professor Longhair; Butler later inspired Big Chief Donald Harrison and both mentored Jon Batiste, who with Butler has imported New Orleans funk to New York. Bloodlines are not as important as they once were; today, many Indians who mask and parade don't have Native American blood.

The same controversy we see elsewhere in this book regarding tradition versus newness affects Mardi Gras Indian music. Bo Dollis died in 2015, and his son, also a Chief, mixes his father's legacy with rap and pop, sometimes performing without an Indian suit. Just as certain fans expect to hear traditional jazz, Indian aficionados revolt at the sight of "Indians" without suits experimenting with contemporary idioms; in the clubs, some fans demand their money back—New Orleans is one place where the latest trend is not always profitable. Bruce Raeburn views this controversy as parallel to the argument in brass-band music: "You find the same conversation in the brass-band world. But the younger generation gets to do what they want with the torch. You pass it on to them—don't tell them what to do."[31] The Indians are adjusting to the times and to a new generation, as they did in the '70s. Once they let the guitars and synthesizers in, why not the rappers?

In fact, scholars now theorize that rapping itself is a variant of Indian call-response. This view is held by admirers of hip hop as well as by antagonists, the most prominent of the latter being Wynton Marsalis: "We called it juba juba, you know, 'My grandma said to your grandma / Iko iko uh nay.' But it dates back long before the Dr. John or Dixie Cups version of that song. Kids would sit on the street corner, improvising stupid rhymes with pornographic lyrics. You know the kind of thing: 'Your old woman got an ass like a truck / Your old woman she likes to fuck' . . . Today's hip hop is just those pornographic rhymes on a grand scale."[32] Whether it's pornographic or mock-scatological, echoes of Indian funk have sounded through hip hop for years, most specifically in samplings of the Meters by groups like Public Enemy and Ultramagnetic MCs. New Orleans hip hop, or "bounce" as its fans call it, began as a movement in the '90s, but it also permeated other traditions. I remember being struck by the prevalence of hip hop in the Rebirth Brass Band when I began hearing their Maple Leaf gigs in those days; when Rebirth went on the road, the New Birth Brass Band, a kind of youthful alter ego, would fill in, and the experience would turn into an even rowdier rap scene. It was only a question of time before groups like the Soul Rebels incorporated hip hop as a basic element. Bounce groups like MC T. Tucker, Lil' Wayne, DJ Irv, Partners in Crime, Juvenile, and Soulja Slim developed their own style of NOLA hip hop that emphasized dancing, chant, call-response, and references to neighborhoods, wards, and projects. Hip hop scholars emphasize how the form is a response to racism, institutionalized poverty, and Jim Crow oppression. As we see throughout this book, many forms of New Orleans music already reflect these realities, so the rappers are part of something much older.

Hip hop scholar Rich Paul Cooper argues that bounce is different from mainstream hip hop in that it is less homophobic, misogynist, and macho, and that it de-emphasizes "elements such as drug culture, sexual exploitation, or violence. DJ Jubilee's music best supports this claim for an emphasis on community and dance that contradicts the sexual exploitation, violence, and unchecked materialism of gangsta rap."[33] As is the case with bebop, hip hop becomes something else when integrated into New Orleans culture. Often it is not conventional hip hop, but part of a complex, varied palette

Skinz N Bonez. © Mark Hertzberg.

where rapping is integrated into other chants, with jazz harmonies and sec-ond-line rhythms.

The new generation of Indians has not abandoned the standards. I found myself parading on Super Sunday 2015 with Bo Dollis Jr., enjoying his robust renditions of "Little Liza Jane" and other familiar songs. The basic rituals and rules remain implacable, though one thing appears to be changing, ever so slightly: the rigidity of gender roles. Skinz N Bonez, for example, an all-female krewe costumed in NOLA-Gothic skeleton suits, plays percussion in Indian parades. "Our queen met Wild Man John Ellis of the Wild Tchoupitoulas a couple of years ago," says Danny Adomaitis, who was parading with Queen Mary Kay Stevenson and her mother, Queen Mercy, when I interviewed her. (Stevenson is the first Queen of the Wild Tchoupitoulas.) "The tribe needed a band, and that's how we grew out of it. Although we're a separate entity, doing thirty or forty gigs a year, we have Monday night crafting and Thursday night rehearsals. Every time the tribes come out, we're there to support them. And we're all very proud and humbled to be part of it." The Indians play percus-sion, and the band intersects with them, adding layers of sound and a female vibe. The old blends with the new, a post-Katrina configuration that integrates women more into Indian practice. It's a delicate balancing act, for the Indians are rule-bound and hierarchical: "It's all about respect. There are lots of rules. We never step in front of them; we follow the hierarchy just like they do, so the Big Chief, Wild Man, and Queen are the big three that we listen to. There are lots of boundaries, and we don't step over them."[34]

The Indians are an immutable force that have witnessed the drama of New Orleans throughout their history. Allen Toussaint believes they are always in the music: "Without even trying, we have that. For the Mardi Gras Indians, whatever it was, it is. If they did a semi-modern tune, it would have that same drive we knew when we were children. We respect them highly, and that music lives, that frenzied beat is around all the time, even when they're not playing it because it's in the fabric, it's in the bricks, it's in the mortar; it seeps up out of the streets." Here again is an obsessive theme that emerges when New Orleans musicians speak: everything comes from the streets, seeping upward, its basis unchangeable. Tampering with it is blasphemy: "None of the guys who are involved in the Indian tradition thinks to move it from where that is. That would be sacrilegious. The Mardi Gras Indians are still there. It's not that they're antiquated. It's a wonderful thing and it lives in our music. Even the guys who are playing something that seems remote from it like the jazz players, they have that in there too."[35] Big Chief Donald Harrison (though he objects to the "percolating from the street" metaphor) is a powerful example, a multi-genre master who carries the Indian beat into whatever he does: "I knew the old Big Chiefs, and they walked beside me and brought me through the old time way. This is what I bring to the table."[36]

Odd things happen when the Indians appear outside New Orleans. At a Lincoln Center outdoor show by Monk Boudreaux, Bo Dollis Jr., and the Golden Eagles, the police moved in on a crowd of happy people celebrating and dancing in the aisles at Damrosch Park, including the three children of the band's drummer. It was one of those times in New York when the city was living up to its myth, when diverse people—young and old, rich and poor, very rich and very poor (this was a free concert), black and white—converged in a communal ecstasy. So, of course, the police had to shut it down. Again and again, the dancers were reprimanded and sent back to their seats after they tried to argue to the law that they were "doing what you're supposed to do with this music." It was a mild version of what happened in the nineteenth century, when authorities put down partiers incited to revelry by the Indians.

The Indians are now sufficiently visible in musical culture that their singularity is starting to be less important than their universality. Seductive percussion and chant united with visual spectacle as homage to one oppressed people by another—all this has broad appeal as a celebration of the human

Mardi Gras Indians. © Mark Hertzberg.

spirit. John Gros quotes saxophone player Tim Green, who "used to say, 'There are only twelve notes; the rest is just music.' There is nothing different when the Indians parade from one end of the street to the other—no different than what Bach, Stravinsky, or Fats were doing: communicating songs to the listener, to make you celebrate or escape life. That's what's great about New Orleans music. It does *all* that."[37]

Chapter Seven

THE CLUBS: SACRED GROUND

You walked in and, even if the joint was empty, it
was a grand theater of life, like New Orleans itself.
—Ned Sublette on the Mother-in-Law Lounge

This is a sacred ground for jazz.
—Charlie Miller on the Little Gem Saloon

The clubs are essential to the city's musical biography. These intimate dives, unique to New Orleans, enable musicians to keep playing, a source of fierce pride for the owners. In the Storyville era, they provided players with a way to develop a style and make a living. Today, they are emblems of survival and renewal. Charlie Sims, owner of Donna's and formerly a chef on the Southern Crescent Railroad, saw the waters of Katrina come up to his door on Rampart Street, then miraculously stop; he was proud to keep the place going, cooking some of the best barbecue in town (free on Monday night) and tending bar, even though he was in his seventies. "We never shut down during the storm," boasts the bartender at the Maple Leaf, and the stubborn determination of owner Hank Staples to keep the club open with his own electricity source is now the stuff of recovery legend.

Also legendary is Joe's Cozy Corner, a small brick place on Ursulines, which every Sunday night beginning in the 1990s hosted the most dynamic shows in the city. For those who remember it, Joe's is a Holy Grail for neighborhood music, a template for what a club can be. Kermit Ruffins would open with "Uncle" Lionel Batiste, Corey Henry, Henry Butler, John Boutte, and whoever happened to be in the neighborhood, then introduce the Rebirth Brass Band, which would parade from North Robertson Street into the tiny juke joint.

Uncle Lionel Batiste, with Kermit Ruffins on trumpet, at Joe's Cozy Corner. Photograph by Jack Sullivan.

Lined up from one end of the small room to the other, their inflated cheeks resembling gargoyles, the band was a formidable spectacle, as was the sprawl of colleagues from different traditions sitting in, including blues singers, swingers, barrel-house pianists, and funksters. By the end of the night, other brass players coming in from the street would crowd onto the stage, blowing their lungs out as the small, packed crowd danced in the cramped corners or on half a dozen small tables. In those days, just before the increase of ethnic diversity in the Tremé, my New Jersey college group was a unique streak of white coming in the door: ("Where did all those damn white people come from?" a woman gasped when we arrived the first Sunday night in 1998.) We were treated with guarded respect, and if anyone gave us trouble, an armed "Papa" Joe Glasper, the towering owner, would glower at the troublemaker, who would back down very fast. Unfortunately, Glasper used his pistol on an unwanted beer vendor outside the bar in 2004 following the jazz funeral of Tuba Fats; he died in jail and Joe's died with him.

Joe's and Donna's are gone and can never be replaced, but many renowned places survived post-Katrina: the trad enclave, Preservation Hall, established in 1961 to preserve jazz from Bourbon Street commercialization; the Tremé mainstays, Sweet Lorraine's and Candlelight; the funk palace, Tipitina's, built in the '70s as a monument to Professor Longhair, a nexus for musicians

Richard Rochester and Cosimo Matassa. Photograph by Jack Sullivan.

devastated by Katrina; the modern jazz hold-out, Snug Harbor, which keeps progressive jazz alive in a town not always sympathetic to its cerebral rumi-nations; the sprawling Howlin' Wolf, which moved across the street from its previous location; the elegant Monteleone and Columns hotel lounges; the zydeco mecca, Rock 'n' Bowl, once one-of-a-kind, then emulated in New York by Brooklyn Bowl; and out-of-the-way dives like Bullet's, Sidney's, Vaughan's, and Le Bon Temps Roule, which have music once or twice a week with some of the greatest talent in the city, otherwise functioning as neighborhood bars.

For those who love New Orleans music, there is a mythological quality to these places and a concomitant disdain for corporate theme parks like the House of Blues and the Dixieland tourist boats. It is de rigueur for people who cultivate "authentic New Orleans music" to denigrate such places, just as they denounce Bourbon Street. Then there is the financial reality: Richard Rochester, who revived the Funky Butt Café in 1995, grudgingly praised the House of Blues when it opened in 1992 because it gave the music scene a lift and paid NOLA musicians a decent wage. The place reeks of marketing and mission statements, but Rochester encouraged me to go there (even though it represented a threat to his own business). Over the years, I've come to see its value, and I've heard wonderful music there, from Mardi Gras Indian bands to Marva Wright. I've also been told by some of NOLA's best musicians—Lucian

Barbarin, Tom McDermott, Phil Frazier, Jon Batiste, John Boutte—that cultural tourism has intrinsic value because it brings out-of-towners into the tradition. It isn't just about economics.

The densest concentration of clubs is on Frenchmen Street, fueling a musical renaissance some say is reminiscent of Bourbon Street in the early twentieth century. Since 2011, this relatively small area, stretching four blocks, has become so surreally crowded with clubs that one can easily hear a dozen groups, old and new, in a single evening, or follow the same performer to different venues. Some are tiny places full of surprises; the Spotted Cat, the smallest and starkest, attracts some of the best swing dancers in the city, and you can hear Meschiya Lake, the Shotgun Jazz Band, Miss Sophie Lee, the Jazz Vipers, and others for no cover. Lee herself presides over Three Muses as jazz singer-restaurateur, serving Moroccan-Asian food and music ranging from the Hot Club of New Orleans, a sensational Django-gypsy band, to the explosive Glen David Andrews, attracting large young crowds. Apple Barrel, even tinier, charges no cover for a diverse music lineup. d.b.a. is more spacious, with two bars in adjoining rooms, but it feels small and welcoming, partly because of the loving care of the owners. Peter Artaserse told me he came down in 1999 to try a new place after his success in New York's East Village. "Tom Thayer and I were looking at Key West and New Orleans, and we discovered that Key West was a giant machine built to separate tourists from their money, and that New Orleans was a place with a soul, a big heart, and just enough craziness and debauchery to make us feel comfortable." The philosophy of d.b.a. is to "give support and encouragement to New Orleanian bands, from funk to brass, from old school to new. We went with what we felt was representative of the heart and soul of New Orleans. We've been successful because we haven't been pretentious, and we have been professional. And we actually like people—otherwise, you shouldn't be in this business. We hardly make any money; the door [from $5 to $15] is for the band. We don't pay them disproportionately, we pay them fairly. We have great local talent, and it needs to be encouraged. You don't play to the flash, the one-visit customer, you play to the heart of New Orleans, and those visitors who have an interest in finding it will discover you. We get them off Bourbon Street—otherwise, they're lost. Oh, please. There are just so many Hurricanes and Grenades you can drink."[1]

One place you can go on Bourbon Street is Irvin Mayfield's Jazz Playhouse. Mayfield, a trumpeter who did a regular gig at Snug Harbor for several years, is now managing this sleek, sexy, place in the Royal Sonesta Hotel, providing a mid-century ambiance modeled after the great hotel jazz parlors of the past. Mayfield focuses on traditional jazz in his programming—Leroy Jones, Germaine Bazzle, and the Tuxedo Jazz Band have regular gigs—but contemporary groups are welcome, and Friday night the place gets down and dirty for a burlesque show. "I don't think of jazz in terms of contemporary or traditional," says Mayfield. "I see it as one continuum. I would say it's thriving. There are more bands playing now than before—more jazz bands, more brass bands, and business is good. This is a great place to be a young jazz musician."[2] Trombonist Michael Watson credits Mayfield and his Playhouse with restoring to Bourbon Street some of its historic luster: "The Playhouse is bringing jazz back to Bourbon Street. It's been how many decades since jazz has been on Bourbon? When Irvin brought the Playhouse here, there were no jazz clubs besides Maison Bourbon and Fritzel's. I'll take three over none—any day, any day!"[3] Fritzel's, where Tom Fischer, Charlie Fardella, and other traditionalists hold forth, has actually been a jazz enclave since 1969, a remarkable achievement given the drunken din of tourists and mediocre music that surrounds it.

The clubs provide musicians not only with a place to perform but a second home, a space to get together after hours. Boutte and his band remain for hours after their gig, lingering in d.b.a.'s humid, atmospheric courtyard with musicians and diehard fans. When Jon Cleary emigrated to New Orleans from England thirty-five years ago, he went immediately to the Maple Leaf, where he still has a regular gig and where he felt "a bit like coming home" the moment he arrived. When music is happening, the Leaf is a cramped, crowded space, but when I spoke with Cleary at 1 a.m. after a performance, it had an eerie, spacious serenity. "This is a beautiful bar," he sighed. "It was my living room my first few years in New Orleans. I lived just around the corner. When I came to America, my first night, I came straight here from the airport, straight to the Maple Leaf. I had a job here playing with Earl King. Imagine! I nearly didn't get here because the cab had to turn on Willow Street; there was a club there that used to be called Jimmy's, and there was a sign outside that said 'Huey Smith and the Clowns,' and I nearly jumped out of the cab."[4] For Bruce Daigrepont, the beloved home club is Tipitina's, where he did a regular Sunday show for over twenty years beginning in 1986 before moving on to Rock 'n' Bowl. There were the usual corporate siren calls; he was lured, for example, by a "huge, huge" place called Mudbugs, offering big crowds and more money, but his loyalty to Tipitina's trumped all. "I'd have had to quit Tipitina's. I thought about it, but I said, 'Tipitina's is a tradition. I'm not going to leave.' And Mudbugs came in, and for a few years it was a hot spot. . . . And as soon as the crowd started dipping, the big corporate place drops them." The funky charm of Tips can't be duplicated, and the owners knew that Daigrepont's couldn't either. The club has everything: historic cachet, good acoustics, excellent sight lines in the balcony, palpable excitement on the floor, lots of dancing, and a seductive ambiance that has somehow not been ruined by renovations and overexposure in popular movies and television. (A French Quarter Tipitina's opened briefly in the '90s, but it was a theme-park version of the real thing, and people knew it.) "We survive at Tipitina's," Daigrepont said proudly, "I'll say that . . . We've outlasted all of them."[5]

This sense of home that players feel for certain clubs is easy to understand once one realizes how geographically small the music scene is. A musician can often walk or bike from one gig to another with ease, appearing at the home club, then others, and this continuity centers the fans as well. The scene has been less stable since Katrina, but one can still more or less count on regular gigs at long-standing places like Preservation Hall and the Palm Court. Musicians travel to Europe, where they feel a sense of home away from home, but they always get back as soon as possible to their favorite gigs. John Boutte, who helped develop the Ascona Jazz Festival in Switzerland, dislikes leaving New Orleans and does so as little as possible. When I talked to him in 2014, he was on his way to Sweden and Denmark: "I always come back to my roots. I envy [Trombone] Shorty and those guys who are on the road, and in another way I say, 'You guys can have it.' They'll drive 500 miles from Kansas City to make Aspen; that's a rough life; it's physically demanding because you don't eat regularly, you don't exercise. The road can take it out of you; it can make you sick. Traveling is nice, but I really love being able to jump on my bicycle and ride to work in ten minutes."[6]

When a great club goes down, musicians have a hard time letting go. Boutte had a deep connection to Donna's, which he speaks of with loving nostalgia and a touch of bitterness. "Oh wow, Donna's is gone, man, and it's something I really miss, and you know what, because a couple of people wanted a quiet neighborhood, and that's what they've got now, a quiet, dead neighborhood, a graveyard. You don't move your head because nobody's on the street. In the Donna's era, with people sitting out on the street, if we saw trouble, we stopped it. Those people are very cowardly anyway and wouldn't try to do anything if people could check them."[7] The closing of clubs because of gentrification and complaining neighbors is a political and economic problem that threatens the life of America's greatest musical city. This is perhaps the single biggest crisis in the current scene. "We need political leadership on this," says David Torkanowsky, speaking for many anxious musicians, but he is not holding his breath. This is a culture war that many fear music is losing.

Nonetheless, New Orleans has a way of resuscitating its tradition for a new era, including the historic clubs. In 2013, Kermit Ruffins told me about the reopening of the Little Gem Saloon in the business district, the joint where Armstrong played as a teenager. Since then, Ruffins and many others have appeared there, none more special than trumpeter Charlie Miller, who regards the Saloon as not just a second home but as sacred ground. The night I heard him, his lyrical trumpet lines, plush piano arpeggios, and gruffly eloquent voice soared through the renovated tiled interior, enhanced by a bright acoustic. The audience was small but adoring, the intimacy so intense that a table of chattering, texting tourists a few feet away almost didn't exist. Upstairs is the darker, more formal Ramp Room, where Ruffins appears Saturday nights. "Do you know about this place?" Miller asked me excitedly. "Louis Armstrong played in this very room. This is the block where jazz was first created. See those beat-up old buildings just outside? Buddy Bolden and Jelly Roll Morton used to play in them. This was their hangout. It was called the Little Gem Saloon 100 years ago, at the turn of the century. They first conceptualized jazz here—let's put this on and let's do this with it. They started strutting around with it, and it caught on. It wasn't called 'jazz' then, but this is where jazz was first played. The next building outside was a big pawn shop owned by the Karnofsky family, a Jewish family that lived in this area, and they mixed in with these black guys in the area who were experimenting and doing this exciting music, and helped them. I believe they gave Louis Armstrong a cornet [his first]. They knew something was going on. They got caught up in the jazz going on in this block. Louis Armstrong came in here as a young boy, following his mentors so he could learn. There was no business then, it didn't exist as a style yet; it wasn't in the public eye. Then, after a while, Storyville came up and became a business, and people started playing jazz with a suit and a tie. I'm honored to be playing in this place; this is one gig I keep. I love being here, I feel good in this room. I don't know why more people don't realize that this is a sacred ground for jazz."[8]

Clubs are a business, of course, and marketers exploit any ground, sacred or otherwise, that will bring in cash. Larry Sieberth, David Torkanowsky, and Aurora Nealand are among those who believe that the marketing of New Orleans is more aggressive now than it was in the '80s and '90s, defining the music in ways that can be constricting. "There is an interesting, dangerous commodification of the culture that I see happening now with traditions after Hurricane Katrina," says Nealand. "The resurrection of clubs on Frenchmen Street hiring traditional jazz bands is great, but also dangerous. Clubs are doing it because, 'Oh, people are coming to New Orleans, and they want to eat red beans and rice, and they want to go to Bourbon Street, and they want to hear this kind of music.' It's dangerous for other types of music that are getting pushed aside." Nealand believes the message is that "'this traditional jazz is New Orleans music, but all that other stuff is not.' That's dangerous to the musician who is living now in New Orleans and creating music, which is therefore New Orleans music. It's dangerous when it's not about the music, but about the money-making. I'm not saying it's about the musicians, but about the opportunities that are there for other types of music. When I speak to older musicians who were here in the '80s and '90s, they talk about how the Klezmer Allstars were playing over there, and this free-jazz group was playing at d.b.a. Ears were more forward-looking then."[9]

Yet, elsewhere in this book, several notable traditionalists—Shannon Powell, Gregg Stafford, Michael White, Katja Toivola—assert that they are the ones being shunted aside, indeed not marketed at all, and that their tradition is barely hanging on. As with everything in the New Orleans scene, the total picture is complex and sometimes contradictory, but one thing is certain: the surge of new people into the city has changed the club scene. "In the nineteen years I've been here," Katja Toivola told me in 2014, "some things have remained the same, but a lot has changed. In 1995, there were five clubs in the Tremé. Now there is one. There were more jazz gigs in those days. A lot of those gigs have shifted from the New Orleans musicians who were born and bred here to younger musicians who have migrated mostly from other parts of the United States and other parts of the world as well." When I pointed out, "That was you," she was quick to reply, "That's me, yeah, but I was here before the floodgates opened. In some ways it's harder now to find the little joints where you get the authentic New Orleans experience, whereas twenty years ago it was very easy." Yet, when I began coming to the city regularly in the early '90s, just before the eruption of social media, I had to work hard to find these authentic places. Toivola attributes this to a lack of publicity: "A lot more of the neighborhood bars had music and the ones that did weren't really publicized anywhere; they were more like local things. Nowadays for example, when Kermit had the Speakeasy on Basin Street, it was a lovely place, but when you went, the audience was not what you would expect in that neighborhood. It was mostly out-of-town people. It was a local joint, but it wasn't a local joint. It's the same with Candlelight. There's a local crowd that somewhat hangs out, but also the out-of-towners."

But if it's only a local joint, musicians will not make money and club owners will get restless. In fact, one wants a place "that's a local joint but not a local joint," so that it will attract tourists—though not too many to ruin the neighborhood feeling. In that sense, Kermit's Speakeasy, which had a strong Tremé atmosphere, was ideal for post-2010 New Orleans, the period when "the floodgates" really opened. Toivola admits that the situation is not black and white: "So things have opened up, which is in some ways really good, but in other ways it takes away from things a little bit. Everybody seems to miss it, the real jazz joint. There aren't that many places that create a jam culture, not necessarily where you would even have to sit in, but where musicians would hang out. That's what Donna's was and Joe's, too. You'd go there late at night and everybody who had their gig in the French Quarter would come here for their little nightcap before heading home. It's weird that there's such a demand for a place like that, but nobody's opened one. I keep forgetting to buy a lottery ticket! If musicians had the money to invest in something like that, it would be a great thing to have a place that would work for the musicians. When a place treats the musicians right, that brings along so many other things."[10]

Nostalgia for the lost clubs is a New Orleans thing. On the other hand, many musicians, from local heroes like Allen Toussaint to newbies like Michael Watson, believe New Orleans is in the middle of a renaissance, with clubs to match. As soon as one place closes, another seems to be opening, and it's always something unique. Siberia and the Hi-Ho Lounge on St. Claude, for example, host contemporary sounds from bounce to sludge metal to Shamarr Allen's "DJ Chicken" show, bringing young people into the Tremé, and other new joints on St. Claude are opening as well, a harbinger, some believe, of a new scene.

And why shouldn't it be? The Frenchmen Street scene started very small. "In the '90s," Toivola recalls, "Snug Harbor was there, and Café Brasil, and Café Istanbul, which is now the Blue Nile. The drummer Kerry Brown was booking the bands at Istanbul. But apart from those, the street was dead." This is hard to imagine today. Frenchmen Street is an Ivesian cacophony of brass bands, bluegrass fiddlers, rappers, and gospel singers, crisscrossing and converging, but I too remember the beautiful quiet of the street, with the sambas from Café Brasil echoing out into an empty silence, occasionally punctuated by more discreet emanations from Café Istanbul, exotic outliers from the central Snug Harbor, whose more cerebral modern beat in the back of the house could not be heard on the street at all. Now Snug is a beacon of sit-down civility in a sprawl of club-hoppers, a place where one can either enjoy the best cheeseburgers in town while watching the show on TV monitors or sit in the small, beautiful room in the back and watch it live. The bar area is cramped and unpleasant (though the bar itself is elegant), but the performance room is comfortable and welcoming. Many musicians regard Snug Harbor as the city's premiere jazz club, a title it has certainly earned.

Just around the corner on Decatur is the Palm Court, housed in a high-ceilinged, nineteenth-century building, boasting a superb Steinway grand piano and an atmospheric mahogany bar, where one can hear traditional jazz for a sense of where the more contemporary sounds on Frenchmen come from. Nina Buck, the ever-present and irrepressible owner, will drag you out of your comfortable chair and thrust you into a second line where people parade around tables waving napkins, an absurd but amiable ritual. The Frenchmen area is more compact and circumscribed than the Bourbon Street scene from the early twentieth century, but rich in repertory and possibility. It is becoming a place where one can experience the history of jazz as well as its many variants and contemporary manifestations—brass band, klezmer, Django-jazz, avant-jazz, R&B, and much else—while only roaming a few blocks.

One club outside this hopping area that has remained remarkably stable given its sheer eccentricity is Rock 'n' Bowl. John Blanchard, the owner, told me in the early '90s that he had just opened this uptown place as an experiment and was as surprised as anyone by its immediate success: "I have no idea why it worked, but it did." He recently renovated the club, doing an elegant job without compromising its funky charm, and getting it closer to the St. Charles streetcar in the process. All types of music happen at Rock 'n' Bowl, but its most important contribution to the scene is a large, regular space for zydeco on Thursday nights. According to Chubby Carrier, a Grammy Award winner whose joyous charisma connects with young and old alike, "zydeco is not from New Orleans, but it's good they brought zydeco here because we need to spread out, and this is more of a Dixieland jazz country right here. They're bringing in zydeco because it's so popular, and people want to hear more of it." The "they" is Rock 'n' Bowl, where one can rock, bowl, drink, and hang out with the affable Blanchard, who mingles with customers at the giant, wrap-around bar, then sits with Buddha-like calm in the back making sure all is well, and finally (if it's the right band) tears his shirt off during the final set and dances onstage. "Thanks to the Rock 'n' Bowl, man!" says Carrier. "The Rock 'n' Bowl do a good thing on Thursday nights, and it's a good thing that they are because if it wasn't for Rock 'n' Bowl, there wouldn't be enough zydeco. The other place doing zydeco is d.b.a. on Frenchmen Street. A lot of young people come to that one." Young people come to Rock 'n' Bowl too; it's a colorful mixture of families, ethnicities, ages, and attire, with cowboy-costumed older fans dancing elaborate zydeco steps and younger ones gyrating to rock 'n' roll, a whirl of musical and visual spectacle.

Who knows what will happen next with the club scene? There is currently a campaign to reopen the legendary Dew Drop, the glamorous black cabaret that shut down in 1972 after a thirty-four-year run. In 2013, the Ooh Pooh Pah Doo Bar opened, located near the Mother-in-Law Lounge in the Tremé, an homage to Jessie Hill and his progeny, including James Andrews and Trombone Shorty. In 2014, Kermit Ruffins took over Ernie K-Doe's Mother-in-Law Lounge, a monument to himself (the self-described "Emperor of the Universe") and the song that made him famous, festooned with K-Doe murals, pictures, and awards. The night I went, K-Doe sang his signature tune, accompanied by his son thumping with deadpan relentlessness on an electric bass; his delightful wife, Antoinette, served ominous-looking shots on the house; and his mother sat next to the restroom with her face to the wall. Once we went in, the door was locked behind us, the final Tremé-Gothic touch. It was a bizarre and enchanting night, with people dancing on tables and K-Doe, after receiving obsequies to the Emperor, mingling happily with the crowd, full of fun and mischief. He was one of the most charismatic R&B singers in the history of the city, and he wanted you to know it. The Mother-in-Law Lounge is a telling example of how even the smallest joints expand into something larger than life once you walk in the door, both within the club and outside as well, as Ned Sublette vividly documents: "You walked in and, even if the joint was empty, it was some grand theater of life, like New Orleans itself. Antoinette and everyone else had been made bigger by their participation in the spectacle of Ernie. New Orleans was bigger because it had the Mother-in-Law Lounge."[11]

Kermit Ruffins is now the proprietor. He feeds his fans while playing for them, something he started at Vaughan's every Thursday beginning in 1991. There, he presided over his cooking-trumpeting extravaganza late at night, sometimes all night, then in 2011 suddenly changed to a dismayingly early 7 p.m. gig so he could get to bed before 3 a.m. in order to spend time with his family. ("I never get to see them," he told me wearily one night.) Cindy Wood, Vaughan's shrewd, spirited owner, told me that she did not think the early gig would sit well with New Orleanians, who are basically nightcrawlers, and she was right.

Vaughan's still blasts on every Thursday, back to being late, with a show featuring the incendiary trombonist Corey Henry and his Tremé Funktet. This is a neighborhood bar on the outer reaches of Dauphine Street in the Bywater, with music only on Thursday evenings. The owner has worked out an uneasy truce with local residents, an increasingly dicey proposition as this once-shunned neighborhood becomes gentrified. So far, Vaughan's has survived the musical ravages of gentrification, a tribute to the toughness of its owner and the loyalty of its fans. Jon Batiste is one of several musicians who told me he still regards Vaughan's as one of the city's great music spots, yet it has no marketing or advertising. The tiny bandstand is down a step from a crowded, friendly bar full of locals, college students, and an increasing number of knowing tourists, a gift (or curse) of the internet. The quintessential New Orleans joint, Vaughan's is ostentatiously funky and densely crowded, yet oddly civilized and comfortable; there are no frills and only a few tables

Soul's Seafood. © Mark Hertzberg.

and chairs, but everyone is friendly, and you can get real wine glasses at the bar. On the upper left are huge, simmering bowls of soul food: red beans and rice and a hearty cabbage and pork stew, on the house. According to Wood, the long-standing Thursday night was "very good for Kermit: he's been steadfast with this single gig all these years. It's something unique."[12] It was good for fans as well, who could look forward to the real thing on a regular basis.

At his various jazz-barbecue joints—Vaughan's, Sidney's, Kermit's Treme Speakeasy, and Kermit's Treme Mother-in-Law Lounge—Ruffins personifies the traditional link between New Orleans music and cooking. At the Speakeasy, he began preparing red beans, fried chicken, and rabbit stew at 7:30 a.m., enjoyed family time in the afternoon, and concluded with a three-hour gig Sunday and Monday at 7 p.m. "I finally have a day job," he told me just before a show in 2014. "I never had one." He was running a terrific soul food restaurant and presiding over some of the greatest music in the city, but his satisfaction was undercut by a gnawing feeling that these terribly grown-up activities were not really him: "I always wanted to run one, but now that I've scratched that itch, I may close it down any day. It's hard work. I've been giving away food for thirty years from my barbecue grill; now I'm selling it. I think I'd rather give it away than sell it." Within a few months, the itch was apparently scratched; he did close it down, and Kermit's Treme Speakeasy, the greatest joint in the Tremé since Joe's Cozy Corner, vanished. I was fortunate to enjoy the place while it lasted.

On one occasion, blues singer Guitar Slim and gospel-funk sensation Glen David Andrews sat in, the former bringing down the happy swing of Ruffins's band with a melancholy delta growl, the latter working the crowd into a chaotic frenzy with one of his signature twelve-step recovery songs, conscious no doubt that by this time everyone in the joint had much to recover from. When I asked Ruffins why he was shutting this glorious place down, he answered: "Because I couldn't make any damn money." He was ready to launch Caledonia's before Katrina blew in, but that project was scuttled as well. "Now I've got Ernie K-Doe's Mother-in-Law Lounge, opening tomorrow. I've finally got it all together. I'll have a guy selling barbecue there, too." Apparently, the itch hasn't been scratched after all.

The day after we spoke, Martin Luther King Day, Ruffins opened his tiny joint with a big parade—yet another excuse for a street party. This anarchy in the midst of stability typifies the club scene. Wonderful places come and go, sometimes very quickly, and others always rise, often feted by a second line. Meantime, indomitable clubs like Preservation Hall, Snug Harbor, the Maple Leaf, Tipitina's, Vaughan's, and the Palm Court rock on, lifelines to a tradition that refuses to die.

Chapter Eight

AFTER THE FLOOD

It's not a break, it's a continuation.
—Davell Crawford on the new New Orleans

We're durable.
—Charlie Sims, owner of Donna's

The first year I took students on an American Studies trip to New Orleans was 1990, shortly before the emergence of the small joints on Rampart Street and the big ones like House of Blues, and long before the Frenchmen Street renaissance. My knowledge of venues was limited to Tipitina's, Preservation Hall, the Maple Leaf, and a few others. Experiencing the accretion of clubs and styles through the decade and into the next century with young people eager to absorb, dance, and sit in was a life-changing musical education—for me as much as my students—and a barometer of the changing scene. Before the ravages of Hurricane Katrina, we visited artists in their homes, attended jam sessions, paraded in Sunday second lines, and sang on celebrated stages. We visited sacred shrines such as the site (a Chinese laundry on Rampart Street) where Fats Domino and Little Richard cut their first records, and met with their irrepressible producer, Cosima Matassa; we crowded into the cramped WWOZ studio in Louis Armstrong Park, a remarkable radio station that began playing New Orleans music decades before it was popular, and one which always invited us on the air. Kermit Ruffins took us into his home and cooked barbecue on his porch. Jack Belsom lectured on French Quarter history and showed us his formidable opera LP collection in his shotgun single on Barrack Street. Richard Rochester, who opened the Funky Butt Café in 1995, initiated us into the nuances of the club scene. In the smaller joints, we were greeted the minute we walked in the door; one year when we arrived at Donna's, the owner introduced us to Mayor Ray Nagin at the bar—and where else should the mayor of New Orleans be? The mayor interrupted the music to make a raucous speech on our behalf.

In 2005, I approached the trip with trepidation. The course schedule was due in October, a month after Katrina had struck, and the class was slated for January intercession. How can you take students to a place that no longer exists, the dean's office wanted to know? The city was in ruins, and January seemed too early. So I held my breath and scheduled the trip for May, right after exams. Mardi Gras and Jazz Fest are credited with bringing in a temporary infusion of business, but the critical question was how the music scene was going to do during a normal downtime. Many commentators had already declared that New Orleans's unique musical heritage was either dead or irrevocably changed for the worst. The neighborhoods from which jazz and brass bands emerged were precisely those destroyed by Katrina, the argument went; the displacement of the people who support the music meant the tradition may never be back. As Ben Sandmel, author of *Zydeco!*, told me, "a lot of people said New Orleans was finished, that the music was washed away by the water."[1]

At first, it appeared the doomsayers might be right. When we arrived on May 13, the airport was a ghostly shell, especially dismaying for a Saturday, and the city streets were empty; even the French Quarter had an eerie tranquility. The smell of stale beer and vomit on Bourbon Street was shockingly absent. But the minute we got into the clubs, everything burst into life, and it was clear that New Orleans was not over. The best of the splendid little dives—Vaughan's, Donna's, the Maple Leaf, Rock 'n' Bowl, Snug Harbor, The Spotted Cat, d.b.a.—were all up and running and packed with exultant, grateful locals. New Orleans rocked on, an adventure that exists and changes in the moment, as it always has. Some 300,000 people were apparently not coming back, an unimaginable tragedy, but the fanatical followers of New Orleans music were mainly a mixture of middle-class blacks and whites, locals, and out-of-town regulars, and they continued to stream into the clubs; the players were either back or commuting in from nearby. If there were fewer drunks from Ohio and Texas lurching about in the Quarter, that was just as well. "Those aren't the people who support music," said bass player Peter Harris of the New Orleans Hot Club, "Those are the people who support Bourbon Street."[2]

And even Bourbon Street, in its tawdry indestructability, played a significant role in the recovery, proving that the music was not dead. Its crowds and noise were dramatically diminished, but some of the clubs were still alive, and I remember experiencing a strange intimacy all the more attractive for

being so out of context. As early as October, Big Al Carson was back in business, a larger-than-life premonition of good times to come. I heard Les Getrex
perform for two people, one of them myself, in a desolate, half-ruined bar, a
haunting and beautiful experience. The rapid comeback of Bourbon Street
showed the world, writes Richard Campanella, that "not only was the city still
alive, it was plucky and resourceful. The cheerful defiance of adversity has
universal appeal, and Bourbon Street was the first to demonstrate that local
ethos, which would become the essential narrative of the recovery to the rest
of humanity. 'Music was important then,' reflected Big Al of the Katrina aftermath. 'It was important for people to know that Bourbon Street was back in
action, that New Orleans hadn't lost its culture. It meant everything.'"[3]

For a few years, the contrast between the emptiness in the streets and
the ecstasy in the music bars was the bittersweet signature of the new New
Orleans. The clubs on Bourbon were not the only ones to come back in October. "We're durable," said Charlie Sims, the owner of Donna's, which reopened
on October 15 to celebrate its tenth anniversary. Jazz veteran Germaine Bazzle
remembers Donna's as a lifesaver after the hurricane: "I worked at Donna's
Monday night quite a bit, and I remember after the hurricane I was living in
Slidell, and one of my friends was there, and there was no live music, and I tell
you, I was all messed up, and he says, 'Germaine, I'm going to New Orleans, to
Donna's,' and I say, 'Pick me up.' So we'd make the drive down and listen to the
set, and I was happy because Donna's was supplying some fuel for us."[4] Sims
told me that the sports bar around the corner remained open throughout the
hurricane's aftermath; George Porter Jr. and Walter "Wolfman" Washington
played gigs at the Maple Leaf before and after the devastation, using electric
generators when everything went dark, as club owner Hank Staples guarded
the door (and the door of the fabulous Jacques-Imo's restaurant next door)
with a shotgun. John Blanchard's Rock 'n' Bowl remained the only business
open in the huge, devastated Tulane-Carrolton area; he was on the verge of
shutting down in the fall, but stuck it out when electricity was miraculously
restored in October.

The scene was certainly different in the years immediately following the
flood: more intimate, more focused, and with unpredictable configurations.
You never knew who you were going to hear, which made club hopping
more of a New Orleans experience than ever. At Preservation Hall, which
for forty-five years played only traditional sit-down jazz, we heard gospel—
Davell Crawford leading a group of local shouters and tambourine rattlers.
At the Maple Leaf Bar, the Rebirth Brass Band was joined by their younger
colleagues, the New Birth Brass Band, for a spectacular jam session. The
Rebirth—all nine of whom lost their homes—had four of its members in New

Bob French, with Jack Sullivan. Photographer unknown, courtesy of the author.

York for a gig, a typical situation for these musicians in exile, so we got to hear different generations blasting together through the club's narrow, New Orleans-red hallway. The crowd, the biggest I've seen at this bar, consisted of young locals. At Vaughan's Thursday night show, Kermit Ruffins was supposed to play, but Trombone Shorty showed up instead, apologizing that half his band was still in Nashville. No problem; half of this charismatic young group playing in a rocking place like Vaughan's has twenty times the voltage of anything we are likely to hear in the northeast.

Afterward, I told my friends in the New York music community not to believe the claim made by many in the press that New Orleans music now has an "angry edge." Certainly, New Orleans residents were stunned and enraged by the magnitude of George W. Bush-era governmental incompetence; funk and hip hop lyrics savagely satirized the villainy of these and other political scoundrels, as they always have. Local after local reminded me that this city has survived not only corrupt politicians, but yellow fever, bubonic plague, two all-consuming fires, and numerous floods. Nonetheless, the life-affirming spirit of the music—the jazz funeral tradition of looking death in the eye and then partying anyway—was intact, with the tragic backdrop of the hurricane adding a subtle poignancy. Davell Crawford's rendition of "Amazing Grace," caressed by his silken piano glissandos, took on a new sweetness, especially at "I once was lost, but now I'm found." "We're in exile," he said of his band, several of whom commuted from Houston for a gig that brought in $8 a person at the door, "but we're here." Trumpet player Leon "Kid Chocolate" Brown, another lost NOLA soul, was exiled in Atlanta for months, but moved back to the Big Easy to live in a trailer because he couldn't bear being away from the music: "I had to get back," he told me, "because I love New Orleans too much to be away from it long."⁵ Richard Moten was in Mobile, Alabama, for four years, and he played mainly bebop because that's what they wanted.

The message musicians had in early 2006 was that, regardless of what else was lost, the music was back. As guitarist Todd Duke told me, "It's important for people on the outside to realize that there is still a lot happening musically and culturally; a lot of musicians are here, and a lot of cats that aren't here are still coming into town and playing gigs and are on their way back."⁶ Bob French, leader of the Tuxedo Jazz Band, added a New Orleans flourish: "We'll be here, drunk or sober."⁷

It's impossible to answer the question of how much the city as a whole has "recovered" since then. Locals have expressed extraordinarily different views, from near-apocalyptic reports of environmental and political degradation, police brutality, income inequality, and persistent racism, to glowing statements about more restaurants, less crime, better schools, more entrepreneurs, and a new spirit of renewal. Leroy Jones has a nuanced view. "Overall, the post-Katrina scene is positive, although in reference to infrastructure, the city should have better footing by now. Six years after the levees failed," he wrote in 2011, "there's still visible evidence of the damage residential neighborhoods sustained around the city, as well as bugs within our civil service departments. Isn't the city of New Orleans supposed to be a part of the United States of America, one of the wealthiest countries in the world? Despite it all, we are still rocking! We've got a professional sports team that finally won a championship title, a new hit TV series, HBO's *Tremé*, that tells a good story about the resilience of the local people and the hope and promise for an even better NOLA."⁸

Jones is not the only musician who believes that *Treme* presents a relatively accurate portrayal of the musical life in post-Katrina New Orleans. With its depiction of brass-band and Mardi Gras Indian musicians, it offers a glimmer of what was really happening after the hurricane and today. Much of the show is like opera, with long takes of musical performances presented as an intrinsic part of the story, with the players sublimely apart in their own space. A depiction of music-making, cooking, Mardi Gras Indian customs, and the struggle against racism, it has a meandering structure, loose but intense, that embodies the city. Neighborhood residents, Mardi Gras Indians, restaurant managers, and brass-band families occupy center stage, treated not as exotic objects but as everyday New Orleanians struggling to make a living. The show

Uncle Lionel Batiste. Photograph by Jack
Sullivan.

put the real music scene on the map of popular culture, and it also accomplished something that could not have been predicted. "You know what *Treme*
did?" asks John Boutte. "Which I'm so grateful for, something no one has ever
done before: David Simon and Eric Overmyer archived the New Orleans
musicians, and a lot of those people are no longer with us. We lost Juanita
Brooks, we lost Bunchy Johnson, we lost Uncle Lionel [Batiste]—I don't even
want to go on. You would never have those people archived musically, and
not through some studio—all that sound was done live. No other music show
did that. You got the real thing. They archived the jazz community, the R&B
community, the zydeco community, and most importantly, the Mardi Gras
Indians. And it doesn't have an ending, only a new beginning. They said we
couldn't survive, some didn't want us to survive, but we did survive."[9]

Whether the city is doing more than merely surviving depends on who one
asks; the politicians say the city is now what it always should have been. The
musicians are largely upbeat, citing greater diversity and more young people
in the music scene, with the dissenters complaining about precisely the same
things. Adding to the confusion is that many on the outside believe that the
city is still flooded, a source of dismay to musicians. "A lot of the time when
we go out on the road, people expect New Orleans is under water," Christie

Jordain of the Original Pinettes said in 2015. "So we need to show the world that we're still here and this music is still alive. The scene is growing. People are trying to promote the brass-band sound. We're trying to get it more national and international and promote New Orleans to the world."[10] You can't promote something if people continue to think you're floating around in a flood from 2005. As Nathaniel Rich puts it, "New Orleans has always been a place where utopian fantasies and dystopian realities mingle harmoniously. May New Orleans always remain so. Or at least may it always remain."[11]

New Orleans is full of stories about musicians who were driven from their homes, sojourned elsewhere for a long while, then returned with a new appreciation of the city and a new broadness of vision—a maturity gained in exile. John Boutte migrated to Florida, North Carolina, Brazil, Canada, and other places before coming back, absorbing traditions and making them his own. "I went up to Canada and did world music; I had a sitar player and a tabla. I did gospel music for John Scofield. But I always come back to my roots, which are New Orleans jazz and Mardi Gras music and local R&B artists like Allen Toussaint or the Nevilles or Irma Thomas. I had to work. The government gave me $2,000 after everything was destroyed. That's a good start, isn't it? Big money, baby! There have been a whole lot more collaborations and an openness to new types of music. When I did bluegrass back in the '90s, people said, 'What are you doing'? When I did Cubanismo, they said, 'What are you doing?' But I was doing what Danny Barker taught me: 'You keep all your pockets open.'"

The storm also gave Boutte an unexpected boost: "I was throwing out some shit after Katrina, then I realized, 'I've got to look through this stuff.' I was about to toss the original manuscript to 'Tremé,' which I wrote in 1993. A friend said, 'Don't throw it out!' I'd written the 'Tremé' song while living on St. Claude Street between St. Philip and Ursuline. I was having my morning coffee on my front porch as a funeral procession was leaving St. Augustine Church. I was moved to describe what I was seeing and immediately wrote lyrics of what I observed. I then put the lyrics to a simple blues progression and New Orleans clave groove." The song has helped him recover in more ways than one: "It garnered me lots of attention. I used to hang out in dives, not give a shit, wasted all the time. Then I realized people recognized me on the street. Am I a wanted poster? People expected something of me. I had to straighten up."[12]

Some musicians relocated and never returned, but others, like Wendell Brunious and Charlie Miller, migrated to Europe, where they have always been more respected and better paid than in America, then felt an irresistible urge to come back. "I'm thankful to be playing music," Miller told me. "I'm

Wendell Brunious. Photograph by Katja Toivola.

an old New Orleans musician, still playing music in New Orleans. Katrina taught me one thing good: I was trying to get out of here, maybe move to France; they have a lot of acceptance in France. I've played a lot of festivals over there and all over Europe. I was grieving so heavily I hated New Orleans; it came out that way—very deep grief translating into hate. I was thinking, 'I'll just move over there and get away from all this.' But when I was forced to be away for four years, I wasn't myself; I was totally lost. I was confused and depressed, and I didn't know it. I finally moved to a Cajun town an hour away and started doing Sunday brunches, and as soon as I did, I started to feel I was myself again. When I recognized that, I immediately moved back. When I finally came back, I realized this is where I need to be. When I was in Jackson, Mississippi, after the storm in a festival and I played 'Do You Know What It Means to Miss New Orleans,' I'd cry. I didn't like that New Orleans was hit. It wasn't that I had lost something, it's because the town had been hit. It's very precious to us. The people up there started requesting the song because they wanted to see me cry."[13]

The confusion and despair Miller experienced is shared by many New Orleanians, who continue to suffer from various forms of post-traumatic stress.[14] For those like Miller, making the decision to return meant they could feel themselves again: New Orleans is not just a place to make music, but an essential component of identity.

For some, the journey back was a lengthy process. Displaced by Katrina for seven years, trumpeter Wendell Brunious returned because there was no other place that fully affirms the pleasure principle. "I'll do any gig as long as it's fun. I'm through with struggling and struggling music. I'm through with that. I'm sixty years old, I raised my children, and I want gigs that's gonna have fun, whether they are traditional or modern. The other day, I played a great gig with a stride piano player and a bass saxophone player, but they knew that old-style music. I enjoyed it *so much* because you can make a statement with that. But then tonight I played a great job with George French, David Torkanowsky, and Troy Davis, and we played all modern music. I enjoyed it *so much.*" For Brunious, what's important is "to have something to say. If you've got nothing to say, leave the horn in the case." Having something to say is inseparable from the pleasure of saying it, and very different from cool attitudinizing—definitely not a New Orleans thing. "If you're going to say it with an attitude or some kind of belittling of what you're doing, then you're not having fun. Don't come. Don't come here."[15]

Katrina did not create the need to gravitate back to New Orleans; it merely dramatized it. As Jason Marsalis and others have pointed out in this book, the hurricane merely accelerated patterns already in place. Terence Blanchard, for example, moved to New York for music school, formed his own quintet, and became Spike Lee's house composer (the sound of Denzel Washington's trumpet). His diamond-hard sonority suited the edgy excitement of the city, and in the early '80s, he immersed himself in bebop. By the '90s, however, he was becoming increasingly restive, haunted by the wall separating business from pleasure, and finally moved back to New Orleans in 1995: "Whenever I would come to New Orleans and hear guys play, that reminded me of why I got in the music industry—because I had fun playing music. Living in New York, it had started becoming a business for me after awhile." New York was a place to make one's fortune, but the ache of a fundamental loss made the journey back inevitable. Even with success and money, "you're always looking for the day you can just come down and be glad. Coming back to New Orleans really helped me refocus myself. A lot of it really didn't have anything to do with the music industry. It's just that the city itself is a nice place to be."[16] Musicians like Blanchard and Harold Battiste, who had a significant career in Los Angeles, invariably gravitate back, "vaccinated by the city," as Irma Thomas puts it. "Once you're vaccinated by the city of New Orleans, you cannot leave. You can go away and spend some time away, but you always come back home. You manage to find your way back here some kind of way . . . your visits get longer and longer, and you usually end up coming back permanently."[17] Even with short tours, artists experience coming back as an enormous relief. "I might leave 100 times," Glen David Andrews says, "but I'll be back 101 times."[18] In 2007, when author Keith Spera asked Fats Domino, just before boarding the flight back from a tour what was the best part, he said, "Right now."[19]

Some regard Katrina as a baptism. "It's a wonderful scene in New Orleans right now," Allen Toussaint told me in 2014. "And I might say that going through that big event let some people know how grateful to be with what we have, that things can come along and interfere, but it makes you realize what was there, especially when you begin to lose some things, mostly things, not people. I say that because I consider Katrina to be a baptism rather than a drowning, and I appreciate all the good residual effects in the aftermath of Katrina. A lot of good things happened: collaborations that never would have taken place before; there were more musicians working right after Katrina than in other times because they all had to be in different places where they wouldn't have been called to be. Now they were in those cities, and proprietors could say, 'Hey, one of those New Orleans musicians are right down the street now. Let's have them in on a Thursday night.'" I tell Toussaint that it's a boon to New Yorkers because we get to hear New Orleans music much more frequently now. "That, too. We like venturing about, too. But, of course, wherever we venture, New Orleans has such a strong magnetic pull. I will always live in New Orleans, though I appreciate having a place in New York. I don't have to look for hotels, but I will always have to live in New Orleans."

Between the flood and his death in 2015, Toussaint spent most of his time in New Orleans, coming to New York "when I have things to do. I'm here on this run for a month now; I'm doing Joe's Pub, four in a row this time, and it feels good because I really love that place. It was an initiation for me to start doing these solo performances. That happened right after Katrina. My business partner Josh Feigenbaum told me, 'You have to go somewhere, so come to New York. It's a great place to be, it's an inspiration for you all the time.' So I came here, and Joe's Pub put me right to work for Sunday brunches, and that was kind of new for me. Something a little shaky was going on."

Toussaint broke through his natural shyness—another aspect to his charm—and began doing solo performances at Joe's, backed first by a small ensemble, then only his piano. Consisting of songs old and new—jazz classics like "St. James Infirmary," his own hits like "Mother-in-Law," "Southern Nights," and "Lipstick Traces," and new tunes like "It's a New Orleans Thing"—his post-Katrina gigs were uniquely intimate and personal. His gentle tenor voice and rippling piano arpeggios caressed the audience. If "something a little shaky" was still going on, it provided a compelling tension. These were some of the most elegant shows to rise from the flood, proof that funk can be suave. These gigs were a testament to how deeply Toussaint internalized the NOLA vibe. "Anywhere I am," he sang, "there's a bit of Tipitina's. Anyone from New Orleans knows exactly what I mean; anywhere I go, there's the sound of the Crescent City in me. It's a New Orleans thing, it doesn't leave you just because you leave town."[20]

The renaissance after Katrina had a paradoxical effect; the new money and diversity of people created excitement but also concern and a bit of grumbling. New Orleans experienced a surge of educators, FEMA people, and social workers, who came and went after the storm, then a much larger and more permanent series of migrations beginning around 2010. Novelist Nathaniel Rich, himself among the latter, says that these transplants "tend to exhibit an almost slavish obeisance to New Orleans cultural institutions. They are frequent attendees of second-line parades and Mardi Gras Indians celebrations, are among the most ardent defenders of the Lower Ninth Ward from redevelopment plans, have become devoted Saints fans, and . . . tend to avoid the French Quarter, reserving particular disdain for Bourbon Street."[21] What more could an "authentic New Orleans" enthusiast ask? These young transplants from New York, Los Angeles, Mississippi, Texas, Nashville, and other places would appear to be as close as one can get to ideal new blood.

Yet several established musicians express resentment and trepidation, particularly since many of the new wave are young musicians with whom they must compete. "Now we have a huge influx of people posing as New Orleans musicians," says Charlie Miller. "They come in and quote things from the old records—literally. That's fine; people have to make a living. I'm not complaining, I'm just stating the difference." This charge of literalism is the inversion of the complaint by Michael White and his colleagues that young players are ahistorical and don't know the "old records" at all. "There is always change," Miller admits. "When I was fourteen and fifteen in the '50s, R&B came out. That was the new music, and it became our music. We were attracted to it and loved it—there was no other reason. We weren't making a living from it. Now we have these multimillion-dollar festivals: people making decisions about music who never felt a moment of music in their life—they know some facts, but they haven't felt the music. It's about the heart, not about facts. So that's a big difference. As soon as there was a lot of money involved, the whole scene changed."[22]

This complaint fits a pattern: the slight backing away, the admission that "there is always change," combined with the argument that it's different this time, and "I'm just stating the difference." The fear of being besieged and displaced isn't easily exorcised. It's not just the kids off the street tainting things but also the big shots running Jazz Fest—again, outsiders—who don't "feel the music."

Jon Batiste, who lives in New York but regards New Orleans as his home, has a different take: "The lifestyle and the scene in New Orleans are desirable for a musician, and after Katrina especially there was an opportunity for everyone to come together and be a part of the whole ethos that is New Orleans. And I think over time, the New Orleans musicians who left created a space for other people to come in. And it's always gonna be that way."[23]

Established NOLA musicians often believe that outsiders need to be mentored by the "real" players. Trumpeter Wendell Brunious is open to the newbies as long as they're "listening to older musicians, like we did, I did, Gregg did, Michael White did, Leroy Jones did, Freddie Lonzo did. We listened to guys with respect. They should be observing experienced, real New Orleans musicians. Somebody come from Battle Creek, Michigan, or somewhere, move here, they got a trombone and they wear a pair of glasses with sparkles in it, and all of a sudden they're somebody—and a real trombone player from New Orleans can't get a job." When I told Brunious I'd heard lots of players recently who had style but not the whole sensibility, he snapped, "You can't. We grew up with this shit, man. You can't have it. Sorry. You can study it, like if you have a Ph.D. in carpentry, but you never built a dog house, you don't know how to build it: sorry, you got your Ph.D., but you don't know how to build a dog house. You've got these people and they've made seven records, and there have been times when someone has learned a record, and the label has been on the wrong side, so they say, 'Next song, "Muskrat Ramble,"' and then they play 'Bourbon Street Parade.' The problem is, they come here, they play on the corner with some twelve-year-old kids, just blowin' high notes and blowin' loud. They think they're playing New Orleans! Come play with me and Freddie Lonzo and Michael White and Herlin Riley and Shannon [Powell], and Richard Moten—real people; then you're going to learn something and not just skate on top of the ice."[24]

For those who deliver this type of scathing commentary, "real people" and "real playing" are common refrains. "The lineage of this town is what sets it apart," says pianist David Torkanowsky. "Since Katrina, the film industry, new restaurants, and outside infusions of money have boosted this town up a bit, but the real playing that has its roots in New Orleans history is now more the exception than the rule." Increasingly, tourism drives the music, moving it "more toward entertainment, less toward the purely musical." In song after song, "a trumpet player will hold a trill, and people will jump." Easy sensationalism is increasingly the rule, he believes. "Where does musicianship end and showmanship begin?" Even the Preservation Hall Jazz Band, once a bastion of tradition, has become a "postcard," a "parody of itself" that "doesn't celebrate the purity" it purports to represent. In Torkanowsky's view, the city is full of institutions that threaten to turn the city into a theme park: "Whenever I hear mission statements about culture, I run the other way." Aurora Nealand and others, as we see elsewhere in this book, also express alarm about theme park appropriation and cynical marketers, a sign, ironically, of the city's rebound. Torkanowsky is quick to point out that he doesn't believe the tradition has vanished: "It's still here, but you have to know where to find it." He admits that the new music offers "more diversity" and "all kinds of creativity," including hip hop, a "really cool" phenomenon. But he worries that New Orleans is "less and less about indigenous people, more and more about people who have adopted the culture."[25]

This post-Katrina worry about the influx of new people in the city, imposing alien values, displacing "indigenous" and "authentic" music, afflicts many musicians—some, ironically, from places other than New Orleans, like Torkanowsky himself. The complaint about invaders is not new, but as old as the Louisiana Purchase, when the culturally conservative French were horrified by the new wave of *les Americains*, a barbarous threat, they believed, to their language, customs, and music. Soon, the new outsiders were refugees from Haiti and other Caribbean islands who flooded into the city by the thousands, a lasting contribution to the city's Afro-Latin musical beat, but another perceived threat to the cultures already there. Each new wave of immigrants—whether German, Irish, Italian, or Vietnamese—has brought challenges and resentments, but also new contributions. It's hard to find any ethnicity that did not arrive from somewhere else, "adopt" New Orleans culture, and redefine it in ways that moved music forward. Who could have predicted that the French would have erected the New World's premiere opera scene in a swamp or that African Americans would create jazz or that Hispanics would inaugurate bands like the Iguanas? Now the immigrants who cause the most ruckus are the tattooed hobo crowd who play for tips on Royal and Frenchmen Streets and compete with the more established musicians once they make it into the clubs. Perhaps more significant, however, is a large contingent of Latin Americans and Asians that began coming around 2010, comprising a potentially new audience and talent pool. As in classical music, Asians are changing the culture, giving bands a different vibe, and offering unstinting professionalism.

Not all established musicians experience immigrant anxiety. For John Boutte, the "invasion" is an affirmation of what the city is about. As we have seen, he regards the ever-changing ethnic complexity as a key reason the music always stays fresh. He likes to remind people that the original New Orleans musicians were not native: "They came from Africa, Albania, Yugoslavia—the only indigenous folks were the Indians. The doors have opened a little bit more. We've had such an influx of players; they may be familiar with the New Orleans style of music, but they weren't really brought up in it—which is no problem because everybody can learn. We had banjos in Preservation Hall, but we have them all over the street now—a lot of people from the folk and bluegrass scenes—the kids who grew up with that music and brought it down with them after the storm. This is not the Caribbean-African instrument the banjo is originally derived from. But the feeling is there, and the sincerity is there. They're out there busting in the streets. Often I don't know who they are. Before the levees failed, I could say with pride that I knew just about everyone who was an active musician, the younger cats as well as the older; you always knew who they were. Now there's always somebody new—with talent."

Boutte admits that not all of the new players can cut it and that not everyone in the musical community is happy, but he has a generous assessment of the risks: "When you increase the talent pool, you have the negative and the positive. I've got to be positive. If you're making music, if you're not making guns, not hurting people, if you're making things that make people feel better in their souls and in their hearts and in their lives, music to help them make it through—if you're not giving grief, you're fine with me."[26]

Allen Toussaint, who regarded Boutte as "the best vocalist we have now," was also fine with the new arrivals, though he sympathized with those who feel threatened. "I understand that, and I even understand people who feel threatened by that in one way or another, not by the spirit of it, but by the gigs all the time, but I don't ever really think that would be a factor. There's enough audience and room for all of that. I do understand it for the guys who take it so very seriously that we're really home, and there's a big world out there that's really busy and speeding, but we down here are just moseying along, minding our own business. We don't feel the usual worldly rush like people coming who visit from New York or LA. I think it's fine to have people come in, and I understand it because there is something special about New Orleans, and I can see a person falling in love, and thought they were going to be there for a week and noticed it's been ten years now."[27]

Jason Marsalis believes the "worldly rush"—the siren calls of money and materialism—are louder in New Orleans now, but not to the point of drowning out the culture: "There are many more outsiders now, and it's symptomatic of America overall. We're at a point now where everybody thinks about themselves, and no one thinks about their own communities. They look for wherever they can make the easiest buck or the most money: 'Hey, let's go there—we can make more money!' But New Orleans is still definitely more of a community than New York, even with out-of-towners. Folks are still going to come together. It still has that."

As we have seen throughout this book, musicians view the '90s as representing the start of a significant shift. "In the late '90s, people in New York and other places started saying, 'Maybe we should go down to New Orleans and check it out.' They started to see the value of learning here. Recently, a drummer said on Facebook, 'Man, I can't deal with New York anymore. It's too much for me,' and another commented, 'I never knew what the big deal was.' So I chimed in, 'You have to go back thirty years.' Did you see the new Patti Smith book about the New York scene then? You could go to New York and become a starving artist, but it isn't that kind of place now." New Orleans, Marsalis believes, is "far more mainstream" now, but it still retains its character. It's a place where serious jazz players from around the world are finding a home.[28]

The claim that the new New Orleans has become a parody of the old one has generated ongoing controversy and has been heavily promoted in the media. According to drummer and folklorist Ben Sandmel, author of the zestful biography *Ernie K-Doe*, pundits have pushed the idea that the city has become "a faint, theme-park depiction of its former self that could only appeal to tourists." He doesn't buy it: "This notion made for a juicy, tragic story but proved to be wildly inaccurate. Despite all the adversity, loss, death, and devastation suffered by the city, New Orleans' musical and cultural community rebuilt itself from the ground up. Some charities and philanthropic agencies helped significantly—but musicians, Mardi Gras Indians, and social aid and pleasure clubs did the heavy lifting. Today the city's long-standing traditions remain alive, vibrant, and ever-evolving."[29]

Victor Goines has concerns about the new immigrants and marketers, but his tone is measured, neither as skeptical as Torkanowsky and Brunious nor as welcoming as Boutte and Toussaint: "From a musical point of view, there's a lot going on in the city, but there is a challenge in the new scene because there are several musicians from New Orleans and those who have come in from other cities and states and other parts of the world who have taken advantage of playing in New Orleans for the door or the hat and not on a scale type of compensation, which creates a very difficult challenge for the musicians in New Orleans I've spoken with who are my peers and colleagues I've grown up with."

Goines does not believe his colleagues dislike the younger musicians and their contributions; they simply would like the economics to be more fair: "Everybody would be equally supportive of the scene if everybody would actually establish a level of excellence and occupational consistency throughout. We can be our own worst enemies when we undercut each other on the music scene, and as a result, promoters or club owners or vendors who call to hire pin us against each other if we're not careful. So when I consider what David is talking about or contrary to what Allen Toussaint is speaking about—I've known Allen Toussaint all my life; I went to school with his son— Mr. Toussaint makes his money in a different way than a David Torkanowsky. So does John, who does a lot of his work in New Orleans, but a lot in Europe. So when you consider where the bulk of your revenue comes from, you have two different types of people looking at it from two different vantage points."[30]

It's hard to imagine "occupational consistency" in a town where anarchic inconsistency is the norm. Still, some semblance of musician-pay rationality would appear to be in order since many musicians end up working for free, as Katja Toivola explains: "There are different ways for gigs to work: guarantee versus commission versus door and combinations of the above. Where we work (Preservation Hall, Bombay, Playhouse, Hermes), we have a guaranteed payment that is not affected by business, for better or for worse—some places the ticket price has increased fivefold, but musicians' pay has remained the same. Some places the band works for tips plus 20 percent of the bar sales. On busy nights this can be better than a flat guarantee, on slow nights you'll end up working for free(ish). Some places the band keeps the door or majority of it. Again, if the place is big and busy, this can be great, but the band assumes the risk and as you've seen, for example, on Frenchmen, sometimes there just isn't enough crowd to go around. And all these no-cover places have trained the audience to be reluctant towards paying one. I've heard people complain about the $5 at the Palm Court. Club owners are willing to pay for all other expenses (rent, insurance, bar stock, food inventory, cleaning services, door men and sound men), but for some reason assume that musicians and waiters can be made to work for free! Welcome to America."[31]

The image of anyone complaining about a $5 cover at the Palm Court is certainly depressing, but musicians have long put up with this kind of crassness, whether they are old or new, "authentic" or "fakers," and the ones who just arrived are simply happy to be playing. Walter "Wolfman" Washington, who sang blues in his early days, then funk and soul, couldn't imagine living anywhere else: "In New Orleans, we have a variety of different types of music. If you're somewhere else, everybody's playing the same style of music. Here you can play any style you want to play in—as long as you do it good.... That's why I'm so glad I'm from here. I wouldn't want go stay nowhere else. They got people saying, 'Man, you can't find no work in New Orleans.' I say, 'If you come here, they got more work than anywhere else.'"[32] They find work no matter how tough it gets. The gifted pianist and preacher Fredrick Sanders, who bounces between Texas and Louisiana, told me that while Katrina slowed the flow of people in the clubs, he nonetheless eked out a meaningful living banging the piano in the French Quarter. He could save souls anywhere; he could only be a jazz musician in New Orleans.

A variety of artists told me that only in New Orleans could they earn a living as jazz musicians. The most active musicians do seven or eight gigs a week plus more lucrative private events such as weddings, corporate parties, and tours; this is a town where people always need a band, and a good one is usually just down the street. "I tried New York," says Lawrence Sieberth, who plays every conceivable style of jazz piano (as well as country music). "This is the only city I could make a living in."[33] Trombonist Michael Watson is emphatic: "I've been around the country and the world, and I've never found a place where I can play music full-time and make a living as a musician other than New Orleans. This is the *only* city. It's the truth. "[34] Philippine-born Antoine Reynaldo Diel, who has an opera background, fell in love with jazz (to the consternation of his teachers) and came to New Orleans from Los Angeles because he "couldn't get work as a singer, and so I had to find a different place. It was between Boston, Chicago, and New Orleans. In New Orleans, I can be a full-time singer. I don't have a day job—this is what I do." [35] Charlie Halloran, a Northwestern University-trained trombonist in the Panorama Jazz Band, says he came to New Orleans from St. Louis because, while "we have a significant jazz history too," only in New Orleans can he continually play. "I could never make a living in St. Louis," he said during a break at the tiny Spotted Cat, where a young crowd was spilling out onto Frenchmen Street. And what could a living possibly be, since the Spotted Cat charges no cover? Enough, apparently, to keep playing: "I play continually; I couldn't anywhere else. I make enough to pay my rent, and I have a great time." He uttered the last sentence with a weary smile; his band had been playing for hours before we arrived at 1 a.m. and was still rocking when we left.[36]

When I spoke with David Torkanowsky a year after his acerbic critique, he was more upbeat, an indication of how quickly the scene can change: "I'm glad we're talking again because the situation has changed. On the gig scene, you have a lot of out-of-towners who have shrouded themselves in this culture and pretended to be legitimate, and they get gigs by imitating, not necessarily honoring the ancestors. But there is a new wave of young players coming up. An example is a young man named Eric Bloom, who plays with a band called

Lettuce and a DJ called Pretty Lights. This guy makes the music sound like Aaron Copland or Harry James—amazingly deep player. Roland Guerin is a bass player from here; his son, Morgan, is sixteen and already sounds like a grown man on tenor saxophone. The only person I ever heard as advanced at that age is Nicholas Payton. So there is a whole crop of younger players that have an absolute reverence for the ancestors and are doing it correctly. In any town or culture there's going to be pretenders and those who carry the mantle; since we spoke last, the latter category has really stepped up."[37]

Eric "Benny" Bloom is indeed one of many younger players who honors the ancestors, even though he plays a great deal of modern music. Torkanowsky's Copland analogy is telling: Bloom's sound has a gleaming clarity and natural flow that makes even the most recondite material sound easygoing and welcoming. One of the reasons Bloom emigrated to New Orleans, he told me, was because "nothing in the modern world has all the things New Orleans has. The elders are still here in the clubs. Everyone is gone in the other cities; there is no more direct lineage to the music."[38] As for Guerin, he regards New Orleans as "an oasis. It's very special because all these different grooves and fields can coexist in any time period and they never get old."[39] His restless bass, which throbs through everything from zydeco to his own highly contemporary compositions, embodies the city's variety. "The people who are in New Orleans want to be in New Orleans," he says, "because the city isn't just about traditional music, there's all kinds of music, all kinds of fluency."[40]

Many of the newcomers respect New Orleans's history and sympathize with the skepticism of Torkanowsky, Brunious, and other elders. "What Wendell was talking about with the newer people," says Diel, "is a lack of respect for the tradition they are entering. Hey, you're coming to this place that has a wonderful tradition; don't just disregard it, you've got to respect it. You've got to learn it and be true to it as it connects to you. That was a good lesson I learned early on even before coming here: that there is an existing beautiful culture. How do I fit? And how do I embrace what is there while putting my own identity and stamp on what I do?"

Diel, like Bloom, has made it his business to gig with established musicians who know the tradition. The night I heard him at Buffa's Lounge in the Marigny, he was singing a hugely variegated repertory with Tom McDermott on piano: "With somebody like Tom, he's already a train that's going, and I just have to jump on. He is more traditional than many of the rising generation from the clandestine jazz families in New Orleans. I know a lot of them that are born here. They want to do something different. They don't just want to do the traditional jazz thing. So they'll go into funk or rap, but that's part of the identity of New Orleans. It was always a gumbo of musical styles. Just because we're not in the 1800s anymore, there is no reason why growth and change cannot occur. It has to occur, but how do you keep the tradition going? I'm forty-one, and people want me to do the modern stuff, but my heart is in the old songs. I write my own, but that's not going to stop me from singing 'Skylark.'"[41]

Interviews with younger musicians confirm that "the rising generation from the clandestine jazz families in New Orleans" insist on moving the tradition forward, mixing funk, rap, and whatever else works for them, including classical. Chadrick Honore, who went to elementary school with Trombone Shorty and Jon Batiste, embodies both tradition and an omnivorous eclecticism: "I do movie scores and lots of productions for different artists. In jazz there's not a lot of money, and right now, families are poor and kids look to see how they can make money. If you stay one-dimensional, like just brass band, then that's what you get. So I try to teach my kids [his students] a little bit of everything: a little bit of classical, a little bit of funk, a little bit of jazz, a little bit of rock 'n' roll—everything. You've got to have a full circle if you want to be a musician."[42]

This coexistence of the old and the new is a hallmark of post-Katrina reality. "When I see the scene now," says Victor Goines, "I see that more activity on our main strip where 'contemporary, modern jazz' used to take place, which is Frenchmen, the street Snug Harbor is on. It's tremendously vibrant—so vibrant you have to park blocks and blocks away to go down there and check out the music. There are still a lot of great musicians in New Orleans making their living playing New Orleans music and contemporary music. A lot have come from around the world after Katrina for a variety of reasons: to be part of the opportunity of the rebuilding process because musicians were given opportunities in terms of rebuilding the city and getting gigs to help out."[43]

According to Allen Toussaint, "New Orleans now is in great shape. It's 2014 now, so it's been a while since our big event, our main attraction you might say, in the recent past, the, Katrina event, but New Orleans's spirits are very high, the musicians are happy, they're doing what they do. Right now, as we speak, there are some guys in front of Jackson Square with their arms out and their hats on the ground, and some youngsters picking up their horns for the first time, and some guys a little bit ahead of them helping them out."[44]

The stories of the newcomers are as varied as the music they make. Michael Watson, from Ohio, spent four years in the Marine Corps and played his trombone for Irvin Mayfield's open mic night at Snug Harbor during his "sitting in years" whenever he was in town. He moved to New Orleans after the flood, and Mayfield hired him for his band; he now plays at the Jazz Playhouse every week and at the Spotted Cat with Kristina Morales and the

Bayou Shufflers, as well as with a fusion ensemble that started in 2015 called the Soul Brass Band (not to be confused with the Soul Rebels). "The city is very healthy now," he says. "Music is providing for the city as it always has, pre- and post-Katrina. It brings people together."[45] Saxophonist Joe Braun learned the repertory by playing in Jackson Square with Tuba Fats, Uncle Lionel Batiste, and members of the Andrews family. His band became the New Orleans Jazz Vipers, playing on Decatur Street in 1999. "We were playing for tattooed junkies and punk rockers," Braun says. After appearing on John Sinclair's WWOZ radio show, the Vipers became the first jazz band to play at the Spotted Cat on Frenchmen Street. "I'm from New York, three of us are from New Orleans, and one from California," Braun told me in his gruff, gravelly voice, a reflection of the Vipers' sound. "When we started at the Spotted Cat, there was nothing happening on this street. Now it's over the top. They don't even need us anymore. They could put anything in here and make money. We started it—the musicians started it. Now a lot of young people are doing it, which is great."[46]

One of the most encouraging stories is that of the Shotgun Jazz Band, from Canada and various parts of the United States. They started on the street in 2010 and gradually became a beacon of traditional jazz, wowing both the hipsters and the old-timers, playing with soul and impeccable style. They have studied the old songs but have also made them their own. "We started by ourselves on the streets," says trumpeter Marla Dixon, who sings the blues with heart-stopping intensity. "My husband plays banjo and I played sousaphone. In high school in Canada, my music teachers were trying to get me to play different kinds of jazz, but none of it spoke to me. I put it down for a long time. Then, in my mid-twenties, I walked into a bar where a gentleman named Cliff Bastien was leading his band called the Happy Pals; he had been coming down here since the '60s, hearing Kid Thomas and getting his inspiration from him. I heard him with his band, and I said, 'Oh, this is it! This is the music I've been looking for my whole life.' I asked him for trumpet lessons, and then he died that week."[47]

As we have seen with Phil Frazier hearing the Dirty Dozen for the first time and James Evans hearing Rebirth, this kind of jazz epiphany, sudden and dramatic, is not uncommon, and can have life-changing consequences. Shotgun is one of the new bands praised by the older musicians, not only because of their devotion to "real" New Orleans music but because Shotgun seeks them out as mentors. Barry Martyn, one of the great champions of traditional jazz, says, "They are the one exception to the rule. Fabulous, they are—that lady, Marla, and her husband on banjo, and the bass player, Tyler Thomson; he's twenty-eight years old, and he's playing like all the classic bass players I

Marla Dixon. Photograph by Jack Sullivan.

came up with. They're trying to play that kind of music because that's what their mission is."[48]

The debate about the old guard versus the new will never get resolved. Nor should it be. "You're dealing with different personalities," says Bruce Raeburn. "It's not like there's some ontological issue that's objective. With Dave [Torkanowsky] and Wendell [Brunious], part of mentorship is stepping on the guys coming up. Allen [Toussaint] has written songs about that: 'On the Way Down.' Look at those lyrics, they're a lot of fun. And that's part of the process too. You don't just coddle the people coming up. You show them that they have to work. And that is part of the criticism. A lot of the guys want to try to do it the easy way, and there is no easy way. It's part of the process. Makes you tough!"[49]

Anyone who thinks there is an "easy way" is in for hard times. The career of a jazz musician is like jazz itself—often improvised, full of unexpected ups and downs. Victor Goines believes the "next-gig" mentality can be perilous for young musicians who lack a sense of what it takes to sustain a career, "not only in a musical sense but in a business sense as well. What will it take for them to be professional musicians over a career as opposed to 'Where is our next gig at?' It's difficult if they're just jumping on a fast-moving train. If you jump on a train at that pace, you're gonna get hurt."[50] Ellis Marsalis also frets: "A lot of the kids don't take the effort to learn the tradition. They'll put together a band and put the hat out, make some change, and that becomes the crux of what they do."[51]

It's easy to form one's own view on the new migrants. Just wander on Royal or Frenchmen Streets or go to Jackson Square or the French Market and hear the bewildering variety of street music, some of it terrible or mediocre, a lot of it sensational. Country, bluegrass, brass band, Cajun, Gypsy, Greek, R&B—all of these styles resound through the Quarter. One afternoon, I heard a group that had arrived the day before, cohering into an ensemble they called the Coyote String Band, including a native New Orleanian tap dancer who "dances all kinds of music"; the others, she said, were "drifting in from various places" (she wouldn't say where—"just drifting through"), including a solid trumpet player. They performed traditional music ("Has Anybody Seen My Gal?") with sound technique and lots of soul. Later, I heard a Cuban string player living in Albuquerque who told me he hopes to move to New Orleans with his friend from New Mexico. This duo performs a variety of ethnic music—including snappy Greek and Hungarian dances—and they hope to get two more string players so they will have a quartet and can move to New Orleans.

Some of the new street people are just out of music school, hoping to move to the city and establish themselves. There are also older musicians—like clarinetist Doreen Ketchens, who has gigged professionally—who have been on the street for years. Afternoons, you can hear her commanding virtuosity on Royal Street next to the Russian grocery store. On the next level are those who get occasional gigs, playing in new bands that are good enough to land jobs in venues hospitable to newbies because club owners get away with paying them little or no money. Gypsy-jazz artist Josh LeBlanc plays in Vagabond Swing, a Django-style Gypsy band. "Yes, we're part of the new influx here," he told me. "We've been in existence three years. There was a big influx of musicians and talent once Katrina happened, and where I lived, Lafayette, a lot of jazz musicians came to find work." The band now plays in the Blue Nile, One Eyed Jacks, and various places in the French Quarter. Gypsy jazz may not be indigenous, but "it's close enough because it's French; anything that's French-influenced is accepted here, especially where we're from, Acadiana—French culture is highly regarded. This place here, New Orleans, was owned by the French before it was America, with all the debauchery and unacceptance of the laws here." LeBlanc also plays in a pop group, the Givers: "People would say it's an indie group, but I also do the jazz thing." All of what he does, he believes, comes from Armstrong, "'the house that Pops built.' He built that whole structure, the foundation."[52] Like many of the new immigrants, LeBlanc has a clear sense of history and his place in it.

Some of the new players are frequent guests who hope to make a permanent move. Jesse Duplechain, a young guitarist, is in the process of relocating to New Orleans. "It's really cool. I like the direction New Orleans is taking," he told me in 2015 at the pool table in the Maple Leaf. His favorite form, zydeco, has taken off since Katrina, and he has landed a gig with Nathan Williams Jr., who "mixes a lot of things: zydeco, hip hop, soul, R&B. The way I met him actually was, we were both going to school for jazz at the same time. He mixes jazz chords and progressions in there too. He can do anything, really." Duplechain is not impressed with technical wizardry for its own sake, which he regards as a cover-up for a lack of lyricism: "I've seen guys who could play really articulate technical stuff for days. I do it too if I don't know the melody. I mean, it's good every now and then to do something flashy. If you really know a tune and can close your eyes, you can just feel it and hear what you play—that's the real thing, if you emulate a vocal melody, play like a vocalist and try to get something across." He believes melody is in better shape south of the Mason Dixon line: "That's what the South has on everybody else. You can't really speak about it. They try to, but they're like, 'Man, what are these guys doing? They're playing the same notes I'm playing, but it doesn't sound the same.'"[53]

The most visible change is the new wave of female performers, representing a dizzying array of style and sensibility. Prior to the '70s, Irma Thomas reminds us, women were at best second-class citizens on the stage: "We were just 'here.' There was an assumption we did what we did and we weren't looked upon as an entity in itself. We were looked upon as a convenience or an inconvenience."[54] This is no longer the case. Meschiya Lake, now a fixture on Frenchmen Street, is typical of a new breed of singer. She has been in the city "for fifteen years, long enough to feel like a New Orleanian," singing traditional jazz with happy abandon and no need for a microphone, mostly at the Spotted Cat, her artfully restrained vibrato weaving out onto Frenchmen Street. Originally from Oregon, she began as a singer and circus performer, fell in love with New Orleans while on a circus tour, sang for tips on Royal Street, and now has an international career. Her band, the Little Big Horns, which she started in 2009, evokes early twentieth-century jazz and blues, though much of the material consists of Lake's compositions. All this sounds too good to be true, but it is and anyone who catches her gig will discover that the actual music is as good as the backstory.[55]

The new generation is adding a new layer on the rich tradition of female blues singers and piano bangers who have prospered in the city for generations. Meghan Swartz, whose scintillating piano has rocked New Orleans since she arrived from Seattle in 2003, has blended into the jazz world with relative ease, performing regularly with Leroy Jones, Lucien Barbarin, and many others. Black female piano players are not at all unusual, but white ones are, especially those who land regular gigs with renowned players. "People ask me about this a lot," she said when I asked her about sexism in the jazz world. "I don't encounter issues. I've had great experiences with people looking out for me, walking me to my car, and treating me like a professional on the bandstand."[56]

More unusual yet are female horn players, who are coming to New Orleans from around the world. Canadian trumpeter Marla Dixon says she has encountered few gender obstacles. "I think it's quite the opposite. People are very taken with it, and are kind of rooting for the underdog. Among some of the older musicians, it might be a bit of a thing. I've had some of the older gentlemen try to talk to other members of the band about tipping and money and things, and I'll just sit there and wait until they realize it's me that does that. But the younger generation, and even most of the older, they know. If you can play, you can hang. It doesn't matter who you are or what you play."[57] It doesn't hurt that Dixon is a gutsy singer as well as trumpeter; her singing has helped her get gigs, but once the bandleader realizes she plays trumpet, she does both.

Trombonist Haruka Kikuchi, who came to New Orleans in 2013, sings only occasionally, but by 2014, she was already playing with the Shotgun Jazz Band and Kermit Ruffins's Barbecue Swingers. With Shotgun, she blends seamlessly, but with the Swingers, she often steals the show, and Ruffins is happy to let her do so. Kikuchi is a small woman with big charisma and a powerful sound. The first time I heard her, she was sitting in at Kermit's Treme Speakeasy just after her move. The stage was crowded with popular, in-your-face male performers, but Kikuchi made a huge impression. When I heard her play with the Swingers in 2017 at the Little Gem Saloon, she had become a focal point of the ensemble, her sound bolder than ever. "Many women now play trombone and trumpet," she told me during a break at the Spotted Cat. "I played both in high school and junior high school brass bands in Tokyo. We Japanese love music, especially the music of New Orleans. I first learned from old records and CDs. I listened and practiced, practiced, practiced. Now I'm here, and

Topsy Chapman. Photograph by Brandon Xeureb, Xistence Photography.

I hope I'll always be here. I love New Orleans."[58] Senior players criticize a stifling literalism that comes from listening to "old records and CDs," but the unpredictability and dynamism of Kikuchi's playing tell a different story.

Topsy Chapman, whose powerful voice has quickened her audience's blood for over thirty years, is a matriarch in her musical family: "We do all right. We do all the repertory—gospel, jazz, blues. People want to hear singing, not just R&B. I've done well, and my sisters have done well."[59] When I asked her whether females had trouble in the business, she was hesitant to weigh in: "It depends on who it is." Her daughter, Yolanda Windsay, is less reticent: "Yes, it's harder for women. It helps if you come from a musical family or if you have somebody before you who was involved. But if you don't have anybody in the music business, like a mother or father or grandparent or nothing like that, it's going to be tough. Yes. Yes." Nonetheless, she believes the current scene is less male dominated than before: "It's getting a lot better. A lot more females are getting involved with it. We put our foot down a little bit. Yeah! You've gotta be tough. Look at the Pinettes. Man, they are awesome, those ladies."[60] One of the Pinettes' most fervid admirers is Germaine Bazzle, who is heartened by the group's recent success: "That's a wonderful group of young ladies. And you know, they're accepted. *They're accepted.*" The field may still be male-heavy, but "the young ladies that are playing, they are making a statement." Bazzle is also encouraged by jazz bands headed up by women like Aurora Nealand and

Marla Dixon: "There are lots of young instrumentalists, and those girl bands are really good—they're not backing down."[61]

One who is definitely not backing down is Arsène DeLay, John Boutte's niece, whose operatic soprano threatened to engulf the small back room at Buffa's Lounge on the night I heard her. "It's absolutely harder being a woman, across the board," she told me after the show. "If you look at the festivals, the headlines, a lot of the lineups are very, very male-heavy. Even though the women are here and we're fighting, and we work and we are great, a lot of the time the spotlight does not shine on us. The attention tends to go more male-centric. We're here, it's just that people are not necessarily paying attention. I've been in conversations with people who have said, 'Are there any female vocalists here?', and I just kind of looked at them and laughed and said, 'You're not looking hard enough if you don't know because we're out here; there's a lot of us doing our own thing and doing our own music.'"[62]

Indeed they are. Drummer Cori Walters is one of a growing number who is playing music on a traditionally male instrument. She does mainly traditional, but also "rock, pop, funk, and everything else" with numerous groups, including Lena Prima, (Louis Prima's daughter), Tom Fischer, and Lucien Barbarin, and has started her own ensemble, Cori Walters and the Universe Jazz Band. She is a magnetic presence, both to hear and to watch on stage, but as a woman in a man's world, she has to work hard to survive. For her, at least, the scene has gradually improved: "There aren't many female drummers here—maybe four. I've been through a lot of stuff, but not anymore, at least not for me. Not in New Orleans. The people who would give you trouble about it are not very good anyway. They're not!"[63] Female musicians in New Orleans tend to be even more scathingly dismissive of those who would dismiss them. "Musicians tend to not take you seriously because you're a woman," says Charmaine Neville. "I'll never forget—I fired a musician one time because he told me, 'Huh? Who's the leader of this band? You? I'm not taking no check from a woman . . . You lead this band? I don't want to work' . . . I say, 'I'll tell you what then. Don't worry about it, you're fired.' 'You can't fire me.' I say, 'Oh, okay. Yah. Watch.'"[64]

Even after they become successful, female players must continually prove themselves. As "Saxy Lady" Natasha Harris of the Original Pinettes puts it, "It's definitely hard being a female. I would tell anybody that. From my experience over the years, even in developmental phases, when I was studying music [with Jon Batiste at NOCCA], I was always the only female, or one or two, so it was always harder; you had to prove that you belong. Now that the Pinettes are an all-female band, it's hard to break that barrier because the music itself is a male-dominated industry—and then to have women playing instruments, that's something you don't see. You may see a lot of female vocalists, maybe a few pianists, but not many instrumentalists the way you see drummers or horns. So when people see us, they are really amazed and surprised because the first thing they see, of course, is that we're all women and then when they listen, they say, 'Hey, y'all sound as good as the guys!' And so there's always that comparison."[65] Harris's stance is typical of the Pinettes: they are shrewd and canny about the male-dominated world they inhabit, but also upbeat and straight-ahead.

Hip hop artists are also making it in the post-Katrina scene. Bounce rapper Big Freedia, a gay black man with a female stage persona, says that Katrina helped give her music a larger audience: "Katrina helped us with that," says Big Freedia. "We were all displaced, and it brought our music to a lot of different areas. And people were like, 'What is that?' I traveled a lot [after] Katrina, trying to make people feel at home away from home. It was just way overdue to get the exposure anyway." Now she feels she can "go anywhere from uptown to downtown, from the West Bank to East Bank to Kenner, and I'm gonna get the same respect as a female or a male rapper."[66] As a rapper who is also a twerker, she gets not only respect, but a national fan base and the inevitable plagiarism from white celebrities: "Every time we do something, people want to snatch it and run with it and put their name on it. And they still don't even have the moves down yet."[67]

This statement echoes similar complaints by Dave Bartholomew about white rock 'n' rollers in the 1950s who "snatched up" black music even though they "didn't have the moves." Cultural appropriation happens all the time in America, but is more noticeable in New Orleans because the town offers so much innovation from so many African Americans—there is so much to appropriate. It started with Dixieland and has never stopped. Even a venue as lively and attractive as the Spotted Cat often showcases bands that many regard as white appropriations of African American music.

The defining characteristic of the post-Katrina scene is greater gender and racial diversity. "I can guarantee you there are a lot more racially diverse bands," says John Boutte. "Years ago, when I first started playing, folks would come up to me and ask me, 'Why you got all them white boys in your band? Used to be black guys, jazzmen. Are they white?' I said, 'Yes, they are—because they can play.'" Segregation and the legacy of "race music" are so stubbornly part of American society that some tourists, according to Boutte, have become literally color-blind. "I had a woman come up to me three months ago, and I'd overheard her ask my guitar player Todd [Duke], who is white, 'I notice John doesn't have any black people in his band. They're all white.' And my bass player says, 'I'm not white,' and I turn around and I say, 'You're sure not, and

Lucien Barbarin, Freddie Lonzo, and Wendell Brunious at Preservation Hall. Photograph by
Jack Sullivan.

Wendell's not white either." But it don't make a difference because you know,
what most people don't get: the queen of soul, Aretha Franklin, her biggest
hits were with an all-white band. The soul records that popped out from that
scene were all white. And then they started doing what they do here, mixing
the soul guys with the country guys with the classical guys during the sessions, and it's all music, man. Music doesn't have a color. You could say it's
black and white: black notes on white paper. It's not in the color; it's in your
musicality."[68]

One of the most moving and painful stories I heard on the subject came
from Lucien Barbarin: "In the early '80s, I was often the only black guy up
there [on the bandstand]. There was a lot of segregation back then. Every night
when I played with those white bands, I'd have to play 'Dixie:' 'Oh, I wish I was
in the land of cotton.' Slavery—not great. But I had to do it because I was with
the band: I had to work. Segregation has always played a big part. In the '90s,
things pretty much started changing, and hopefully things are getting better,
but we still have a lot of Confederate statues here that we need to tear down,
just like we need to tear down that flag."[69] Barbarin is not the only musician
who feels this way: Terence Blanchard, Topsy Chapman, and others have hailed
Mayor Mitch Landrieu's controversial removal of Confederate monuments.

Some of the spiciest ingredients in the new gumbo are the Cajuns, who
came to New Orleans by way of Canada, France, and Lafayette, and have

emerged as a formidable presence in the contemporary scene. Tourists who
enjoy Cajun food and players in clubs on Bourbon Street often think this is
a New Orleans thing. It actually has more to do with Nashville and country. Cajun guitarist Jack LeBlanc, for example, got his start with the Grand
Ole Opry, has never done a New Orleans gig, and "never got close to New
Orleans." The one exception was his work with Irma Thomas, who was "easy
to get along with and sang in tune and in time—more than most zydeco singers."[70] Yet Cajun music is making inroads. Bruce Daigrepont is from New
Orleans, and his Sunday afternoon gig at Tipitina's was for many years a joyous fixture. "I play the music of southwest Louisiana," he says, "and that's my
heritage. And yet I'm based in New Orleans. I don't feel like I'm part of the
inner circle in southwest Louisiana, in Acadia . . . And I'm not part of New
Orleans's inner circle either. I haven't been in the *Tremé* series. . . . But I think
I'm respected in both places. I'm kind of like an independent."[71]

An "independent" is what a New Orleans musician often is. The city is a
mecca for outsiders, interlopers, and independents of all kinds, who somehow manage to form a community. When I began traveling regularly to New
Orleans in the 1980s, Daigrepont was already a regular presence; he was my
introduction to Cajun music (could there be a better one?) and I assumed
his sound was native to New Orleans. Given the increasing number of young
Cajun and zydeco musicians flocking to New Orleans, it actually is a scene
now, thanks in part to Daigrepont's pioneering gigs, first in the Maple Leaf in
the '80s, then at Tipitina's.

Now prominent jazz and funk players show up at places like Rock 'n' Bowl
to enjoy Cajun and zydeco bands, doing moves on the dance floor with the
best of them. Zydeco, a black Creole form that is looser and more open to
innovation than Cajun music, faces the usual issue of how far to push the
boundaries without losing its soul. Chubby Carrier is happy to serve the rockers and funksters, but he is deeply attuned to tradition: "My heart is in traditional zydeco. I grew up in the '70s, listening to James Brown and all those
guys, man, but I also grew up with zydeco with my grandfather and my daddy
teaching me—I was listening to disco too, you know? And I kind of incorporated it into my sound; that's why people hear that funky sound, you know? It
works real good together. I don't want to be known just as a zydeco musician.
I want to be known as a musician."

Musicians like Rockin' Dopsie, Little Nathan, and Corey Ledet overlay
zydeco with country, rock, and contemporary pop, creating unpredictable
mélanges. Rock classics by the Who, Jimi Hendrix, and the Beatles take on an
entirely new personality when sung in French and embellished by accordions.
Since the early '90s, I've seen Dopsie do everything from Hank Williams to

hip hop, incorporating new indie sounds and pop songs with relentless eclecticism. Dopsie has few boundaries; those washboards can work with anything. For Carrier, however, crossover can only cross so far. "A lot of people are trying to do a crossover, but I don't like to go too far and get too mainstream. I want to keep the traditional sound, but I still want to incorporate some of the funkier sounds in my riffs. There's a line somewhere; don't cross over that border and get too far. You know what I'm saying? Get right where people say, 'Wow, that's a Chubby Carrier song' because you can hear the funky guitar riffs, you can hear the beat, but it's still Carrier carrying the tradition from his grandfather and his father."[72] That tradition, including the preservation of French language and customs, is incredibly important to musicians, who feel it is constantly under siege. The zydeco-Cajun community walks the same fine line as jazz musicians, creating new repertory and experimenting with modern trends while clinging to its heritage and guarding against the temptation to "go too far and get too mainstream." This balancing act evokes a subtle anxiety, keener with someone like Carrier and Ledet than with Dopsie and his Zydeco Twisters: "There's a line somewhere" not to be crossed, elusive and constantly redefined.

For the fiercest traditionalists, it was crossed long ago. "I'm very strict about what's happening in New Orleans," says Shannon Powell. "I take a lot of things, and I don't take a lot of things. I can't control a lot of things, but I'm very much into trying to keep the traditional style of New Orleans music alive, and I'm not having the help at all. I'm not having any help at all. I seem to be on the fringe. I'm really trying to keep this culture alive, but you know— time moves on. Time moves on."[73] There is a long pause before those last three words, which Powell utters with weary fatality, then repeats. The irony (as we have seen repeatedly) is that numerous NOLA musicians, young and old, traditional and modern, revere Powell, and go out of their way to get him in their gigs. If he's the fringe, it's one they want to get on.

Even the sternest traditionalists recognize the mandate of history—a new generation will always have its own agenda—and admit it grudgingly. "Younger players and groups like Rebirth have all the spirit of New Orleans," says Gregg Stafford. "And they play soulfully, but they have not been attempting to play the old music because they are so busy doing their own thing, so they haven't put forth a concerted effort to learn the old stuff. I think if they put forth some effort—even if they learn five or six songs—they can do it." I asked Stafford if the younger groups knew "Panama," a personal favorite of mine that he and his band had just played with blazing intensity. "No, I don't think they have even attempted it. The Hot 8 attempted it because Michael [White] was working with them. He tried to train them and get them interested. It's like anything else, the more you do it, the better you become at it." When I asked Stafford whether some of his gripes might be generational—even the earliest jazz players were accused of "messing up music"— he admitted, "Yes, it evolves. People come with new ideas, you know. Pops was experiencing the same thing with Dizzy and those guys who came over with the bebop. But New Orleans was still doing its thing because the culture was so different from anywhere else in the United States."[74] It still is, and a confluence of old and new is still what it's about. Bassist Richard Moten, a serene presence onstage or off, puts the critiques of White, Stafford, and others into perspective: "When Michael and Gregg talk, what they really mean is that they wish there were more traditional jazz bands, but we do have them. They still exist."[75]

More than ever, musicians insist on defining New Orleans tradition for themselves, and for many it lies in multiplicity. Aurora Nealand, a tireless experimenter, believes there's "a very vibrant creative music/improvising music scene in New Orleans" exemplified by the Open Ears series and the HIP festival, organizations that constantly expand what we think of as New Orleans music.[76] Keiko Komaki, keyboard player for the Brass-A-Holics, believes "there are no walls or barriers. I do jazz, blues, funk, hip hop—it's all one flavor." Her playing ripples serenely from Jelly Roll Morton and Professor Longhair to black Baptist and soul.[77] Singer-pianist Davell Crawford, who specializes in gospel and blues, welcomes the newness: "Musically, New Orleans will always be a thriving community of artists. Every time I come back there's new young brass band—guys on a new corner I didn't even know existed. Winston [Turner], who just formed the Brass-A-Holics, is a wonderful musician and a great person; he has such a passion for New Orleans and the music, the contemporary brass-band sound and the traditional. Right now that's what New Orleans is and is really what New Orleans has always been about; we hold onto tradition here, but it's also a very innovative sort of place when it comes to what we do with the tradition, how we move it forth. It's not a break, it's a continuation. Look at Trombone Shorty, look at Big Sam: they can sit and play 'Bugaloosa Strut' and 'Muskrat Ramble'—Trombone Shorty knows the whole song book. Many of the musicians here hold onto and value the traditions of the past, and then they put their own new life into it. I've tried to do a little of that with my music—not as much as I should have, perhaps."[78] The wistful note at the end is typical of Crawford, exemplifying a certain type of thoughtful eclecticist who frets about getting the balance between old and new just right, not allowing one to displace the other.

The youngest and most innovative musicians are often the ones most deeply tied to the tradition. Jon Batiste regards himself as "an educator and a humanitarian. Ultimately the purpose of any culture is to educate and teach the next generation about things of value we've already learned. So, for me, education is a key component in that and also humanitarianism, because, at the center of it, all comes from a place of deep love and truth. That's ultimately what guides me in everything I'm doing: trying to stay connected to the source of that. When people are creating and it resonates with other people, it takes so much from them that in a lot of ways, it *is* an act of love." The ideal models for young musicians, Batiste believes, are Trombone Shorty and Kermit Ruffins: "Yeah, man, Troy and I have grown up together. When I was fifteen, we had a band, Argo Nuevo. Now he tours every year nonstop. I learned a lot from being around him because he represents something in the contemporary generation that is very rare in that he grew up in the brass-band culture and took that Tremé brass-band aesthetic and then went to NOCCA and studied in a jazz context and figured out a way to take these influences and put them in a more accessible package in terms of his music and his presentation on stage and showmanship. For a lot of people who come from New Orleans, he's a very important figure to study: younger musicians coming up—I always encourage horn players to check him out, see what he's done with this different approach to the music that is basically traditional music of New Orleans. Kermit is interesting too. He came from the same era, that same brass-band culture—not that many people come from that anymore. Kermit is something rare."[79]

Musicians "coming up" also look to the Rebirth Brass Band, which has been showing the way since the '80s: "Yeah, Kermit was in the band then," says Phil Frazier. "Since the hurricane, there are more young people who appreciate the music. More people care about it, love it. Ain't that they didn't love it before, but now it's larger: they can't get enough of it." Do the new "nonindigenous" bands crowding into the city bother him? "Oh, no, no, I love all kinds of music. There's room for everybody." Is he a traditionalist or a modernist? "I'm both at the same time."[80] Rebirth is a template for how to blend tradition with newness. Musicians as different as James Evans and the Original Pinettes told me Rebirth was their chief inspiration. "People like Rebirth are doing the traditional thing," says Josh LeBlanc, "but they do it in a way that's . . . I hate to use the word, 'hip.' I'm a big Miles fan. Miles Davis is my top pop culture icon. I like how he made himself relevant but stayed true to himself. And that's what Rebirth does; they do it really well."[81]

There is no single template. For Shamarr Allen, even Rebirth was too confining. He began with the group, left to establish his own band, the Underdawgs ("Thank God I'm out of there!" he told me right after he left), and gradually moved from traditional jazz and brass band to something he can't

Shamarr Allen. Photograph by Jack Sullivan.

quite define. Allen can still do as gripping a version of "St. James Infirmary" as
anyone, and when he gigs with the tradition-oriented Treme Brass Band, he
blends in seamlessly, yet for the most part he's "so far away from traditional
jazz right now, it's ridiculous." The song he sang just before this interview was
"Happy Together" by the Turtles. It sounded to me like the Turtles reconfig-
ured as jazz, but he would have none of it: "The minute you see a trumpet,
you automatically assume it's going to be some type of jazz, but it's so far away
from that. If I didn't have a trumpet, what would you call that music? You
wouldn't call it jazz. This is another stereotype that I get from doing what I
do." Surely, I insisted, jazz doesn't disappear: you did have a trumpet, and you
did play jazz-inflected riffs. After reflecting on the question, he said, "I guess
there are still elements of jazz, but you can't call it that because there's not
enough of it. You can't call it rock because it's not rock, you can't call it hip
hop because it's not hip hop—but it has elements of all of that in it. It's just
my personal view on it." So what would he call it? "I don't know what to call it,
man, that's the crazy part about it—which is good, all of those elements I use.
It's everything that has to do with New Orleans music." So it's "New Orleans
music," the term so many musicians actually prefer? "No. It's not New Orleans
music, it's the *new* New Orleans music. New Orleans created all American
music: you've got jazz, the older guys who created jazz here—Sidney Bechet,
Louis Armstrong, all the music of that era; David Bartholomew, Fats Domino—the rock music of that time. It evolved into Aerosmith, the Beatles, and

the Rolling Stones, those guys were the pioneers of that music, you know what I'm saying? You have people like the Meters, the Neville Brothers, they created a sound, funky, funky, funky—and all of it came from here. Right now there is another whole generation of musicians changing everything about New Orleans music. New Orleans is so different from the rest of the world. You can't describe it to somebody. You have to see it in order to understand it."[82]

Given the city's tumultuous eclecticism, it is more important than ever, says David Torkanowsky, to forge a personal style: "If you're trying to play, find your own voice. It's one thing to acquire the vocabulary by transcribing and imitating and impersonating players, but it's important to find your own voice. You never know where that voice is going to come from or how it's going to present itself. Nicholas Payton said jazz stopped being cool in 1959; there are many layers of truth to that, but in contemporary American music there are no boundaries. You can play whatever it is you want to play, and the demise of the record business means you must make it your personal mission to connect with the common man. It puts more pressure on you economically and spiritually." So you can't unload on the record companies anymore? "That's right. You can't blame it on the record companies: it's just you."[83]

Davell Crawford also feels a certain liberation in the decline of record companies. His searing vocals and explosive pianism resist confinement: "I'm so glad to be alive at this time in our history because I like so many things. Gospel has inspired me so much, and classical, country, funk, and R&B. Record companies, when I was a child, told me I was not focused enough. They told me that, and I said *you're* not focused enough; I'm focused: I like everything—so you're not focused on what the hell I'm not focused on. It's your job as a record company to focus yourselves and market me as an artist that will try and do everything. And there's a market for that, especially now. Most of these guys are in charge of their own careers now; they have a little bit more say-so, and they're musicians, and a musician such as Stevie Wonder, Prince, Ray Charles, Aretha, Donny Hathaway, Johnny Guitar—every now and then the industry has let a musician grow, but for the most part, the music industry and the media have stifled a lot of that because you put out one record, your first, and they want you to remain there for the next sixty years. Well, hell, I change my clothes every day—I'm a few pounds bigger or lighter. God has given us this great earth to experience and to love and enjoy all the gifts, but the greatest gift is the ability to learn, to learn and grow, and so that's what we have to do with the arts.[84]

Openness to all types of music is becoming the rule rather than the exception, but it was not always easy to be a Jon Batiste. Batiste's mentor, Donald Harrison, embraced eclecticism early in the game and regards it as an important part of his legacy: "I am exploring all the possibilities that I can with the sound of many types of music and have been doing that since the 80s. I taught my students all kinds of music never taught them to have musical prejudice as many music teachers tried to teach me. I figure if you learn as much as possible, then you have the option of choosing what you want to do with music."[85]

Pianist Jeff Franzel, who has written songs for everyone from Shawn Colvin to Placido Domingo, also has an expansive view. Grounded in jazz, he gobbles up other idioms while maintaining a consistent style. In the French Quarter during the '70s, he learned a bit of everything, with jazz at the center: "The French Quarter was hopping: jazz trios, pop groups, Cajun, great musicians—not big names, just people who were local—but there was plenty of jazz; it was very jazzy in that time. On Bourbon Street, there was so much music going on all the time." Although Franzel prefers the rhythm and "greater harmonic freedom" of jazz, he writes and plays pop as well, which allows him to make a comfortable living around the world. "I want my music to be widely appreciated, and economically as well. I've finally found a balance. Many jazz players can't write pop music. They're not able to cross over. I think there's a real art to it. I put a lot of my heart into pop as well as jazz. It's not about selling out or dumbing down, it's about the beauty of writing a simple song. John Houston said, 'The hardest thing is being simple.' There is a simplicity to pop music. The common denominator to all these styles is putting your own voice into every idiom that you're doing. It's like what you do as a writer: it has to be from your perspective rather than copied. That's the key."[86]

Many younger musicians look to the internet for new possibilities. Jon Batiste believes that the story this book tells could only have happened in New Orleans, and that technology is making the rest of the world catch up to what the Crescent City always was. "The internet is in a lot of ways making the world become what New Orleans was at the turn of the century. New Orleans was the global city, a global port city where everything was coming together, a confluence of cultures, and you have it now in the world for the first time; we're more connected than ever in the sense that you can press a button and talk to someone in Japan; you can know what's happening in your neighborhood or on videos across the world; you have streaming, social media, and people are just now figuring out how to embrace it and how to accommodate all this connectivity—and what is the music coming from that going to sound like? What's going to happen because of this?"[87]

It's a world Batiste and his younger colleagues embrace, but "all this connectivity" makes it harder to create new repertory standards. "The way music is spread around is very different from the way Irving Berlin's stuff was spread around," says Antoine Diel. "It was easier back then because there was a limited style. People would write for musical theater, then Frank Sinatra or Barbra Streisand would pick that up and make it famous, and then it became a standard. Now there are so many different kinds of music—younger folks look at something and say, 'I like that song, it's kind of a rock 'n' roll song, but let me try and change it and make it more of a jazz tune.' It's harder to spread that around. There isn't that one thing everybody looks at and goes, 'Oh! Look what they're doing! Let's put our stamp on that song!' It's harder to find those songs."[88]

Tom McDermott shares Diel's worries about the lack of new standards, but he is also full of optimism: "There might be fewer clubs than before Katrina, but the core elements—brass bands, gospel choirs, Mardi Gras Indians marching bands—are very much in place. And *Treme* really raised the visibility of all that. Just today I was walking down Frenchmen Street, and there was a new trad jazz band called Up Up Up and Go, all twenty-year-olds and thirty-year-olds. I've sat in with the Shotgun Jazz Band—I really like them. They do traditional repertory, but off the beaten path. I'm very open-minded about that type of thing; I try not to be critical about younger players who play it not exactly like the recording or play notes outside what the players from the '30s would have played or mess around with the arrangement in whatever way they care to. I find that a very healthy thing. But there are some very puritanical guys, especially older guys who feel threatened, who made their whole life playing—but they get good gigs. I consider myself one of these older guys. We do get good gigs because we've been around for thirty years; on the other hand, these twenty- and thirty-year-old bands are drawing in other twenty- and thirty-year-olds. They want to see their own tribe. That's what *they* want."[89]

Even the strictest traditionalists often express a keen sense of realism about the reality of change. In his evocative memoir, *Song for My Fathers*, clarinetist Tom Sancton expresses regret about the passing of "the mens" (the old Preservation Hall generation) and what they represent, but his tone is one of equanimity rather than bitterness: "Out on the street, vibrant young groups like the Dirty Dozen and the Rebirth Brass Band have transformed the old marching-band tradition, with its proud uniforms and harmonized voicings and regimental grace, into a brasher, funkier sound. They bear little resemblance to their predecessors—apart from their exuberance and the unmistakable New Orleans beat that underpins their music and delights new generations of second-liners. And that's okay. As much as I regret the passing of the old guard, I know that a living culture must be in tune with its times. Only a fool could expect a musical tradition rooted in the late nineteenth century, tempered by the Jim Crow era and the hardscrabble Depression years, to survive intact into the twenty-first century. Yet something still survives."[90]

A majority of the musicians covered in this book are not threatened by the challenge of the new. "There are a lot of young cats playing their butts off," says Kermit Ruffins, his big eyes beaming, "especially at NOCCA and in the high schools. They're playing brass-band music, and they're writing music, and they're studying the way music is supposed to be played for its chord changes and *all* that good stuff. So it's a big scene in the city right now. I mean it's hundreds of kids whippin' my butt right now. It's the truth!"[91]

Some of the most seasoned words on the scene come from Germaine Bazzle, who has been around long enough to comment on several scenes: "The New Orleans music scene is coming back, it's coming back in the way I knew it to be. I'm proud of the young people who are doing this because so many of us are leaving. Many of the great musicians have passed on, and we're looking to the young people to keep it going. I'm hoping that they will always remember us and what we shared, and keep the spirit. Some of them are still exploring, but the interest is there. They are still doing the traditional music, but bringing their own concepts to it, being creative, not just playing things as they've heard them before, but expressing themselves through that. They're keeping the spirit, but keeping their minds open and developing it even more. I think they're very serious. We've got Big Sam, the Hot 8, Troy Andrews, the Pinettes, so many others. We have many more women now playing brass instruments, making a statement that's very empowering. It's young people who are doing all this: taking the tradition and moving it forward."

Bazzle dismisses the grumbles about a lack of authenticity, but not in a hostile way. Her commentary has a commanding objectivity, like the jazz version of a Greek chorus: she's been there before. "There are always going to be people who complain or see a negative side, but that's the way things go, that's the way things grow. They said the same things about me when I was younger. I don't put down what they're doing, because this is their concept of traditional music." Bazzle believes the process is not linear; one can begin with the new, then discover the old, a pattern we have seen with Wynton Marsalis and Kermit Ruffins, and which continues with younger groups: "I don't think we should try to stifle that because sooner or later they will discover something else about traditional music. As long as you're performing, you're always discovering something new, and maybe they'll go back to the standards, to Cole Porter or Gershwin, and say, 'All of these things we've been doing all along, we can now apply it to this.' Every generation has its own impact. I've always done what I'm doing now. I came up at a time during Ella Fitzgerald, Sarah Vaughan, Betty Carter, June Christy, Chris Connor—those were the vocalists that influenced me. I liked the other music, but I wasn't comfortable with it. I could not feel free with it, whereas with this, the door was open. I understand what they are saying about the young people, but I still say, 'Give them a chance. Give them a chance.'"[92]

The new generation is going to do its thing whether the older gives them a chance or not. The essence of a great city is its embrace of innovation, even if the embrace is a reluctant one. New Orleans always moves forward even as it holds tightly onto its ancestors. "The balance between tradition and innovation is always going to be the focal point in New Orleans music," says Bruce Raeburn. "You can't have exclusively one or the other. You always have to have a nexus of tradition and innovation. That's where the surprises are."[93] And surprises are the essence of New Orleans, every day, every gig.

NOTES

INTRODUCTION

1. Thomas W. Jacobsen, *The New Orleans Jazz Scene, 1970–2000* (Lafayette: Louisiana State University Press, 2014), 96.

2. Jason Marsalis, interview with the author, January 10, 2016.

3. Bruce Boyd Raeburn, *New Orleans Style and the Writing of American Jazz History* (Ann Arbor: University of Michigan Press, 2009).

4. Leroy Jones, interview with the author, January 11, 2015.

5. Chris Edmunds, interview with the author, January 20, 2009

6. Jon Cleary, interview with the author, June 24, 2014.

7. Charlie Miller, interview with the author, June 24, 2014.

8. Bruce Raeburn, interview with the author, April 18, 2014.

9. Quoted in Burt Feintuch, *Talking New Orleans Music* (Jackson: University Press of Mississippi, 2015), 54.

10. Quoted in Jason Berry, Jonathan Foose, and Tad Jones, *Up from the Cradle of Jazz: New Orleans Music since World War II* (Lafayette: University of Louisiana at Lafayette Press, 1986; rpt. 2009), 323.

11. Leroy Jones, interview with the author, January 11, 2015.

12. Feintuch, *Talking New Orleans Music*, 93.

13. Chris Edmunds, interview with the author, January 20, 2009

14. Jonathan Foose, Tad Jones, interview with Dave Bartholomew, October 23, 1981, Hogan Jazz Archive.

15. Allen Toussaint, interview with the author, August 8, 2015.

16. Ben Sandmel, interview with Eddie Bo, December 19, 1981, Hogan Jazz Archive.

17. Eddie Bo, remarks made at the Conference on Black Music Research, April 19, 2008.

18. John Boutte, interview with the author, June 23, 2014.

19. Henry Kmen, *Music in New Orleans: The Formative Years, 1791–1841* (Baton Rouge: Louisiana State University Press, 1966), 245

20. Connie Atkinson, "Louis Armstrong and the Image of New Orleans," in Reinhold Wagnleitner, ed., *Satchmo Meets Amadeus* (Innsbruck, Austria: Studien Verlag, 2007), 49.

21. Berry, Foose, and Jones, *Up from the Cradle of Jazz*, 11.

22. Michael G. White, "The New Orleans Brass Band: A Cultural Tradition," in Ferdinand Jones and Arthur C. Jones, eds., *The Triumph of the Soul: Cultural and Psychological Aspects of African American Music* (Westport, CT: Praeger, 2001), 95.

23. Todd Duke, interview with the author, January 12, 2012.

24. Chris Edmunds, interview with the author, January 20, 2009

25. Barry Martyn, interview with the author, March 17, 2015.

26. Jesse Serwer, "New Galactic Album is a Taste of Classic New Orleans," *Washington Post*, February 6, 2010.

27. John Boutte, interview with the author, July 21, 2013; "Memorable Jazz Quotes: Rate Your Music," http://rateyourmusic.com/list/Count5/memorable_jazz_quotes/.

28. Quoted in Richard Scheinin, "A+E Interactive: The Complete Nicholas Payton," October 4, 2013.

29. Interview with the author.

30. Billy Collins, "Seventy-Five Needles in the Haystack of Poetry," *The Best American Poetry, 2006* (New York: Scribner, 2006), 23.

31. Victor Goines, interview with the author, November 14, 2014.

32. Lucia Micarelli, correspondence with the author, October 14, 2014.

CHAPTER ONE

1. Barry Martyn, interview with Olivia Cook, August 30, 1999, Hogan Jazz Archive, video.

2. Antoine Reynaldo Diel, interview with the author, March 19, 2015.

3. Jon Batiste, interview with the author, Mardi Gras Day, 2015.

4. John Boutte, interview with the author, June 23, 2014.

5. John Gros, interview with the author, February 5, 2013.

6. Ellis Marsalis, interview with the author, November 14, 2014.

7. Allen Toussaint, interview with the author, August 8, 2015.

8. John Boutte, interview with the author, July 21, 2013.

9. John Boutte, interview with the author, June 23, 2014.

10. John Batiste, interview with the author, Mardi Gras Day, 2015.

11. S. Frederick Starr, "Amadeus and Satchmo," in Wagnleitner, ed., *Satchmo Meets Amadeus*, 49.

12. Terry Teachout, *Pops: A Life of Louis Armstong* (New York: Houghton Mifflin Harcourt, 2009), 9, 13, 14.

13. Joshua Berrett, "Louis Armstrong and Opera," *Musical Quarterly* 76/2 (summer 1992), 226–41.

14. Barry Martyn, interview with the author, March 17, 2015.

15. Quoted in Carolyn Kolb, "A City of Great Voices," *New Orleans Magazine*, June 2012, online.

16. Charles E. Kinzer, "The Tios of New Orleans and Their Pedagogical Influence on the Early Jazz Clarinet Style," *Black Music Research Journal* (Fall 1996), 280.

17. Jack Belsom, *Opera in New Orleans* (New Orleans, 1993). I am deeply indebted to Jack Belsom for his exhaustive knowledge, both in his book and in conversations and correspondences with him over a twenty-year period.

18. Jack Belsom, *The American Record Guide* (March/April 2015), 44.

19. Renée Fleming, in conversation with André Previn, "A Streetcar Named Desire," March 7, 2013, Carnegie Hall video, YouTube.

20. Jack Belsom, *Opera* (August 2006), 959.

21. Bruce Boyd Raeburn, "Beyond the Spanish Tinge," in Luca Cerchiari, Laurent Cugny, Franz Kerschbaumer, eds., *Eurojazzland* (Lebanon, NH: Northeastern University Press, 2012), 22.

22. Joshua Berrett, "Louis Armstrong and Opera," *Musical Quarterly* 76/2 (summer 1992), 226–41.

23. For additional information on Paoletti and the "Milano Conservatory," see Bruce Raeburn, "Stars of David and Sons of Sicily," *Jazz Perspectives* (August 2009), 136, 143.

24. Jon Batiste, interview with the author, Mardi Gras Day, 2015.

25. Jack Sullivan, *New World Symphonies: How American Culture Changed European Music* (New Haven, CT: Yale University Press, 1999), 196–98.

26. Louis Moreau Gottschalk, *Notes of a Pianist* (1881; rpt. Princeton: Princeton University Press, 2006), 99.

27. Francois Lesure and Richard Langham-Smith, eds., *Debussy on Music* (New York: Knopf, 1977), 278, 275, 323.

28. Cited in Dean Alger, *Encyclopedia of Jazz Musicians*, Jazz.com,

29. Kim Kowalke, ed., *A New Orpheus* (New Haven, CT: Yale University Press, 1986), 331.

30. Paul Rosenfeld, *Musical Impressions* (New York: Hill and Wang, 1969), 221–22.

31. Cited in Arbie Ornstein, ed., *A Ravel Reader* (New York: Columbia University Press, 1990), 390, 472.

32. Cited in Vera Stravinsky and Robert Craft, *Stravinsky in Pictures and Documents* (New York: Simon & Schuster, 1978), 203.

33. Constant Lambert, *Music Ho!* (1934; rpt. New York: October House, 1967), 177–99.

34. Teachout, *Pops*, 13.

35. Leroy Jones, interview with the author, January 11, 2015.

36. Teachout, *Pops*, 9.

37. Donald Harrison, interview with the author, March 8, 2016.

38. Tom McDermott, interview with the author, March 19, 2015.

CHAPTER TWO

1. Phil Frazier, interview with the author, July 29, 2013.

2. Kermit Ruffins, interview with the author, January 5, 2011.

3. Quoted in Mick Burns, *Keeping the Beat on the Street* (Baton Rouge: Louisiana State University Press, 2006), 109–110.

4. Keith Anderson, interview with Katja Toivola, January 23, 2002, Hogan Jazz Archive.

5. Quoted in Burns, *Keeping the Beat*, 112.

6. Keith Anderson, interview, Hogan Jazz Archive.

7. Phil Frazier, interview with the author, January 7, 2015.

8. Phil Frazier, interview with the author, July 29, 2013.

9. Matt Sakakeeny, "New Orleans Music as a Circulatory System," *Black Music Research Journal* 31/2 (Fall 2011), 28.

10. *Satchmo the Great*, CBS television documentary, 1956.

11. Keith Anderson, Hogan Jazz Archive.

12. Ned Sublette, *The World That Made New Orleans* (Chicago: Chicago Review Press, 2008), 110.

13. Quoted in Joseph Roach, *Cities of the Dead* (New York: Columbia University Press, 1996), 61–62.

14. Matt Sakakeeny, *Roll With It: Brass Bands in the Streets of New Orleans* (Durham, NC: Duke University Press, 2013), 167.

15. Roach, *Cities*, 61–62.

16. Quoted in Sakakeeny, *Roll With It*, 167,

17. Leroy Jones, interview with the author, March 22, 2011.

18. Quoted in Geraldine Wyckoff, "Meet Me At the Second Line," *Offbeat* (September 2012), 24.

19. Phil Frazier, interview with the author, July 29, 2013.

20. Christie Jordain, interview with the author, March 13, 2015.

21. James Evans, interview with the author, April 18, 2011.

22. John Boutte, interview with the author, June 23, 2014.

23. Michael White, interview with Danny Barker, January 1995, Hogan Jazz Archive.

24. Shannon Powell, interview with Stanton Moore and Paul Siegel, September 9, 2011, YouTube.

25. Gregg Stafford, interview with the author, January 7, 2015.

26. Michael White, interview with Danny Barker, 1995, Hogan Jazz Archive.

27. Sakakeeny, *Roll With It*, 117.

28. Quoted in Burns, *Keeping the Beat*, 109.

29. Victor Goines, interview with the author, November 14, 2014.

30. Christie Jordain, interview with the author, March 13, 2015.

31. Quoted in Burns, *Keeping the Beat*, 17.

32. Richard Rochester, interview with the author, January 5, 1995.

33. David Hood, interview with the author, August 8, 2013.

34. Quoted in Samuel Charters, *Playing a Jazz Chorus* (London: Marion Boyars, 2006), 212.

35. Leroy Jones, correspondence with the author, August 23, 2011.

36. Gregg Stafford, interview with the author, January 5, 2015.

37. Quoted in Burns, *Keeping the Beat*, 171–72.

38. Phil Frazier, interview with the author, July 2013.

39. Ellis Marsalis, interview with the author, November 14, 2014.

40. Christie Jordain, interview with the author, March 13, 2015.

41. Veronique Dorsey and Christie Jordain, interview with the author, March 13, 2015

42. Jon Batiste, interview with the author, Mardi Gras Day, 2015.

43. Leroy Jones, correspondence with the author, August 8, 2011.

44. White, "The Brass Band Tradition in New Orleans," 91–92.

45. Michael White, interview with the author, January 1, 2014.

46. Victor Goines, interview with the author, November 14, 2014.

47. Gregg Stafford, interview with Katja Toivola, November 24, 2000, Hogan Jazz Archive.

48. Gregg Stafford, interview with the author, December 26, 2013.

49. Barry Martyn, interview with the author, March 17, 2015.

50. Christie Jordain, interview with the author, March 13, 2015.

51. Shamarr Allen, interview with the author, October 25, 2013.

52. Burns, *Keeping the Beat*, 11.

53. Robin Clabby, interview with the author, October 25, 2013.

CHAPTER THREE

1. "Jass and Jassism," *Times-Picayune*, June 20, 1918, 4.

2. Wendell Brunious, interview with the author, March 17, 2015.

3. Barry Martyn, interview with the author, March 17, 2015.

4. Jon Batiste, interview with the author, Mardi Gras Day, 2015.

5. Jeff Franzel, interview with the author, April 24, 2015

6. Johnny Vidacovich, "Secrets of Second Line Drumming," October 30, 2013, www.creseentcymbals.com.

7. Shannon Powell, interview with the author, January 9, 2016.

8. Cited in Homer N. Bartlett, "First of American Pianists to Gain Recognition Abroad," *Musical America*, January 30, 1915, online.

9. "A Candid conversation with Delfeayo Marsalis," October 18, 2013, irockjazzmusictv, YouTube.

10. Earl Palmer interview, November 7, 1981, Hogan Jazz Archive.

11. Lawrence Sieberth, interview with the author, June 23, 2014.

12. John Boutte, interview with the author, July 21, 2013.

13. Germaine Bazzle, interview with the author, March 16, 2015.

14. Thomas Fiehrer, "From Quadrille to Stomp: The Creole Origins of Jazz," *Popular Music* (January 1991), 23

15. Lawrence Gushee, "Nineteenth Century Origins of Jazz," *Black Music Research Journal*, vol. 22 (2002), 153, 163.

16. Barry Martyn, interview with the author, March 17, 2015.

17. Cornel West, interview with the author, March 2, 1992.

18. White, "The Brass Band Tradition," 91, 77.

19. See especially Lawrence Gushee, "Nineteenth Century Origins of Jazz"; Bruce Boyd Raeburn, "Stars of David and Sons of Sicily," *Jazz Perspectives* (August 2009).

20. Wynton Marsalis, lecture delivered at Harvard University, January 9, 2014.

21. Jon Batiste, interview with the author, Mardi Gras Day, 2015.

22. John Boutte, interview with the author, July 21, 2013.

23. Bruce Raeburn, foreword, Sally Newhart, *The Original Tuxedo Jazz Band* (Charleston, SC: History Press, 2013), 9.

24. Raeburn, foreword, 10.

25. Gregg Stafford, interview with the author, January 7, 2015.

26. Kermit Ruffins, interview with the author, January 9, 2008.

27. Leroy Jones, correspondence with the author, July 19, 2014.

28. Ben Sandmel, *Ernie K-Doe: The R&B Emperor of New Orleans* (New Orleans: Historic New Orleans Connection, 2012), 42–44. This book offers not only an excellent biography of K-Doe, but astute coverage of the NOLA R&B scene.

29. Tom McDermott, interview with the author, July 3, 2013.

30. Richard Moten, interview with the author, January 15, 2014.

31. Lars Edegran, interview with the author, January 20, 2014.

32. Paul Longstreth, interview with the author, January 12, 2014.

33. Eric Bloom, interview with the author, August 21, 2015.

34. Barry Martyn, interview with the author, March 17, 2015.

35. Tom Fischer, interview with the author, January 11, 2015.

36. Katja Toivola, interview with the author, June 25, 2014.

37. Marla and John Dixon, interview with the author, March 14, 2015.

38. Jack Fine, interview with the author, January 16, 2014.

39. John Boutte, interview with the author, June 23, 2014.

40. Jason Marsalis, interview with the author, January 14, 2013.

41. Ben Ratliff, *Coltrane* (New York: Picador, 2008), 208.

42. Ellis Marsalis, interview with the author, November 14, 2014.

43. Bruce Raeburn, interview with the author, February 23, 2013.

44. Leroy Jones, interview with the author, January 10, 2015.

45. Katja Toivola, interview with the author, January 8, 2015.

46. Victor Goines, interview with the author, November 14, 2014.

47. Charters, *Playing a Jazz Chorus*, 62.

48. Tom McDermott, interview with the author, July 3, 2014.

49. White, "The Brass Band Tradition in New Orleans," 92.

50. Michael White, interview with the author, April 9, 2008.

51. Michael White, interview with the author, October 25, 2013.

52. Feintuch, *Talking New Orleans Music*, 46.

53. Evan Christopher, interview with Floyd Levin, October 23, 1993, Hogan Jazz Archive.

54. Lolis Eric Elie, "An Interview with Wynton Marsalis," *Callaloo* 13/2 (Spring 1990), 284.

55. Ivan Hewitt, "Interview with Wynton Marsalis," *Telegraph*, July 5, 2012, online.

56. Malcom X. Abram, "Marsalis to Lead Lincoln Center Orchestra at Akron Civic," *Akron Beacon Journal*, June 14, 2013, Ohio.com.

57. Howard Mandell, "Wynton Marsalis, Musician of the Year," *Musical America Directory*, 2004, 14.

58. Wynton Marsalis, interview with the author, December 7, 2004.

59. David Torkanowsky, interview with the author, March 9, 2015.

60. Barry Martyn, interview with the author, March 17, 2015.

61. Jason Berry, "Doc Paulin's Long Goodbye," *Gambit*, December 4, 2007, online.

62. Geraldine Wyckoff, "Meet Me at the Second Line," *Offbeat* (September 2012), 2.

63. Les Getrex, interview with the author, May 13, 2006.

64. Christie Jordain, interview with the author, March 13, 2015.

65. Chris Edmunds, interview with the author, January 20, 2009.

66. Roland Guerin, interview with the author, April 20, 2014.

67. Ellis Marsalis, interview with the author, November 14, 2014.

68. Tom McDermott, interview with the author, March 19, 2015.

69. Ellis Marsalis, interview with the author, November 14, 2014.

70. Robin Clabby, interview with the author, January 11, 2014.

71. Feintuch, *Talking New Orleans Music*, 76.

72. John Blanchard, interview with the author, January 9, 2009.

73. Bruce Raeburn, interview with the author, October 24, 2013.

74. Victor Goines, interview with the author, November 11, 2014.

75. Leroy Jones, correspondence with the author, March 3, 2013.

76. Jon Cleary, interview with the author, June 24, 2014.

77. Yolanda Windsay, interview with the author, January 15, 2014.

78. John Boutte, interview with the author, July 21, 2013.

79. Scheinin, "A+E Interactive."

80. Chris Edmunds, interview with the author, January 20, 2009.

81. Lucien Barbarin, interview with the author, January 15, 2012.

82. Lionel Ferbos, interview with Richard B. Allen, August 3, 1964, Hogan Jazz Archive.

83. Bruce Raeburn, interview with the author, September 26, 2013.

84. Eric Bloom, interview with the author, August 21, 2015.

85. Elliot Hoffman, program annotation, Preservation Hall Jazz Band, vol. 4, Sony, 1988, 4.

86. Leroy Jones, January 28, 2001, Hogan Jazz Archive.

87. Joseph Irrera, interview with the author, July 16, 2013.

88. Alan Light, "Band's Goal: Keep History and Make It," *New York Times*, July 6, 2013, C1.

89. Bruce Raeburn, interview with the author, October 24, 2013.

90. Quoted in Roger Hahn, "Pres Hall 2.0," *Offbeat* (May 2013), 58.

91. Mark Braud, interview with the author, January 20, 2014.

92. James Evans, interview with the author, January 17, 2014.

93. David Torkanowsky, interview with the author, March 9, 2015.

94. Jon Batiste, interview with the author, Mardi Grs Day, 2015.

95. Jon Cleary, interview with the author, June 24, 2014.

96. Wendell Brunious, interview with the author, March 17, 2015.

97. Richard Moten, interview with the author, June 25, 2014.

98. John Boutte, interview with the author, June 23, 2014.

99. John Gros, interview with the author, February 3, 2015
100. Shannon Powell, interview with the author, April 20, 2014.
101. John Boutte, interview with the author, June 23, 2014.
102. Katja Toivola, interview with the author, June 25, 2014.
103. Tom Fischer, interview with the author, January 7, 2015.
104. Victor Goines, interview with the author, November 14, 2014.
105. Lawrence Sieberth, interview with the author, May 19, 2014.
106. James Evans, interview with the author, January 17, 2014.
107. Leroy Jones, interview with the author, January 11, 2015.

CHAPTER FOUR

1. Leroy Jones, January 28, 2001, Hogan Jazz Archive.
2. Les Getrex, interview with the author.
3. Quoted in Larry Blumenfeld, "At Jazz Standard, New Orleans' Loss is New York's Gain," *Wall Street Journal*, November 2, 2011.
4. John Boutte, interview with the author, March 15, 2015.
5. Allen Toussaint, interview with the author, August 8, 2015.
6. Quoted in Feintuch, *Talking New Orleans Music*, 62.
7. Aurora Nealand, interview with the author, January 11, 2016.
8. Meghan Swartz, interview with the author, January 10, 2015.
9. Donald Harrison, interview with the author, March 8, 2016.
10. Stoogis Brass Band, interview with the author, January 10, 2016.
11. Tom Sancton, interview with the author, January 7, 2015.
12. John Boutte, interview with the author, March 14, 2015.
13. Joachim Berendt, *The Jazz Book, From New Orleans to Rock and Free Jazz* (revised edition, New York: L. Hill, 1975), 131.
14. Eric Bloom, interview with the author.
15. Jeff Franzel, interview with the author, December 23, 2015.
16. Chadrick Honore, interview with the author, January 6, 2016.
17. Phil Frazier, interview with the author, January 7, 2015.
18. Burns, *Keeping the Beat*, 14.
19. See, for example, James Lincoln Collier, *Jazz: The American Theme Song* (Oxford: Oxford University Press, 1993), 30.
20. Neville Brothers, interview with Robert Palmer, circa 1990s, Hogan Jazz Archive.
21. Interview with Earl Turbinton, September 1, 1990, Hogan Jazz Archive.
22. James Drew, interview with Jason Berry, January 4, 1982, Hogan Jazz Archive.
23. Cited in Keith Spera, obituary for Earl Turbinton, *Times-Picayune*, August 8, 2007, online.
24. Richard Motin, interview with the author, January 17, 2014.
25. James Evans, interview with the author, April 14, 2014.
26. Robin Clabby, interview with the author, October 25, 2013.
27. Jason Marsalis, interview with the author, January 10, 2016.
28. *Icons Among Us*, dir. Michael Rivoira, Lars Larson, and Peter J. Vogt, 2009.

CHAPTER FIVE

1. Teachout, *Pops*, 6, 280.

2. Quoted in Dave Gelly, *Being Prez: The Life and Music of Lester Young* (New York: Oxford University Press, 2007), 119.

3. Tom McDermott, interview with the author, July 3, 2013.

4. Jon Batiste, interview with the author, Mardi Gras Day 2015.

5. Tom Fischer, interview with the author, January 7, 2015.

6. Katja Toivola, interview with the author, June 25, 2014.

7. Wendell Brunious, interview with the author, March 14, 2015.

8. John Gros, interview with the author, March 17, 2015.

9. Irvin Mayfield, interview with the author, March 19, 2015.

10. Henry Butler, interview with the author, January 1, 2010.

11. John Boutte, interview with the author, June 23, 2014.

12. Danny Barker, interview with Michael White, Hogan Jazz Archive.

13. Herlin Riley, interview with the author, November 14, 2014.

14. Professor Longhair, interview with Shepard Samuels, Alison Miner Kaslow, fall 1978, Hogan Jazz Archive.

15. Keith Anderson, Hogan Jazz Archive.

16. Kermit Ruffins, interview with Katja Toivola, January 22, 2002, Hogan Jazz Archive.

17. Elie, "An Interview with Wynton Marsalis," 285, 286.

18. Gregg Stafford, interview with the author, December 26, 2013.

19. Charters, *Playing a Jazz Chorus*, 154.

20. Quoted in Brett Milano, "Simple Lessons," *Offbeat* (June 2015), 33.

21. Quoted in Scheinin, *A+E Interactive*.

22. Interview, Beausoleil Live at Johnny D's, October 17, 2007, Hogan Jazz Archive.

23. James Evans, interview with the author, January 17, 2014.

24. John Boutte, interview with the author, July 21, 2013.

25. Quoted in Adam Schatz, "Bird," *New York Review of Books*, November 7, 2013, 71.

26. Interview with the author, July 21, 2013.

27. Danny Barker, interview with Michael White, 1995, Hogan Jazz Archive.

28. Barry Martyn, interview with the author, March 17, 2015.

29. Leroy Jones, interview with the author, January 11, 2015.

30. Katja Toivola, interview with the author, June 25, 2014.

31. Herlin Riley, interview with the author, January 15, 2015.

32. Samuel Charters, *A Trumpet around the Corner* (Jackson: University Press of Mississippi 2008), 338. For more information on *Jazzmen* and the jazz schism, see Raeburn, *New Orleans Style and the Writing of American Jazz History*.

33. David Torkanowsky, interview with the author, March 19, 2015.

34. Katja Toivola, interview with the author, June 25, 2014.

35. Herlin Riley, interview with the author, November 14, 2014.

36. Lawrence Sieberth, interview with the author, June 22, 2014.

37. Eddie Bo, interview with Ben Sandmel, December 19, 1981, Hogan Jazz Archive.

38. Keith Frazier, interview with the author, July 29, 2011.

39. Phil Frazier, interview with the author, January 7, 2015.

40. Troy Andrews, interview with the author, January 14, 2010.

CHAPTER SIX

1. "Queen B: Portrait of Littdell Banister," Hogan Jazz Archive, video.

2. Quoted in Feintuch, *Talking New Orleans Music*, 51–2.

3. Donald Harrison, interview with the author, March 8, 2016.

4. John Sinclair, "They Call Us Wild: The Mardi Gras Indians of New Orleans," *Offbeat* (July 1, 1988).

5. Jon Batiste, interview with the author, February 17, 2016.

6. Allen Toussaint, interview with the author, August 18, 2014.

7. Donald Harrison, interview with the author, March 8, 2016.

8. John Gros, interview with the author, February 3, 2015.

9. John Gros, interview with Abigail Lucas, December 2014, Vimeo, video.

10. Quoted in Geraldine Wyckoff, "The Song Remains the Same?" *Offbeat* (February 2013), 20.

11. Allen Toussaint, interview with the author, August 18, 2014.

12. Lawrence Sieberth, interview with the author, January 6, 2015.

13. Quoted in Jeff Hanusch, "James 'Sugar Boy' Crawford," *Offbeat* (February 1, 2002), online.

14. Bruce Raeburn, interview with the author, September 26, 2013.

15. Bruce Raeburn, interview with the author, April 18, 2014.

16. Robert Silvers, conversation with the author, March 15, 2015.

17. Neville Brothers, interviewed by Robert Palmer, circa 1980s, Hogan Jazz Archive.

18. Quoted in Geraldine Wyckoff, "A Decidedly Different Drummer," *Offbeat* (August 1, 2005).

19. Eddie Bo, interview with Ben Sandmel and Jonathan Foose, February 19, 1981, Hogan Jazz Archive.

20. Danny Barker, interview with Michael White, February 23, 1995, Hogan Jazz Archive.

21. Bruce Raeburn, correspondence with the author, April 27, 2015.

22. Clarke Peters, interview with the author, August 10, 2014.

23. Dave Bartholomew, interview with Jonathan Foose and Tad Jones, October 23, 1981, Hogan Jazz Archive.

24. Allen Toussaint, interview with Robert Palmer, 1987, Hogan Jazz Archive.

25. James Evans, interview with the author, April 14, 2014.

26. Neville Brothers, interview with Robert Palmer, Hogan Jazz Archive.

27. Don Snowden, CD annotation, "A History of the Neville Brothers," Disc 2, Rhino Records, 1988.

28. George Porter Jr., interview with Brian Turk, *Offbeat*, June 1, 2014, online.

29. Neville Brothers, interview with Robert Palmer.

30. Bruce Raeburn, interview with the author, April 18, 2014.

31. Bruce Raeburn, interview with the author, March 18, 2015.

32. John Lewis, "Shock of the New," *Guardian*, March 1, 2007, online.

33. Rich Paul Cooper, "Bouncin Straight Out the Dirty Dirty: Community and Dance in New Orleans Rap," in Mickey Hess, ed., *Hip Hop in America*, vol. 2 (Santa Barbara, CA: Greenwood, 2009), 530.

34. Danny Adomaitis, interview with the author, March 15, 2015.

35. Allen Toussaint, interview with the author, August 18, 2014.

36. Donald Harrison, correspondence with the author, December 1, 2015.

37. John Gros, interview with the author, February 3. 2015.

CHAPTER SEVEN

1. Peter Artaserse, interview with the author, March 18, 2015. d.b.a. bands are booked by Tom Thayer, who moved from New York to New Orleans.

2. Irvin Mayfield, interview with the author, January 5, 2015.

3. Michael Watson, interview with the author, March 19, 2015.

4. John Boutte, interview with the author, June 23, 2014.

5. Quoted in Feintuch, *Talking New Orleans Music*, 94.

6. John Boutte, interview with the author, March 14, 2015.

7. John Boutte, interview with the author, June 23, 2014.

8. Charlie Miller, interview with the author, June 24, 2014.

9. Aurora Nealand, interview with the author, January 11, 2016.

10. Katja Toivola, interview with the author, June 25, 2014.

11. Ned Sublette, *The Year Before the Flood* (Chicago: Chicago Review Press, 2009), 111.

12. Cindy Wood, interview with the author, January 13, 2011.

CHAPTER EIGHT

1. Ben Sandmel, interview with the author, May 16, 2006.

2. Peter Harris, interview with the author, May 13, 2006.

3. Richard Campanella, *Bourbon Street: A History* (Baton Rouge: Louisiana State University Press, 2014), 312.

4. Germaine Bazzle, interview with the author, March 15, 2015.

5. Leon "Kid Chocolate" Brown, interview with the author, May 14, 2006.

6. Todd Duke, interview with the author, May 14, 2006.

7. Bob French, interview with the author, May 14, 2006.

8. Leroy Jones, correspondence with the author, August 23, 2011.

9. John Boutte, interview with the author, June 23, 2014.

10. Christie Jordain, interview with the author, March 13, 2015.

11. Nathaniel Rich, "Hurricane's Wake," *New York Times Book Review*, August 5, 2015, online.

12. John Boutte, interviews with the author, July 21, 2013; June 23, 2014.

13. Charlie Miller, interview with the author, June 24, 2014.

14. Jan Ramsey, editor's note, *Offbeat* (August 2015), online.

15. Wendell Brunious, interview with the author, March 14, 2015.

16. Quoted in Keith Spera, *Groove Interrupted* (New York: Picador, 2011), 114.

17. Irma Thomas, unidentified video interview, Hogan Jazz Archive.

18. Quoted in John Swenson, *New Atlantis* (New York: Oxford University Press, 2010), 24.

19. Quoted in Spera, *Groove Interrupted*, 88.

20. Allen Toussaint, interview with the author, August 8, 2014.

21. Nathaniel Rich, "The Heart of New Orleans," *New York Review of Books*, July 10, 2014, 22.

22. Charlie Miller, interview with the author, June 24, 2014.

23. Jon Batiste, interview with the author, February 17, 2015.

24. Wendell Brunious, interview with the author, March 14, 2015.

25. David Torkanowsky, interview with the author, April 20, 2014.

26. John Boutte, interview with the author, March 14, 2015.

27. Allen Toussaint, interview with the author, August 8, 2015.

28. Jason Marsalis, interview with the author, January 7, 2016.

29. Ben Sandmel, correspondence with the author, October 10, 2015.

30. Victor Goines, interview with the author, November 15, 2014.

31. Katja Toivola, correspondence with the author, July 16, 2014.

32. Quoted in Feintuch, *Talking New Orleans Music*, 79.

33. Larry Sieberth, interview with the author, April 21, 2014.

34. Michael Watson, interview with the author, March 17, 2015.

35. Antoine Reynaldo Diel, interview with the author, March 19, 2015.

36. Charlie Halloran, interview with the author, January 9, 2009.

37. Ibid., March 19, 2015.

38. Eric Bloom, interview with the author, August 21, 2015.

39. Darren Hoffman, dir., *Tradition Is a Temple*, 2011, video.

40. Darren Hoffman, dir., "The Shotgun Waltz Presents Roland Guerin," September 1, 2013, https://www.youtube.com/watch?v=6pFDXYIT_jQ.

41. Antoine Reynaldo Diel, interview with the author, march 19, 2015.

42. Chadrick Honore, interview with the author, January 6, 2016.

43. Victor Goines, interview with the author, November 14, 2014.

44. Allen Toussaint, interview with the author August 6, 2015.

45. Michael Watson, interview with the author, March 9, 2015.

46. Joe Braun, interview with the author, January 11, 2016, http://www.neworleansjazzvipers.com/about.

47. Marla Dixon, interview with the author, March 18, 2015.

48. Barry Martyn, interview with the author, March 17, 2015.

49. Bruce Raeburn, interview with the author, March 18, 2015.

50. Victor Goines, interview with the author, November 14, 2014.

51. Ellis Marsalis, interview with the author, November 14, 2014.

52. Josh LeBlanc, interview with the author, January 7, 2015.

53. Jesse Duplechain, interview with the author, January 7, 2015.

54. Irma Thomas interview, unidentified interviewer, January 5, 1995, Hogan Jazz Archive.

55. Meschiya Lake, interview with the author, March 17, 2015.

56. Meghan Swartz, interview with the author, January 10, 2015.

57. Mara Dixon, interview with the author, March 14, 2015.

58. Haruka Kikuchi, interview with the author, March 14, 2015.

59. Topsy Chapman, interview with the author, January 15, 2014.

60. Yolanda Windsay, interview with the author, January 5, 2015.

61. Germaine Bazzle, interview with the author, March 5, 2015.

62. Arsène DeLay, interview with the author, March 19, 2015.

63. Cori Walters, interview with the author, January 10, 2016.

64. Quoted in Feintuch, *Talking New Orleans Music*, 61.

65. Natasha Harris, interview with the author, March 15, 2015.

66. Quoted in Jesse Serwer, review of Y-Ka May, *Washington Post*, February 6, 2010, online.

67. Quoted in in "The Morning Mix," *Washington Post*, June 12, 2014, online.

68. John Boutte, interview with the author, June 23, 2014.

69. Lucien Barbarin, interview with the author, January 10, 2016.

70. Jack LeBlanc, interview with the author, February 20, 2016.

71. Quoted in Feintuch, *Talking New Orleans Music*, 85.

72. Chubby Carrier, interview with the author, January 8, 2015.

73. Shannon Powell, interview with the author, January 9, 2016.

74. Gregg Stafford, interview with the author, December 26, 2013.

75. Richard Moten, interview with the author, January 17, 2014.

76. Aurora Nealand, correspondence with the author, November 13, 2014.

77. Keiko Komaki, interview with the author, January 18, 2014.

78. Davell Crawford, interview with the author, October 25, 2013.

79. Jon Batiste, interview with the author, Mardi Gras Day, 2015.

80. Phil Frazier, interview with the author, January 7, 2015.

81. Josh LeBlanc, interview with the author, January 15, 2015.

82. Shamarr Allen, interview with the author, October 25, 2013.

83. David Torkanowsky, interview with the author, March 19, 2015.

84. Davell Crawford, interview with the author, October 25, 2013.

85. Donald Harrison, correspondence with the author, December 1, 2015, March 5, 2016.

86. Jeff Franzel, interview with the author, April 24, 2015.

87. Jon Batiste, interview with the author, Mardi Gras Day, 2015.

88. Antoine Reynaldo Diel, interview with the author, March 19, 2015.

89. Tom McDermott, interview with the author, March 19, 2015.

90. Tom Sancton, *Song for My Fathers* (New York: Other Press, 2006), 293.

91. Kermit Ruffins, interview with the author, February 19, 2015.

92. Germaine Bazzle, interview with the author March 5, 2015.

93. Bruce Raeburn, interview with the author, January 18, 2015.

INDEX

Page numbers in **bold** refer to illustrations.

Trombone Shorty (Troy Andrews), 8, 13, 18,
  43, 70, 118–19, 124, **124**, 148, 152, 159, 174,
  186–87, 192
Tuba Fats (Anthony Lacen), 51, 144, 175
Tucker, Ira, 75
Tulane University, 26, 87
Turbinton, Earl, 106–7
Turbinton, Wilson (Willie Tee), 6, 131
Turner, Winston, 61, 186
Turtles, 188
Tuxedo Brass Band (Tuxedo Jazz Band),
  45, 60, 69–72, **71**, 79, 117, 120, 122, 146,
  160
Twain, Mark, 33

Ultramagnetic MCs, 139
Underdawgs, 187
Universe Jazz Band, 181
University of New Orleans, 87
Uptown Jazz Orchestra, 78
Up Up Up and Go, 191

Vagabond Swing, 177
Vanguard, 81
Vanguard Records, 37
Vappie, Don, 76, 87
Varese, Edgard, 37
Vaughan, Sarah, 35, 66, 192
Vaughan's Lounge, 63, 77, 89, 145, 153–55,
  157, 159
Ventry, Kevin (MC T. Tucker), 139
Verdi, Giuseppe, 21, 23, 29
Verrett, Shirley, 25
Victor Talking Machine Company, 21
Vidacovich, Johnny, 54, 64
Vienna Philharmonic, 35, 77
Voices from the Morning of the Earth, 36
von Karajan, Herbert, 35
von Stade, Frederica, 26
Von Suppe, Franz, 20–21

Wagner, Richard, 21, 24, 35
Waller, Thomas Wright "Fats," 114

Walters, Cori, 181
Wantanabe, Mari, 70
Ward, Michael, 132
Warren Easton High School, 27
Washington, Denzel, 164
Washington, Isidore "Tuts," 50
Washington, Walter "Wolfman," 9–10, 13, 74,
  88, 158, 171–72
Watson, Michael, 147, 151, 172, 174–75
Weber, Carl Maria von, 23
Webster, Ben, 98
Weill, Kurt, 33, 35
Weinberg, Meyer, 27
Welk, Lawrence, 100
West, Cornel, 67–68
Westminster Choir College, 70
Wexford Festival Opera, 33
White, Michael, 11, 13, 49, 51, 55, 59–60, 64,
  67, 68, 74, 82, 86–87, 94, 115, 120, 150,
  166–67, 185–86
white musicians, 12–13, 34, 116, 179, 182–83
Whitman, Walt, 21, 33
Who, 184
Wild Magnolias, 123, 130, 132
Wild Tchoupitoulas, 128, 132, 136, 140
Williams, Clarence, 103
Williams, Hank, 184
Williams, Nathan, Jr., 178
Williams, Sammie (Big Sam), 186, 192
Williams, Tennessee, 3, 25–26, 42, 68
Williams, Tony, 121
Willie Tee (Wilson Turbinton), 6, 131
Willis, Jack, 50, 91
Wilson, Gran, 25
Winchester, Lawrence, 91
Windsay, Yolanda, 70, 92, 180
Wonder, Stevie, 61, 92, 189
Wood, Cindy, 153–54
world music, 34, 37, 83, 162
World That Made New Orleans, The, 22
Wright, Frank Lloyd, 64
Wright, Marva, 145
WWOZ, 156, 175